THIS IS NOT A LOVE SONG

AMBER PETTY

First published in 2021

Text © Amber Petty 2021

The moral rights of the author have been asserted.

This work is copyright. Apart from any use as permitted under the Copyright Act 1968 (Cth), no part of this publication may be used or reproduced by any process, electronic or otherwise, without the prior written permission of the copyright holder. Neither may information be stored electronically in any form whatsoever without such permission.

A catalogue entry is for this work is available from the National Library of Australia.

This Is Not A Love Song

978-1-922267-58-0 (print)

978-1-393245-19-3 (digital)

Book production by Noble Books, a division of Brio Books

Printed and bound in Australia by SOS

Cover illustration: Bob Freeman (occultdetective.com)

CONTENTS

Chapter One. 1
Ghosts of Airports Past 1
The Carpet Kingdom 7
Ding Dong the Bitch is Dead 12

Chapter Two. 21
Learning to Run 21
Gold Medals & Hot Pants 30
Where There's Smoke 37

Chapter Three. 42
Goodbye My Friend 42
Wrong Way, Go Back 46
I'm a Survivor 56

Chapter Four. 62
Poker Face 62
Playing in the Dark 72
A Love Story 80

Chapter Five. **91**
Angel Sarah 91
When You're Gone 100
A Window of Time 106

Chapter Six. **114**
I Want to Learn a Love Song 114
Daisy, Daisy 123
Bearing Gifts 128

Chapter Seven. **136**
Behind the Green Door 136
Send Me An Angel 147
The Weatherman Called for a Twister 158

Chapter Eight. **166**
Somewhere Out There 166
Check, One, Two 171
Chasing a Fairy Tale 180

Chapter Nine. **190**
The Long Goodbye 190
Love Comes in, Love Goes Out 196
All My Life's A Circle 208

Chapter Ten. **212**
Take It to the Bridge 212

CHAPTER ONE.

GHOSTS OF AIRPORTS PAST

It's easy to waste a lot of time in Los Angeles staring at people and wondering if they're *someone*. It can be as stupid as losing 15 minutes on the five-foot-tall tanned dude in his 60s wearing a tangerine short-sleeve shirt, smoking a fag out the front of a cafe: *Hang on, did I see that guy on Seinfeld?* Or maybe it's the grey-haired guy in the white sneakers and trench coat, gliding at a suspicious pace through LAX like he might be trying to avoid attention: *Was that Richard Gere?* Five minutes later and along comes a blonde wearing a plain white T-shirt and jeans, moving fast and I think: *Wow. Was that Sharon Stone?* Then I realise: *Holy shit! That was Sharon Stone.*

It can pay off being alert in LA. It can also waste you a *shit-load* of time. Which is precisely what I was doing while queuing at the Burger King at LAX behind a tall, long-haired guy in a brown leather jacket (to be honest, my type). I wondered: *Is that the guy who just won American Idol?* My bloodshot eyes must have been burning lasers into his right temple because he suddenly looked over his shoulder. I whipped my eyes back up to the Burger King menu overhead. Back to my other dilemma: *Will my hangover get better or way, way worse with a Whopper with the lot and, given I'm boarding in ten minutes, is this going to be the greatest mistake of my life, or just one of them?*

I go for the Whopper Junior and give up on my need to know the deal with the guy in front. It'd been a hectic week attending the Golden Globes after-parties (the perks of being a magazine columnist) surrounded by certified stars like Morgan Freeman and Halle Berry. I thought my fashion industry buddy Aaron, in town for G'day LA, was going to have a panic attack when I mentioned Debra Messing was standing a metre away. 'Oh. My. God. It's fucking *Grace*!' he shrieked loud enough to make me want to knee him in the groin.

My flight gate to Sydney was conveniently located in front of Burger King and I could see people starting to queue. Waiting for my order to be called out my eyes drifted to a little girl standing next to a guy in his early forties. The girl, who was eight or nine, was wearing a purple T-shirt with Dora the Explorer on it, denim shorts and a small silver backpack over one shoulder. Whatever the man was saying was making her giggle.

I wonder if they're going on holiday together. Or maybe they've just finished one? Perhaps they're going home to her Mum? I found myself getting lost in their moment, watching that magical connection between daughters and their dads.

'128? Order 128?' I swung away from the Burger King bench to retrieve the order I was already regretting. Bag in hand I sat down and began unpacking the burger I had three minutes to devour. As the taste of meat and melted cheese, mayonnaise and pickle filled my mouth and heart with joy, I looked back to where the girl and her father had been. She had her back towards me now so I couldn't see her face. Her Dad was stroking her hair lovingly, only stopping to plant kisses on the top of her head. And then he leaned down closer to her face and appeared to whisper. All of a sudden it hit me. This wasn't what I thought it was. *Oh, god, no. They're not saying goodbye, are they?* At that very second, she turned her head back into view as she looked up at her Dad. The smile that had danced across her cheeks minutes earlier was gone. Now the man was kneeling in front of her. She put her head down, shaking it back and forth, crying. Like she was trying to make something go away. I wanted to vomit. I knew exactly the pain that little girl was in. I could feel it in every part of my body. That girl was once me. Memories from so long ago flooded back like it was yesterday.

I never understood why my dad chose to move from Melbourne to Sydney when my brother Myles and I were just two and three years old – or why he chose to live with another woman and her son. *Why did they get him, not us?* Divorce wasn't common in 1971 so it was hard not to feel different from other kids. There was no 'one week on, one week off' arrangement back then. We got short bursts with Dad. A couple of weeks during the year or when he came to Melbourne. It was never enough. I was obsessed with my dad. I thought he was the most amazing person in the entire world. I'd overhear people telling Mum we were better off never having lived with Dad so we didn't notice his absence. *You don't know what you're talking about*, I'd think. I missed Dad every day. Not that I recall it but Mum and Dad were still together for the first twelve months of my life before splitting when Myles was born. I never stopped wishing he lived with us.

In the early days of their divorce, while we were still toddlers, Mum would fly with us to Sydney so we could see Dad. Which must have been an absolute *shit* of a job. We were legally allowed to fly on our own when we were about four and five. People would stare as Mum would hand us over to the air-hostesses – the pity in their eyes only confirming to my young self that there was something wrong with us.

I credit those TAA and Ansett hosties for their kindness and, *God bless* them, always a promise of 'meeting the captain' and 'taking a look at the cockpit'. My brother loved it but it was always a 'no' from me. I had zero interest in seeing the one windscreen of the plane most likely to reveal a mountain seconds before our faces smashed into it. I'm sure some kids might have found flying a super fabulous and exciting adventure but not me. I hated every goddam second of it.

Once in our seats, strapped in tightly, my head would already be up in the clouds before the plane even left the runway. *What if Mum could tell how much I want to see Dad? Maybe she thinks I don't love her?* And so the game of emotional Twister would begin, fading only as the plane took off when, like clockwork, I'd turn white as a ghost and start sweating profusely. I'd then have about three seconds to grab the sick bag. The whole routine would leave my stomach muscles hurting for days. Only when I was one hundred per cent certain I was done, like squeezing the last of the toothpaste of the tube, would I hold my bag of shame out towards the aisle, waiting for a hostess to grab it like a baton in a relay race. There was not a single flight in my childhood that I didn't think we were going to die. And sometimes, when it was really bumpy, a deep wave of sadness would wash over me as I'd contemplate just how close we were to reaching Dad but weren't going to make it.

'Please fasten your seatbelts as we prepare for landing,' the pilot would announce. Rattled and relieved we'd have to wait for the grown-ups to get off before our hostess could walk us down the airbridge. Peddling fast, annoyed by my lack of sight in this land of giants, my heart would race at a million miles knowing my daddy was out there. Eyes darting left, right, trying to see past their backs, I'd search for his face. I loved the way Dad would be smiling even before he saw us. Our eyes locking, I'd charge as fast as I could at him, launching myself through the air and into his arms. Dad would scoop me up, swing me around, oblivious to the fact we might take someone's eye out with my shoe.

Dad always smelt like a delicious blend of Pierre Cardin aftershave and Rothmans cigarettes. Usually wearing a pair of designer shorts bought my stepmother, his fat wallet bulging from his back pocket, and an XXL long-sleeved polo shirt that looked like it'd been plucked off the floor seconds before racing out of the house.

With bags in tow the three of us would head for the car – Myles and I hanging off his big arms. Dad would swing us back and forth while we laughed hysterically. Once in the car Myles and I'd fight for body space from the back, squish ourselves between the front seats, spill over on to the front console, and start chanting, 'Harry, Harry, Harry'.

Harry Chapin was the man who wrote 'Cat's in The Cradle' and (slightly) lesser hits like (our song) '30,000 Pounds of Bananas' – the greatest song ever written. Two weeks later, on the way back to the airport, not even the lyrics of '30,000 Pounds of Bananas', a song about an out-of-control truck driver spilling a load of bananas on to a slippery, wet road on the way to Scranton, Pennsylvania, was enough to lift the dread of saying goodbye. With dehydration and a flight announcement bringing me back to reality (and my hangover), I realised it had never occurred to me that other little girls all around the world might be doing the same airport goodbyes with their Dads. Shaking out of my time-travelling trance I promised myself, if the little girl was seated anywhere near me, I'd find something to say – anything that might break her out of the feeling I knew only too well. As we inched on board, I watched the passengers around me placing their bags overhead, slotting their belongings under the sleeves in front of them, bums plonking down on seats, and then, *24C, that's me*. With my bags in the overhead locker, buckled in for the long flight, I was almost too scared to look. *What if she is near me? I've vowed to say something but what the hell am I going to say?* Nervously I turned around and there she was – just two rows back, sitting with her head down quietly weeping. I knew how this stuff went: *Hide your feelings. Don't embarrass yourself in front of the adults. Wait for the tears to go.*

I sat contemplating my next move. As the aisles began to clear I decided I had nothing to offer except knowing her pain. So, I got up, crouched down next to her seat, and said, *'Hello sweetie, I just wanted to see if you were OK?'* She looked up at me, wiping her tears away. 'Oh yes,' she said, trying to force out a smile.

'I'm sorry, it's OK, thank you.'

'Have you just said goodbye to your dad?' I asked, trying to be gentle.

'Yes,' she whispered, trying to be brave in front of the stranger.

This Is Not a Love Song 5

'Does your dad live here?'

'Yes,' she whispered.

'And your mum lives in Sydney?'

'Yes.'

I took a breath, trying to hide what I didn't want her to see in her eyes – that once I was just like her and my pain was still there, raw as ever. I wanted her to believe one day all this *Dad stuff* would fade away. Something you grew out of like, *I hoped*, like vomiting into paper bags. I didn't want her to know I still didn't get it. That I didn't understand the ramifications of it all and its effect on who I'd become. And then I came up with a *genius* idea! Or, perhaps, just an idea.

'Wait there, sweetie. I've got something for you. I'll be back.' I moved back to my seat, grabbing all the crappy magazines I'd just bought, and returned to her seat.

'These are just the silliest magazines and you probably won't be interested in them but why don't you look at the pictures? Just until you feel a bit better.'

Just what a distraught little girl needs. A magazine full of celebrities she's never heard of with headlines written by assholes with no conscience. I hoped she was too sweet, too young, to get what they were saying. She just needed a distraction. I knew her tears would go at some point during the flight but I also knew they'd be back. Maybe even thirty years later, when you're all grown up thinking you're ever-so fucking fabulous, working for a magazine, on a flight home after attending the Golden Globes. I went back to 24C and stared at the seat in front of me. I closed my eyes, trying to block out the feeling welling up inside. When I opened them out rushed the tears, streaming down my face in perfectly straight lines – tears that'd waited a long time to run free. And then it hit me: *Oh, my god. I am so damaged.*

I couldn't let her see me – not mid meltdown. I pressed my head hard against the chair so she wouldn't see me. I didn't want her to know that the pain she was in, saying goodbye to her Daddy, might follow her for as long, as I'd just discovered, it had in me.

Two hours later I got a tap on my shoulder. And there she was, this brave kid standing in the aisle next to me. 'Thank you for your magazines,' she said, now smiling.

'Are you feeling a bit better?' I asked, hoping my eyeliner wasn't hinting I'd been having a few of my own issues over in 24C.

'Yes, I'm OK now. Thank you.'

As she went back to her seat, I had a feeling she was going to be OK. For the rest of the flight anyway. She was learning the art of survival. But, as I knew only too well, distractions from pain won't always be as harmless as a few trashy magazines.

THE CARPET KINGDOM

As far as dads went mine was fun, funny and the most outrageously irresponsible man I've ever known. Even by seventies standards he was considered loose. And the problem with having a party boy Dad is everyone wants a piece of him. And when your piece is already too small it creates competition for his attention. Hanging out with Dad was never dull – he lived like it was his birthday every day. He didn't believe in depriving himself of anything – sex (which didn't mix well with marriage), gambling (see previous bracket), travel or food. The latter resulting in a large percentage of my time being spent with my father across a Lazy Susan discussing the merits of steamed dim sims v fried, and the unsung health benefits of a banana split. Despite his daily indulgences, Dad did work. In fact, he owned a relatively large business called The Carpet Kingdom which it appeared, if his Ferrari and our holidays to places like Dunk Island were anything to go by, did pretty well. I found out as an adult that this calculation was entirely off. Dad got his Ferrari after winning a 'quaddie' at the races and his business was mostly hanging by a thread until it went into bankruptcy in the mid-80s.

Someone convinced Dad in the late seventies that he should invest in a TV commercial to advertise his business. The next thing we knew Dad was on TV wearing a red King's robe, a dodgy looking crown and holding a sceptre while he rattled on about his 'carpet empire'. Dad occasionally got recognised, which would embarrass the hell out of him. It embarrassed all of us – especially my stepmother Helen who Dad had met not long after arriving in Sydney. She was attractive, glamorous and not at all the type to go out with an overweight fake king. But Dad was funny and naughty, which most women loved. He was also a 'bloke's bloke' so men loved him too – even while he was making inappropriate remarks about their wives.

Myles and I loved going to work with Dad. We got to jump and climb all over his carpet rolls stacked high on the warehouse shelves despite the fact we could have been crushed at any second by a rolling shag-pile. Dad let us hang from the iron prong on his forklift while his showroom manager Barry raised us to the roof as high as the forklift would go – 'Don't tell your bloody mother,' they'd yell as our bodies dangled five metres above the concrete floor.

We ate pasties with tomato sauce, vanilla slices and drank lemon squash for lunch. It was a feast fit for a Carpet King and the heirs to his throne.

Mum struggled with us being with Dad. She stressed continuously about whether we were getting skin cancer (she was way ahead of her time on the SPF front), how fat we were getting (she had a zero tolerate policy on people over a size ten) or how close we were to dying – she knew Dad well. Thankfully she never found out. Mind you nor did we until many years later, learn Dad had nearly lost us on the Hawkesbury River one night. As the story goes, Dad and Helen left us sleeping on a clipper boat they'd rented for the weekend while they dined with friends at a restaurant on the river bank. At the claret and dinner mints end of the night one of their mates, who had their own boat and a child sleeping alone inside, pointed towards the river as a boat drifted slowly by, 'Oh fuck, is that one of ours?' They managed to stop us before we ended up in New Zealand. Here's the fascinating thing about the seventies

– people got really good at handling emergencies while completely shit-faced drunk.

It wasn't all fun and games with Dad – not when you're a highly sensitive, highly likely to vomit in moving vehicles, kind of kid. Dad rarely said 'no' to us but when he did it made life unbearable. From screeching up the mountain in his Ferrari around corners with no barricades and a hundred-metre drop into the forest, to smoking Rothmans on planes despite me turning broad bean green with his every exhale, Dad didn't like anything that got in his way of having a good time. In what we'll file under karma, his baby girl ended up growing up just like him. I was fourteen in 1984 when Dad and Helen decided to buy a pub in Narrandera in the NSW Riverina – what felt like the middle of goddam nowhere. They left behind their Sydney home (including a pool, a white pool table, and black leather and mirrored bar) and their entire social life. The decision seemed odd, especially for Helen. I could see the benefits for Dad – beer on tap, an in-house Chinese chef and the racing channel on 24/7 – but all Helen got was Dad.

I thought all my Christmases had come at once as I stood in the doorway of the storeroom at their new pub, like Howard Carter discovering Tutankhamun's tomb. I was staring at rows of bottles and cartons of cigarettes. All I could think of was how popular I was going to be if I could get some of it back to my friends. That was the thought process behind me taking several bottles of my favourite brands – Kahlua, Midori and Malibu (all your 80s classics) – along with one packet of each cigarette brand. It took me a couple of shifts to get it all back to my room, but I got there.

Things went pear-shaped when Dad stumbled across my handy-work the next day while I was out. Stupidly I'd left my stash in my suitcase sitting smack bang in the middle of my bedroom floor. When he went to move it out of the way with his foot, he discovered it was only slightly lighter than Ayres Rock.

An hour later I walked into Dad's room ready to flop down beside him on the bed. 'Hi, Daddy!' I said, joyfully. He was propped up against a pillow with the racing form guide draped over his legs like a blanket – his signature spot. Dad looked up at me without speaking. Something was wrong. He'd never looked at me like he did on that day.

After a few painfully long seconds he said, 'So, can I ask you something?' He was squinting as though confused. 'When have you asked for something and not gotten it?' I didn't know what he meant. 'Um ... never?' I replied sheepishly a second or so before the penny dropped.

'So why is it that you feel you need to steal from us?' he said, now staring at me with his piercing blue eyes. I stood at the end of his bed, as shame filled my body. Steal? The word felt like a stab. I stared down at my feet not knowing what to say. I knew what he was talking about and yet, until that very moment, hadn't for a second thought about it that way. Helen walked past the doorway, stopping only to drop me a disdainful look before walking off. Dad waited for her to disappear before telling me they'd fought over her wanting to call the police. The police? Jesus Christ. I knew I'd been an asshole – but calling the cops? What Dad was yet to divulge was he hadn't won the fight entirely. He'd compromised by agreeing I be banned from returning or seeing him for twelve months. I was fourteen and, according to him, once I got on that plane, I wouldn't see him again until I was fifteen.

Not being allowed to see my dad for twelve months felt like a jail sentence. I don't remember much about the year that followed except that I made my first fake ID, went to my first nightclub and, according to Mum, it was the year I became an 'angry little girl'.

Eventually I turned fifteen, finally off the no-fly zone restrictions with Dad, when something else happened that I would not recall until three decades later. It was the day I heard through the school grapevine that Dad was in town. According to these little whispers my dad was staying at his best friend's house, just five minutes from my house. It got back to me via a group of girls at school that included Dad's best mate's daughter, all celebrating the 'hysterical night' they'd had the night before with 'Uncle Ian'. AKA my dad. At first I couldn't believe it was true. I spent the rest of the school day trying to suck back my humiliation and rage, counting the minutes until I could get home and learn the truth.

That afternoon I came through the back door at home like a tornado, throwing my schoolbag down on the kitchen floor. Mum was standing in the doorway from the kitchen to the front hallway. 'Did you know Dad's in town?' I spat, through a tight jaw. I distinctly recall the expression on her face as my eyes bore through her skull as I awaited her response. She looked sad and a little terrified. I was scary. I was in the first year of my new scary self.

Mum started looking up Dad's best friend's phone number. 'I'm going to ring him,' I spat, as she handed me a post-it-note with the number on it. I charged off towards the phone outside my bedroom door. My heart was pounding under my school jumper as I snatched the phone receiver, my finger stabbing each hole, dragging the numbers around forcefully, trying to calm my breathing with each excruciatingly slow dial return. 'Hello!' came an answer from the wife of Dad's best friend. Trying to sound polite and unperturbed I replied, 'Hi. It's Amber. Is my dad there?' *Please say no, please say no, please say no.*

There was a brief pause before she answered, 'Yes, darling, I'll put him on!' I wanted to smash the receiver against the side of my head.

A minute later Dad picked up. 'Hello?' he said as if surprised.

'Dad? So, you are in Melbourne?' I said trying to mask my fury and my disappointment. He sounded nervous. I, however, sounded like a cop who'd just pulled over a P-plate driver doing twenty kilometres over the speed limit. I wanted to sound disconnected, business-like, grown-up.

'Yes, darling. I was just about to ring you,' he said, sounding pathetically upbeat.

'And when did you get here?'

Like a kid about to lose his license he sheepishly replied, 'Last Tuesday.'

He'd been around the corner for almost a week.

'And when are you going back?' I said, still determined to keep my cool.

'Tomorrow, but I can see you tonight?' he replied, hopefully. I slammed the phone down and dropped to the ground like a three-year-old. I bashed my fists onto the carpet until my wrists hurt. I cried and screamed words Mum let me get away with for a day.

DING DONG THE BITCH IS DEAD

It's funny when you're young how you're acutely aware when your mother's footsteps sound a little ominous. Particularly after a phone call you didn't manage to eavesdrop on, and I did pride myself on eavesdropping on most. I was used to being on high alert when the phone rang in our house – a habit I formed as a child waiting for Dad to call. It was a chilly winter's day in the middle of my Year Ten school holidays when we received an unexpected phone call from Mrs Turner, my school principal. She was calling to confirm whether or not I was returning to school the following semester.

'Of course she's coming back. Why wouldn't she be?' my confused and perhaps slightly naïve Mother responded.

'Well, we just think it might be best if she didn't return here. We think it might be time you looked for somewhere else for Amber to go. We feel we've tried our best with her and it hasn't worked out,' the principal said flatly.

Next minute I hear Mum yell, 'Amber, are you there?' I was cross-legged on my bed with my stereo on my lap, hard at work taping my favourite songs from Casey Kasem's American Top 40 while trying to clip out his voice. Stop, start, rewind, record – there was an art to this shit.

Now Mum was at my door, left hand on hip.

'Amber, do you have any idea why Mrs Turner might have just called me wanting to know if you were returning to school after the holidays?' she enquired.

Click, stop, button-down. I rolled my eyes, pissed off I hadn't got to fully record my song, dreading what my intuition told me was not the principal doing a housekeeping ring around on every student at school.

'Nope, no idea,' I answered, trying to sound calmly curious.

'Well, that's the phone call I've just had, and she made it pretty clear she doesn't want you back. What exactly has been going on at school that I don't know about?' she asked.

This was a bit of a tricky one as there might have been a handful of things that had gone down which hadn't entirely made it onto Mum's radar. Mind you, a couple had gotten uncomfortably close. Like the time two rival ratbags at school tried to frame my mate Sabrina and I for sending death threats (I mean, please). Mrs Turner found out after the terrified recipient and her mother brought the letter to her attention. Sabrina and I were immediately hauled into the principal's office and warned that if we didn't come clean by the end of the week, she'd be calling our parents to notify them of suspension. The little bitches behind the letter eventually buckled under mounting pressure from our small but persuasive group of supporters and confessed with about an hour left of the week. I'd also managed to wriggle out of getting busted for selling drugs at school that year after my sports teacher found a suspicious aluminium parcel in the bag of a Year Ten student. I'd made a whopping $15 that week palming off dried rosemary that I may have implied was marijuana. Obviously, there'd been a sprinkling of other incidents that had somewhat cemented my reputation as a nasty little piece. And yet up until Mrs Turner's phone call that day I'd also been in the rather gifted position of my brother making an even bigger asshole of himself at his school, which provided me with the perfect smokescreen.

I was just shy of turning sixteen which I guess is quite old for a feral cat at an Anglican Girls Grammar School. It was time for a fresh start. Conveniently I had it in my head that maybe, given I was so close to being an adult anyway, it might be time I got on with the job of life after education. That, however, was not what Mum had in her head, 'Your dad and I have decided we're not wasting another cent sending you to a good school so that you can sit around being a smart ass all day.'

I didn't like the sound of that. For all my disdain for authority and a boring private school education I most certainly was not ready to get among it at the local high school. I didn't want to be dealing with girls I hadn't had time to scope out and plan a strategy around and I was definitely not ready to share a classroom with the opposite sex.

'We're going to have to try and get you into Brighton High School and see if they'll take you at short notice.' Short notice? I don't want them to notice me full stop. In my mind, Brighton High was where all the bogans went to school and I didn't particularly want my name mentioned in the same sentence, let alone be wearing the same uniform. *I cannot go to this school. I will not go to this school.* I'd been told I had 'a reputation' over at Brighton High for being a little too big for my roman sandals.

The crazy thing was that prior to high school, on my last day at primary school, there'd been a whole gang of us who'd clung to each other howling like babies that we were leaving each other. There were just three of us going to the local private school instead of Brighton High and yet one year later the old gang suddenly shunned us in the streets and branded us 'snobs'. The little bastards turned on us like cut snakes, regardless of whether our mum's bought Black & Gold versus Birdseye fish fingers – which to me said everything about whether your family was rich or poor. So eventually I just played the role I'd been bestowed with – some might say a little too well.

Mum believed if she sent my brother and I to private schools we'd have, as she put it, 'a better shot at life'. But the reality was I'd entered my private school on day one with a raft of insecurities that ranged from being from a divorced family to not being pretty enough and not rich like I assumed everyone else's parents were. I decided my only strategy for saving myself from potential social annihilation would be to present a side of me that would be too intimidating to call out. Which served me well-*ish* for four years until Mrs Turner decided to give me the flick.

After much debate, not with but about me, Mum announced she'd found a new school. One that was 'public', and uniquely, as she PR-ed it, 'an all-girls school'. Proudly adding that the school had a 'surprisingly good reputation' with regard to education. *A surprisingly good education?* As if that was a necessary consideration. The only hiccup, according to Mum, was it was just out of our catchment zone so they didn't have to take me. But why wouldn't they? I mean, I'd just been asked to leave school mid-year, I came armed with grades ranging in the Ds, Es and Fs, not to mention a report card that, if held close to your ear like a shell, echoed the faint cries of my exhausted teachers. I guess it didn't help my cause that on the day of our appointment with the new school's principal I'd arrived wearing my ex-private school uniform. There was nothing accidental about my look; the message was simple, 'Fuck you.'

I was polite enough as Mum and I introduced ourselves before sitting down in front of the principal's laminated, fake wood desk. After about ten minutes of the adults crapping on about stuff I didn't catch, it was suggested I leave the room. Apparently the principal needed to have a 'private chat' with Mum. Guided to a chair outside her office I settled in for what I hoped would be minutes countable on one hand, before we'd leave and never return. Class was in session so the halls were quiet aside from the occasional girl wafting past at seemingly regular intervals, each one glancing my way as my eyes burned back at them. I wasn't embarrassed (or aware how delusional I might've looked) that I was outside the principal's office in my old uniform – because I'd never see anyone in that building again.

Back inside the most unglamorous office I'd ever laid eyes on the principal spoke to my mum, 'As you know Mrs Petty, Amber lives outside this jurisdiction so we are not obligated to take her. And, unfortunately, with her current grades and her teachers' comments I am concerned about what the issues are with Amber.'

'Yes, I understand,' Mum began her carefully thought-out speech. 'You know she was actually always such a good student and loved school prior to the last year or so but she's sadly taken my divorce from her Dad quite hard.'

Back out in the foyer, the bell blared overhead, sharply followed by the eruption of voices and the sound of hundreds of chair legs scraping across classroom floors.

For Christ sakes, Mum, hurry the fuck up, I thought to myself, uncomfortable at the prospect of a sea of high school girls about to spew forth from all directions. There was only so long I could keep my face locked in a snarl. I could hear Mum's favourite piece of advice ringing in my ears, 'Don't do that. You'll give yourself wrinkles.'

In the only highlight so far of that day, Mum suddenly appeared in the foyer, surprisingly upbeat, if not just for show, as she farewelled the woman she was hoping had fallen for her charms. There wasn't much hope she'd fallen for mine. We politely thanked the lady for seeing us then swiftly headed out to the car.

Once inside Mum's yellow Celica, as I attempted to say nothing, Mum proudly announced she believed the *'slight creative license she'd been forced to take'* with the principal regarding, as she recounted – *'why you're such a problem'* – appeared to have had an empathetic reaction from her prey.

'I just explained you used to be a good student but had struggled since your Dad and my divorce.'

'*What?* Did she ask you when you two actually broke up?' I enquired.

'No, no, I just gave the impression that it had been in the last couple of years. She didn't specifically ask when, so it's fine.' She had that air of getting one over and, even better, one over me. God knows she revelled in that shit. *Wow, she's good*, I mused to myself, praying her intuition was as off as her grasp of the truth.

As it turned out Mum had been on her A-game that day and as term three began so too did my new chapter at a school I was convinced I'd never return to. The vain side of me, however, was at least excited about the colour of my new uniform given I'd just spent four and a half long years in army green and American military brown uniform. Not exactly colours that help an already self-conscious girl feel like Kelly Le Brock in Weird Science (AKA, the hottest thing to come out of 1985).

I was totally on my own in a school that had more subgroups than the archives of a decade of 80s music. We had The Wogs who proudly referred to themselves as such and who didn't want me and appeared to passionately loathe every molecule of my being. I'd never been subjected to so much hate in my life. Well, I had, but in the safe space of my last school. This lot would sit huddled together on the cricket pitch in the middle of the oval, dragging away on their Winnie Blues, and yell at me, 'Oi, come over here so we can cut off those little ringlets of yours.' Those girls scared the absolute *shit* out of me.

Next up we had The Head Bangers. Again, not my label. This was an accepted title embraced by the girls themselves. They stared intensely at me through heavily made-up eyes. *Maybe,* I prayed, *if we couldn't bond over their terrible choice of music we'd bond over a mutual understanding of the spiritual importance of hairspray?* I mean, values are at least important, aren't they?

The Bogans – the only group who appeared to have been given their title by all other groups – were quite unaffected by my presence. This I found particularly curious given I'd assumed they'd be the first lot to want to ram my forehead into a locker.

And finally, The Trendy girls – my closest demographic – they made it crystal clear I was categorically not welcome under any circumstances. Unbeknownst to me they'd made a pact to shun me as much as humanly possible. While I was clueless as to why I did suspect it might just have been a classic case of my shit catching up with me.

My new school became such an incredible whirlwind experience as I received a crash course in what would form the foundation of my social beliefs about myself and others. In a divine curve-ball, the first people to show me kindness at my new school were the bogans. With so many teenage girls from varying socio-economic backgrounds vying to find and make their tribes I became fascinated by all that was going on around me. It all felt so authentic in a way I'd never experienced before. And, despite at times feeling like Sissy Spacek with a bucket of blood over her head at prom night, I was finally awake.

Speaking of awake, it's hard not to be when you've just received a threatening, anonymous note in class outlining that the author knows where you live, how you travel home, and stating they're going to meet you somewhere halfway to 're-arrange your pretty little face'.

Clearly designed to rattle my ex-private school cage and my sense of worth I do remember as I read those three little words, pretty little face, that I felt a surprising pang of joy: *Do they think I'm pretty? Shame about the bashed head.* A compliment delivered by a poison arrow. *How totally Snow White? Or was it Cinderella? Whatever.*

As I was reading the note that had been thrown on the desk in front of me as a cluster of girls brushed past me on their way to their seats my face must have revealed I was digesting something more sinister than the sleeve notes to a Madonna single. One of the bogans sitting in the row of seats in front of me looked back and asked, 'Hey, what's that?'

I hesitated before handing the note over, trying to remember what a new cast member on the TV show Prisoner would do in my position. The letter had been creatively written and designed with blood droplets in red biro, dripping off every other word.

Before I could work out what my lone, new girl strategy was going to be on death threats, the bogan in front of me stood up in front of the class, not a brass razoo about our poor maths teacher keen to get stuck into Pythagoras' theorem and a couple of pie charts. She shouted, 'Hey, who's the fuckin' idiot that wrote this letter to Amber?'

There was silence.

'Well, we're not fuckin' going anywhere until the person that wrote this shit stands up right here, right now.' I was gob-smacked. This amazing girl who I'd never spoken a single word to was holding the entire class hostage until the red biro bandit came forward.

The teacher, astoundingly, remained with her back against the blackboard, like a warden in the middle of a prison outbreak, meekly protesting, 'C'mon girls, this is silly, who wrote this to Amber?' She'd lost control of the room. My bogan angel was like Angelina in Maleficent, determined to take the anonymous dragon down with her verbal and energetic chains, threatening to wrap them around her neck. Finally the author piped up. It was the headbanger in the second row from the front. She swung her body around towards us, and snapped, 'I *fuckin'* wrote it, so what? She's a *fuckin'* bitch.'

'Is that right Helen, and what makes her a fuckin' bitch?' My angel shot back while the rest of the class risked whiplash as their heads went from player to player.

'She's come from this *fuckin'* bullshit school, and she lives in *fuckin'* Brighton. She's only *fuckin'* here cause she got kicked out of her other school,' she said, looking furious.

It was like a tennis match and I was the fresh, furry Slazenger ball. Here was this stranger sticking up for me in what might have been me versus the head banger community of Australia. My bogan angel looked her opponent straight in the eye and warned, 'You touch her outside of this classroom, and you'll have to deal with me.'

Axel Rose's cranky girlfriend backed down, shaking her head as she turned away from us, and muttering profanities under her breath. I stayed quiet, taking in an event that I didn't deserve. I didn't deserve my bogan angel. What I deserved was to hear the school bell ring, feel sick with panic knowing I'd have to get home not knowing when my headbanger might come for me. Like a game of Cluedo. What would her weapon be? The candlestick? The knife? The revolver? A Guns N' Roses boxset?

Another revelation came to me in the days after that death threat arrived on my desk. Despite the fact I'd viewed this school in such stark contrast to where I'd come from there were similarities I couldn't ignore. Although the sub-groups or cliques were more pronounced than at my last school, both had girls with innate personal power willing to step ahead of the pack. And it dawned on me I'd used my own personal power to manipulate others in order to protect myself while the girl who'd taken on the headbanger had used hers to protect someone else. This school that I had so hugely dismissed as being of no value to me actually changed my life right when it needed it. And, for the record, I never saw that girl who protected me once I left school but I do remember her name. Her name was Susan and she changed the course of how I would forever treat those that don't look like me, or live like I do. To use words that honour her appropriately I say: What a seriously, fuckin' cool chick.

CHAPTER TWO.

LEARNING TO RUN

Breathe. Ride through the pain. It doesn't make sense. Why would anyone self-destruct after seeing a photo of the baby of an ex-boyfriend from 15 bloody years ago? What's wrong with you? And, excuse me, what happened to the old 'you'll grieve a relationship for exactly half the length of time you were in it?'. Who came up with those fucking miscalculations? Clearly someone (like me) who failed veggie maths.

'It's Julian's baby!' Myles said. As the last words of my brother's unsolicited news update came rolling out his mouth it felt like a knife had been thrust into my belly.

We're not together! You were the one that broke it off because you didn't think you should be together. Don't start second-guessing all that shit now, for god's sake!

How bloody thoughtless Myles. 'Oh hey, have a look at this!' without a hint of *content warning or viewer disclaimer.* And as I stared at the photo on my brother's computer screen of possibly the most beautiful baby I'd ever seen, I wondered *who was lucky enough to give birth to this amazing child?* But I did not need to know it was his. Anybody's but his.

I was twenty-one years old on the day I went strutting down an old cobbled road in Rethymno in Crete. It was my first trip outside Australia, made possible thanks to my dad coming good on his promise to buy me an around-the-world plane ticket for my twenty-first birthday. On my way home from the beach I was wearing an old men's Bonds singlet I'd fashioned into a dress. I'd been discreetly checking out my bum in a shop window as I made my way back to the Youth Hostel when I first saw Julian.

This handsome, shirtless stranger, with a rose tattoo hugging his tanned left bicep, was outside a souvenir shop window checking himself out – meticulously re-arranging individual strands of his long curly hair like he was putting the final touches to a work of art. From what I could make out – *hair, back, shorts, calves, biceps, tattoo* – he was the most beautiful guy I'd ever seen. He ticked boxes I hadn't known were there to tick.

Uncomfortable with unexpected surges of attraction I chose to channel my vulnerability into appearing aloof and sexy, just in case he looked my way. After all, I could quite easily just be a girl searching for a Cretan tea-towel to buy her grandmother and he was simply blocking my view. Half an hour later, back inside the foyer of the youth hostel, I turned around to find my tick-box guy standing right behind me. 'Alright?' he asked, in an English accent, catching me off guard as he stuffed a wad of drachmas into his pocket.

Christ, he's even more gorgeous face to face I thought, suddenly overcome with a rare bout of chronic shyness. I was so embarrassed I wanted to run. Instead I put forward possibly the blandest presentation of myself as I responded, 'Yes, thanks, and you?'

The youth hostel, which I'd decided was not for a girl like me (despite my budget suggesting otherwise), suddenly became my favourite place on the island – because Julian was staying in it. And, to my utter delight, over the next 48 hours it appeared the two of us might have been engaging in some old-fashioned stalking of each other. *'Oh, there you are in the courtyard reading a book in the sun. I was just coming out to do the same.'* I might have been the one with the book in the courtyard first but I'd been staring at the same page for an hour, hoping to be found.

One afternoon while scrubbing my dirty undies and other assorted travel attire, Julian arrived next to me, carrying a pile of his own sweat-stained items. 'Alright?' he asked, again, sidling up next to me at the trough. Quickly throwing my undies into my plastic carry bag, and trying not to blush, Julian and I began chatting, at which point he confessed he was in Greece for the summer on a 'boy's trip'. I knew what that meant. I wasn't stupid. Boy's trips involve a gross amount of drinking and a spike in the chance of catching chlamydia.

'It's a pity you work every night. It'd be nice to hang out,' he said shyly, his biceps bulging as he squeezed the water out of his now clean shorts. Trying not to sound too keen I confessed (some might say *lied*) that the job I'd just landed washing glasses at a busy tourist nightclub in town was giving me the following night off. With that Julian and I had our first hot date locked and loaded. And it was magical. Easily the most romantic night I'd ever had. One date turned into as many as we could fit in around our low paying, cash-in-hand, dodgy nightclub jobs. Fairly soon we both knew it was more than a holiday fling.

Julian and I fell in love just months after meeting and, as we did, I simultaneously become the most hated woman in Crete courtesy of Julian's best mate Guy. According to him, Julian wasn't in Crete to fall in love. He was supposed to be 'getting his end away' with Swedish tourists – then avoiding them the next day. Certainly not getting shacked up with – or spooning in a dorm – with a random Aussie chick and then taking her home to England, which was now our plan. Following a tattooed Englishman wasn't on my original schedule either. I was supposed to be doing the 'London thing' like all my school mates. Not the 'head down to a village near Swindon experience' – a place not even the English want to visit. But I was in love and all bets were off.

Julian and I did not cry on our last day in Crete. We did not spend hours farewelling all the people we'd grown to love in our four months on the island. We grabbed our bags, marched straight to the bus stop to

Heraklion and didn't look back. Julian, ever the gentleman, pretending not to strain under the weight of my backpack or the shame heaped on him as he farewelled the boys after changing his flight home, paused before tossing my bag into the boot of the bus. He whispered a little breathlessly, 'Thank fuck we're leaving this shit-hole, sweetheart!' Julian did not like strangers, tourists or Greek nightclub owners.

After a ferry ride from hell during which I spent six of the eight and half hours it took to get to Athens vomiting off the side of the boat, we arrived in Plaka. After aimlessly walking around for an hour or so we found a cute (but tiny) room with a perfect view of fifty per cent of the Acropolis. It would be our little love nest for an entire six days.

I adored everything about Julian – the way he smelt, his soft curly hair that went dry and golden on the ends, his voice, and his belief in us. I even loved his phobias – the way he'd hold his hands up and wiggle his fingers like he was about to play Beethoven's 'Moonlight Sonata' on the piano – which signified it was time to wash them or the world might end. I loved the way his lips were redder than mine, how he cared more about hair products than I did and that not once did he ever make me feel like I wasn't the most beautiful woman he'd ever seen.

Our first days of freedom together in Athens were incredible. We existed in a romantic bubble that made it easy to forget the outside world. I'd never imagined being in this kind of love. After a week, despite everything feeling like bliss, I sensed Julian was getting excited about returning home. He missed his parents, decent beer, watching his favourite soccer team and his expensive hair products. As for me, I could feel a sense of dread tugging at me about what the future might hold. No matter how hard I tried I kept falling into a funk, staring up at the ceiling and gnawing away at my thumbnail like a starving rodent. Images of awful stuff I might discover about Julian once we got back to his kept flashing through my mind. *Maybe there'll be a girl back there waiting for him?* I thought. Someone he's chosen to conveniently delete from his story. Back and forth I'd churn. *Was I just days away from ending up with egg all over my face once we arrived in his real life?*

When Julian said he was ducking out for an hour to buy a gift for his Mum I lay on our bed listening to an ugly, loud voice in my head urging me to grab my stuff and run. The voice was telling me to leave Julian a note saying, 'I'm so sorry Julian. I'm in love with you but I can't do this.'

The voice was drowning out the hopeful girl inside me, whispering like an evil sister. I tried to counter her. *No! Don't go you lunatic. You have to stay. Stay because you love him.* After an hour of staring at a pen and a small notepad on our bedside table, Julian walked through the door.

'I bought you something,' he said, beaming, as he handed me a small brown box.

It was a necklace I'd admired earlier that day in one of the street stalls we'd passed. It was silver with daisies with turquoise centres threaded through the chain. It was the prettiest necklace I'd ever seen.

'I wanted to buy you something that would always remind us of our first steps together,' he said, looking at the necklace now dangling from my hand.

'I love it so much,' I said, fighting back tears of guilt. All I could think of was my plan to leave, Julian returning to an empty room, gift in hand, only to find my note on the end of the bed. I felt queasy with shame knowing how close I'd gotten to breaking his beautiful heart.

I didn't find out any dirty dark secrets about Julian once we arrived in his home village of Highworth in Wiltshire. Nothing more than a mention of an ex-girlfriend from years ago who, thankfully, we didn't run into at any of the six pubs on the High Street. There had been, however, some bad press doing the rounds about me thanks to his still *cranky-as-hell* best friend Guy. I got used to people viewing me suspiciously.

I told myself, not so romantically, that Julian and I getting engaged after just six months was logical because we loved each other and it'd help our case once we went to Australia. By now we'd discussed applying for a de-facto visa so we could live there permanently. The idea I'd be engaged at twenty-two, given I'd spent the bulk of my life planning for divorce rather than a wedding, was almost unthinkable. But I loved

Julian with all my heart, so when he presented me with a £100 Princess Diana knock-off ring I said yes.

Secretly though I'm not sure 'yes' was really what a girl like me meant.

After a year living with Julian's parents and little brother Danny we decided to head to Australia. Julian needed to see my life back home so, in my mind anyway, we could be properly real (as if a ring wasn't enough). Mum was about ready to combust at the thought of me coming home with a cute English fiancé in tow. When she and my brother Myles picked us up from the airport Mum immediately started fussing over Julian as if he was heir to the throne. She genuinely adored him. He, however, appeared terrified of her, like a new kitten presented to an enthusiastic, cordial-fuelled three-year-old.

Everyone in my life loved Julian. Everyone except my dad. Not that he didn't love him eventually but it took a little longer. Dad loved to tell anyone who'd listen, 'I told Amber not to go overseas and fall in love with anyone short, with long hair, tattooed or English. And what did she do? She came back with the whole box and dice.'

To which I liked to reply, 'Dad, he's not short! Stop exaggerating.' My dad approving of Julian was not quite the same as perhaps other fathers approving of their daughter's new love interest. As far as I was concerned, as much as I utterly adored my dad, he was not in a position to judge on the merits of what comprises a suitable partner. He was, perhaps, the poster boy for what best to avoid. Except, if you wanted someone who could make you laugh. Or find you the best dim sims in town.

Not long after Julian and I arrived in Australia our relationship began to change. I seemed to bring out an insecure side in Julian, especially when he'd get drunk which, as the years went on, was more often. But we were still in love and I hoped it was a side-effect of dealing with too many adult decisions – stuff none of our friends were even close to considering. The kind of things I never imagined being the first to do.

We lived in Melbourne, Australia, for just over a year but with Julian constantly homesick and overwhelmed by the land of loud, super-friendly Aussies, we decided it would be easier if we moved back to England, to the land of pints, Premier League and bird-watching (yes, birds of the winged variety) with his friends. I figured I was tougher, so I'd suffer less.

One night after we'd arrived back to Julian's home, we ended up together on the floor of his bedroom, entwined as if something was coming to tear one of us away. At that moment, as we made love, I put it out to the universe that I wanted the two of us to create a life together. I wanted to be joined together for the rest of eternity. I wanted to have his baby.

About six weeks later and the morning after another big night at the village pubs with Julian's friends, I was more nauseous than I'd ever remembered feeling from a hangover. I naïvely didn't put two and two together until a week later when another wave of nausea knocked me over one morning. Only this time there'd been no half a dozen pints of cider or a pack of Embassy ciggies to blame it on.

We decided to take a pregnancy test later that day, both of us terrified at what might be the result. The test turned up positive. Our first thoughts were *Holy fucking shit, this is amazing! Look what our beautiful love has created together!* And then, like two petrified kids, the gears shifted into *Oh Jesus, what the hell are we going to do now?*

Julian was working full-time for a large insurance firm and I was working part-time near the High Street for a mad but strangely lovable artist who looked like he'd spent his youth getting shit-faced with Keith Richards. His rock and roll links, in reality, consisted of being famous in the village for screen-printing Vivienne Westwood T-shirts and regularly going berserk and smashing up his own studio.

My unconventional workday would finish around 3pm so, with Julian working, I'd be home hours before his return. And, just like in that room back in Athens, I had a lot of time to think. Thinking and pregnant was a match not made in heaven for a girl like me.

Two years into our relationship, with me now pregnant, Julian and I were still deeply in love but we'd been arguing a lot. I was homesick and what used to unite us – love and conquering the world together – was now pushing us apart. I'd begun openly questioning him about whether I should take my engagement ring off. I was uncomfortable with people mentioning it or wanting to congratulate us. We weren't as stable as we should have been given we were planning the rest of our lives together. And then it hit me. I was pregnant with our child and yet there was no way I could honestly say that Julian and I were going to last.

The dread was back only this time it had good reason to stay. I could feel a mistake looming dangerously close. Julian and I had jumped way too far ahead. I had no intention of leaving him but knowing a child was coming into the world and I couldn't guarantee she (strangely I never thought he) wouldn't be in danger of growing up without her Dad started to suffocate me. There was no oxygen, or light, to fight those fears.

In the hours I spent alone in Julian's bedroom waiting for him to come home I became frozen with a fear I couldn't shake. I was so disgusted with myself that I hadn't once considered this vital part of such a life-changing decision. It wasn't Julian's fault – I did this to us. Not once had I considered how cautious we should be in case we didn't make it to forever. It came at me like a tsunami – an all-encompassing panic – as it dawned on me I'd done the one thing I'd vowed my whole life not to do. But I'd never factored in falling in love and I'd been reckless and self-indulgent. Now all I could think was, *If Julian and I don't work out, I can't live with myself being the one who moved my child away from their father.*

The truth was I'd put out a request to the universe and it'd been delivered. But it had reignited wounds from my childhood. And so, with that most distorted, dysfunctional view of what was right, I made the most excruciating decision I've ever made. I came to the conclusion I had to tell Julian that I couldn't bring our child into the world. But there would be no note this time. I'd look at his face while I stabbed him through the heart. As I did, I watched the devastation take hold of the only man, other than my father, that I'd ever dared love. I was never right (in my head or my heart) after that trip to the clinic. It changed everything. Now, living back in Australia for the second time together, I began having panic attacks. They'd start with tiny pinpricks of pain in the lower right side of my stomach.

In the early days I'd try to ignore them and breath through the pain but I never treated them with enough importance. I'd just push through. Then the dizziness would start and I'd know I'd have all of a minute or so to get out of wherever I was, as happened one night when Julian and I were out at a packed pub in Melbourne with friends. I ignored the pain before we left the house but once the dizziness came, I was out of time. I navigated my way with the help of a friend out the front of the pub, hoping the fresh air would fix me. But I blacked out, crashing to the pavement. I came to as Julian was bundling me into the car. He wanted to take me to the hospital but I fought like hell. 'I just want to go home and rest,' I screamed.

When we got home I was sitting on the floor of our bedroom at Mum's house when I caught a glimpse of my hair, a teased looking mess on the side of my head. I patted the area down with my hand. It felt wet and strange. I touched the area with my finger, pulling it away to reveal blood. It wasn't a scrape; it was a gash. 'I think we better go to the hospital,' I said admitting defeat, concussion now kicking in. I ended up with six stitches that night and a bald patch that lasted three years. I had no idea what my panic attacks were trying to tell me. I just knew I felt vulnerable and scared about when they might strike again. A year later we were back in England living in an apartment above a haberdashery shop in the High Street of Highworth. Another decision brought about by Julian's dissatisfaction with living in Melbourne. My Dad called one day when Julian was across the road at the King & Queen getting pissed with his soccer mates. Dad told me Helen was dying of cancer. The news sent shockwaves through me and the last threads of Julian and I being a team fell apart. He responded by sticking his head in the sand, hoping time would heal everything. No matter how often I hinted things were bad, he just headed back across the road to drown himself in Stella Artois.

Imagining what Dad and Helen were facing together, knowing she was going to die and that Dad would be broken-hearted, was something I couldn't disconnect from. I was so far away, so hopelessly unable to help. Dad called one night to tell me he and Helen were cutting off from everyone for a week so they could come to grips with it all. I could barely think or speak to anyone about anything that week. That's when I started drinking heavily on my own.

I knew Julian and I had to end but I would not say goodbye. But I would go. I used Helen's illness as an excuse to tell Julian I had to leave. The idea of leaving Julian felt like another death for me. Because I knew if I left we'd never see each other again and I could not bring myself to say *goodbye*. 'I'm sorry, I have to go,' I finally said. 'I have to be with my dad.' I gutlessly avoided saying a proper goodbye and in doing so I robbed Julian, for the second time, of having a say in another loss thrust upon him. I never consciously factored in what I'd done to him when I was pregnant. When we were pregnant. I couldn't handle the enormity of what I'd done to our child, to Julian, to me. So, I blocked all thoughts and empathy for both of us. Consciously or unconsciously I had to push my baby chapter as far down as it could go. I had to keep running and never look back. That was the plan. I accepted that nothing good I'd ever done in the past, or anything good I'd do in the future, would ever stop me going to hell – a place promoted by a religion I'd never subscribed to but a place I feared nonetheless.

GOLD MEDALS & HOT PANTS

My first job post-Julian was at Mushroom Records in Melbourne in their sales and marketing department. I was over the moon when I'd landed that job. It allowed me to reinvent myself at a time when I thought my only hope of surviving my breakup was to shut the door on that part of my life and go, go, go. The new music industry me was birthed – and the old me laid to rest.

It was at times a completely surreal working environment with a constant stream of Aussie music legends I'd grown up knowing and loving (some of them, anyway), ambling about the building. I was just fourteen when I'd gone to see Brian Mannix from the Uncanny X-Men in concert. My friend Naomi and I had wiggled ourselves as close to the stage as we could get – a move we'd soon regret. Staring up at Brian we'd watched him move from one side of the stage to the next in this drunk crab-like motion while he vomited intermittently between singing *Everybody Wants to Work. No, no, not me*'. A roadie with a keen eye and motor skills frantically chased him across the stage trying to catch his bile in a plastic bucket.

Seeing Brian thirteen years later coming down those Mushroom Records stairs in my first week on the job, with him all spiky bleached hair and smudged eyeliner, it felt like no time had passed at all. I half expected that roadie and his bucket to appear.

It was a weirdly amusing, nostalgic and distracting new world I had landed in.

Six months after starting at Mushroom Records I became promotions manager, a role based in Sydney. I couldn't believe it. With the music industry on the cusp of a digital transformation jobs were evaporating and people who'd been in the industry for decades were getting the chop. The fact I got promoted was both flattering and little uncomfortable.

My new life became one long procession of gigs, driving bands all over town for media interviews then picking up their bar tabs at 4 am from venues like the Iguana Bar in Sydney's seediest suburb, Kings Cross. Bands and their entourages loved going there for all its charming grunginess and infamy. The Iguana Bar was the kind of place that understood how to cater to musicians needs. It wasn't uncommon for 'record company reps' to *rack up* hundreds of dollars on bar bills for

'French Champagne' – despite champagne being the thing least likely to be seen in the hands of its patrons.

But no matter what sort of post-show debauchery unfolded by night it was also my job to drag my sorry ass out of bed the next morning and collect (usually) trashed musicians at their hotels or hustle my media contacts into playing our music.

Little did anyone know, given the dollar value of the cargo I was transporting, I'd had my licence for less than a year and had never owned a car. With driving an essential element of my new job (and the thing I'd lied most about to my new boss), I was like a cat with nine lives when I really should have been sacked in the first three months. There were days I'd have to cancel media appointments after not being able to find my way through a sea of one-way streets. Artists like Shirley Manson from Garbage would ask me to pull over so she could get out of my car to walk herself into a rehearsal after tiring of me driving her around the outside of the largest entertainment venue in Sydney unable to find the gate. Mandawuy Yunupingu from Yothu Yindi, in Sydney from Arnhem Land, would have to point out I was driving the wrong way up a major city street.

But there was the odd occasion when I thought I did very well not to kill a multi-award-winning artist by Thelma and Louise-ing us off the Sydney Harbour Bridge. I'd expertly juggled another iconic Aussie, this one a wild rock legend who lived up to his name by smoking a joint in my car (windows up to keep out the rain), later racking up lines of coke on my street directory while giving me an animated rendition about having sex with a 'young lass' on the bridge. 'There it is! Right there,' he declared, pointing to a spot above our heads.

Amid the constant blur of my cool job there was no time left to contemplate how I felt about life, my health or my heart. I'd vowed to turn my back on love and propel myself at 100 kph into the music industry – the perfect place to heal a broken heart.

When my friend Mary called to say she was coming back from her overseas trip and was weighing up whether to settle in Melbourne or

Sydney I launched a ferocious PR campaign in Sydney's favour, 'Come with me, my little pretty.' I was like the witch in the Wizard of Oz and she was my Dorothy. I had first noticed her, the new girl Mary, while I was working as a receptionist at a marketing agency during another stretch back in Melbourne with Julian. I was stuffing envelopes with robotic precision when I saw her. I glanced up as Mary strode purposely across the far side of the office; a manila folder clutched to her breast.

The boss had announced we had a new girl but we'd yet to have an introduction. Initial impressions were that she walked with a sense of determination, she was pretty in a Linda Blair from *The Exorcist* kind of way (minus the demonic possession), wore designer framed glasses and was fashionable yet by my scale conservatively dressed. Physically she looked like she might do alright in a triathlon – her vibe like she might even enjoy it.

I came to know my new friend Mary for every reason that should have closed the door on us ever becoming friends. She wasn't in the boozy Friday-lunch agency gang like I was. And she wasn't one of the twenty-somethings smartasses who thought they knew a lot more about life than they did.

Several months after she'd started, I was tottering around the agency in the same strappy black sandals I'd taken backpacking, long black pencil skirt and a seventies style shirt that had a terrifying habit of bursting open at the wrong moment when I saw her looking a little down. I swung a hard left towards Mary's desk deciding to plop myself down next to her without invitation. I went straight in, 'Hi. Are you OK?' She wasn't. It turned out she'd just broken up with her boyfriend. Or they were taking a break. She wasn't sure. We continued chatting at her desk when I noticed the picture frame above her head move to the left. Or so I thought.

'Sorry to interrupt you,' I said, pointing above her, 'Am I going mad or did that frame right there just move?'

'I'm not sure, maybe?' she glanced up behind her, clearly not knowing what the hell I was on about.

'Did you feel something? Seriously, did we just have a bloody earthquake?'

Mary started laughing. 'I don't know?' Do *you* think so?' There was something about the way she laughed that suggested she was considering if there was something a little off-kilter about me.

It turned out I was right, about the earthquake anyway. The news channels confirmed that while we'd been bonding over our romantic predicaments the foundations below us had done a little 0.5 on the Richter scale. But there would be another event in the formative days of our friendship that would have a significant impact on Mary, and in a different way, on me.

A year or so later, and me freshly single, I was standing in front of the French doors in the sunroom at home looking out across the slightly overgrown grass in the backyard, when Mary called with some 'news'. She was calling to let me know her mother had died.

I had to sit down – like the world felt heavier and it was a little harder to breathe. I'd never known anyone's mum die. We were still so young – it just wasn't a thing. Mary described how they'd lost her Mum due to complications after a relatively standard heart procedure. Something terrible had happened – and then she was gone.

I struggled to find the right words. Losing a parent had always been my greatest fear, one I'd had since I was little. I'd lay in bed at night sobbing at the thought that one day I might lose Mum or Dad. And now it had happened to someone I knew and cared for. I suddenly felt like the most useless person in the entire universe that she could have shared her news with. She appeared to be handling it in a way that can only be described as stoic – a word I knew nothing about in my twenty-something world.

I was devastated for Mary but secretly I also felt trapped in my own selfish paralysis of fear, imagining losing my parents. And yet somehow our friendship continued to grow. In my mind the day I got that phone call was the real start of our friendship. It was the springboard to me wanting to become whatever she'd seen in me.

In August of 2000, three years after I left Julian, I turned thirty. The week before my birthday I remember staring at myself in the mirror, long and hard, and being shocked by what I saw. I looked old and exhausted. I may have been turning thirty but, in my mind, I could have been a woman at least a decade older. I don't think I'd stopped to acknowledge until that moment just how weighed down I'd become by lifestyle decisions and unprocessed emotions.

The month after my birthday celebrations, which ran across Melbourne and Sydney, the Olympics kicked off in the city I'd called home for the last three years – and oh my god was it fucking fabulous. Little did I know things would never be the same after that.

I'd taken a break from working for record companies that year. I knew enough to know it wasn't great for my health and I wasn't planning on following in the footsteps of my older female colleagues who I knew were paid a pittance despite their age and experience. So, I'd taken one foot out of the music industry, while keeping one in, and started Control Agent 99 my own freelance music PR business.

When the Olympics started, I'd been contracted to work for a friend whose biggest client at the time was Kylie Minogue. Australia's most loved pop princess was in the height of her gold hot pants fame and enjoying success from her seventh album Light Years. Not to mention she was scheduled to perform on a giant thong at the Olympics Closing Ceremony.

It was a truly magical time in Sydney and I made sure I was right in the thick of it all.

Had it not been for Mum, who is obsessed by all sporting competition (except darts), there was a chance the Olympics might have come and gone without me seeing a single sporting event. But Mum had been hot on the heels of the ballot-buying ticket process from the second they were released to the public. She and Myles were staying for the duration of the Games during which time we'd planned on meeting up at events Mum had secured tickets to.

I spent the first week of the Games juggling Kylie and other work commitments while nicking off to catch up with Mum and Myles at the beach volleyball in Bondi, then over to Olympic Park for the swimming. By night I was dolling myself up for laps of the News Limited Club. Hosted and paid for by the Murdoch's exclusively for the Olympics season anyone who was anyone was in that nightclub. There were more prawns, oysters and French champagne than any thirty-year-old on a shitty freelance music industry wage could get down their throats.

With so much going on it'd been almost a week since the Opening Ceremony, which by now was a long time for Mary and me not to have caught up. When she called one sunny morning as I was grabbing my hangover cure at McDonald's I demanded, 'So what's your goss?'

Curiously, she didn't jump in as quickly as our regular phone call beats but then she said, 'I went to a dinner last night, and … I think I met someone quite nice.' It was a decent hook.

Of course, stuff like this between girlfriends isn't unusual but I hadn't heard her speak like that before. There was something in the way she chose her words that felt different. Sure, we'd meet the occasional cute guy here and there – you don't live in Bondi and avoid meeting 'someone' – but a person of substance? That wasn't a given. Not by a long shot.

Just as I was about to demand 1000 details in under ten seconds she added, in a tone I initially took as sounding ominous, 'There's only one problem'. *OK, here we go,* I thought, *the dude's probably married, gay, the lead singer of a successful death metal band returning to Brazil that afternoon, or, all of the above.* This was Sydney after all.

'His name's Frederik, he's the Crown Prince of Denmark and he lives in Denmark – which is a long way away.'

Funnily enough, this had not been a category I'd expected Mr Quite Nice to land in. When Mary had mentioned she'd 'met someone nice' I was as delighted (and hopeful) as a friend should be. But now things sounded a little complicated. And I'd need more than a handful of seconds to work out exactly why. Searching for a response all I could come up with was, 'Oh.' I was buying time, hoping for something more enlightened to spring forth. But all that followed was a slightly lower tone, 'Oh.'

Another trademark genius reply. It wasn't like I wasn't happy but I also wasn't going to turn into a squealing idiot over what might be a double-edged, romantic sword. And I was not your fairy tale girl. But he'd taken her phone number, this Frederik guy, so now the ball was in his royal court.

WHERE THERE'S SMOKE

While my best friend was in the budding days of her new romance, back at my ranch things were also heating up – unfortunately not so much in my favour. My pot-smoking lawyer flat mate Kerry, who held the apartment lease and had the largest room, was heading off for the weekend and had offered me her room while she was away.

I was grateful for the chance to upgrade from my futon and my terribly chic bean bag. The bean bag was just in case I had a visitor – as I did once in the form of a famous six-foot-four Australian rock star. Known for his dangerous degree of sex appeal, the guy had followed me home for an extended drunken chat. The night ended with said star snoring for three hours on my beanbag. When I woke up to see his body hanging off every part of the beanbag I wondered if there was something wrong with me. Was this really what I was supposed to do with a ludicrously sexy singer in the privacy of my room? 'No, dickhead. It is not.'

But one-night stands require intimacy – physically and mentally – and I wasn't wired for any of that (not unless I was so drunk I'd be unlikely to remember it the following day). I'd done intimacy with Julian, but that was then and this was a different now.

It was nice to have a little more space as Kerry headed out the door. I was already getting ready for a party on a large yacht heading around Sydney Harbour to celebrate one of the hottest new music shows in Australia. Guests included a bunch of media, musicians and music industry types (like me) going along for the free booze.

With another warm, spring, mid-Olympics evening unfolding I had a nasty feeling I was going to turn up to the semi-finals of the swimming, to meet my mum, Myles and a friend from Melbourne, with a whopping hangover. If there was one thing I did know about myself it was that fearing a night might escalate meant it *was* categorically going to escalate – with varying degrees of catastrophe ensuing.

As I fell through my door around 4 am my last morsel of a brain cell was telling me, *4 am? That's pretty good. I should be OK by the time I have to get up at 11 am. I won't let the family down too much after all.* I fell on to Kerry's bed feeling sloshed and smug.

The next minute it's 11 am and the sun was blasting into my skull thanks to the blinds being up. I looked down at myself through my clumped mascara crusted eyes and discovered I was still wearing the black-leather skirt and short sleeve black bodysuit I'd worn the night before, while my bag had vomited its contents all over the floor.

Now, not recalling what time I'd come in at nor what quantities I'd drunk, I was lucky I'd even woken up as I hadn't even set my alarm clock. Somehow I had woken at precisely 11 am. I got up and moved slowly towards the door, destination bathroom, for a shower. My eyes were still squinting at the unbearable force of light – Mother Nature's slap for being a naughty girl. I opened the door. Something wasn't right. The hallway was black.

Maybe I'm not awake I thought to myself, stepping slowly into the mysterious darkness. I turned to the left towards the loungeroom. It too was black but not black like the blinds were still drawn. It was nightmare black. Now increasingly convinced I wasn't awake I looked around the room. The large mirror above the fireplace, the ornaments on side tables next to the couch, were all black. The windows out to the balcony – everything black. Then I noticed further down the hall a tiny break in the darkness – a red light that appeared to be moving slowly – dancing from side to side. I moved closer and it dawned on me what it was – flame.

I figured, 'I'll go to the kitchen and get some water to throw on the fire.' I walked down the hall that led to the front door and turned right into the kitchen. The kitchen looked more normal. The nightmare blackness hadn't turned the corner. I grabbed the plastic kettle and filled it with water. I headed back down the black hall towards the loungeroom and back into the blackness. I stood away from the on-fire stereo but close enough to fling water on it. It fizzled a bit before the little dance of flame disappeared. Then I noticed what appeared to be a slither of natural light lining the crack of the bathroom door. The mirror! I need to see how I look. Maybe it will give me a clue to whether I'm awake, I thought to myself. I marched straight towards the mirror. There was no blackness in the bathroom except a film of grey across the mirror itself. I wiped my hand across it, clearing a small space so I could get a glimpse of my face. I barely recognised what was staring back at me. The whites of my eyes were blood red, the green of my pupils as bright as emeralds. The black that was covering everything else was also covering my skin like paint.

I panicked as I looked down at my neck and arms. They were so black I could barely tell where my clothing started. As I took in my bizarre, horrifying self I heard a loud bang from the loungeroom. I turned back. I could see flames. Not small and dancing but tall and clapping, getting louder, like gunshots. With delirium and fear kicking in I decided to try a final test. I would make a phone call to the outside world. I would tell someone what was happening. I decided to call Mary. With hands shaking, I dialled her number. 'Hello?' she answered brightly.

'Hey, it's me. I think my house might be on fire!' I said. She didn't understand what I was on about. Was this the intro to a joke? With a witty punch line on its way? I gave a stuttering recap of what I'd done. 'I made sure the water separated from me and the jug before it landed though,' I assured her.

'You threw water on an electrical fire?' she said in disbelief.

'I guess so,' I responded, brain cells and logic starting to wake up.

'Have you called the fire brigade?' she asked.

'Not yet. I thought I'd call you first.'

'Oh my god, get off the phone. Get out of the apartment and then call the fire brigade,' she said, scolding me like an angry Mum. I agreed and hung up. I rang triple zero, suddenly tripping over my words, realising just how much time I'd lost playing David Lynch in my head with an actual emergency unfolding. The operator told me to get out of the apartment, warn my neighbours and then wait outside for the fire brigade.

Then an image of my Manda Panda teddy bear, given to me by my dad on my first birthday, flashed before my eyes. She was in my bedroom. I raced down the hall as the flames built in intensity. I jumped on the couch, ran across it to my room and threw myself at my closet. I yanked Manda by the paw and raced out. Within seconds the flames flared more furiously. Now I'd have to run along the other side of the couch to get out. With my furry acrylic partner in crime now safe I remembered there was an old woman living in the apartment across the landing. I knocked on her door first. Then the other three on our level. Two tenants came out looking confused. I started to cry, panicking the fire would start travelling towards the door and we'd not yet had a response from the old lady in the apartment across from mine.

'We can't leave if we don't know if she's in there or not,' I said, forgetting they were communicating with a girl completely covered in black ash and holding a black bear with dirty white paws.

The sirens of the fire brigade were coming down the road. Thank god I thought to myself as I began running downstairs and out the front as six firemen were getting out of their truck. Now screaming, I urged them to check on the old lady. As I sat down on the brick fence out the front of my house, my teddy bear lying next to me, I wondered how I was going to explain all this to my mother, who was waiting for me at the swimming. I looked down at my phone, wondering what to do. I decided to text my friend who was with Mum and Myles. I wrote, 'I'm sorry, can you tell Mum I'm not going to make it. Don't tell her but I've been in a fire. I'll call you from the hospital. Don't freak her out.'

I have no idea how I expected my friend to deliver news that involved the words 'fire' and 'hospital' and not freak her out but I do know people around me were getting used to the unpredictable, increasingly dark landscape of my life. I didn't care about myself enough to try to figure out why everything was so chaotic or why I was so self-destructive but what I did know, which only added to my self-loathing, was I couldn't bear the feeling that people who loved me were worried about me. I didn't want to be the girl who people pitied or looked down on but my actions were giving everyone around me ammunition in which to do all of the above. There was no denying it any more – I was a fucking *hot* mess.

CHAPTER THREE.

GOODBYE MY FRIEND

Things between Mary and her new Danish man progressed slowly yet steadily over the next twelve months. The long-distance courtship continued, with Frederik making trips back to Australia to spend time with her. There was no reference point for me to get my head around how life might look like if Mary and Frederik went the distance. Well, there was, but I found it too scary to think about. All I had was my intuition that he, a man from a very different world, appeared sincere and that their connection was growing at a natural pace.

A year or so later Mary decided to leave for Paris. It made perfect sense. She and Frederik needed more time to be in each other's company. With the media in Australia on high alert it was no longer feasible to meet in Sydney. Nor was it in Copenhagen. Paris was the perfect (and romantic) stepping stone.

I felt selfish being down about her going but I hated the idea of her being so far away. I didn't want to lose the light Mary brought to my life, the comfort and security of our friendship. I worried about being left alone in Sydney, knowing how self-destructive I was. How it might affect my mental state. I wasn't good at being kind to myself, as people would constantly remind me.

My heart grew heavier as the day of Mary's departure approached. I was dreading our last 24 hours together but they were creeping towards us regardless. We promised to spend as much time as we could together before she left but as I sat on her bed watching her pack I wanted to cry like an angry child. I wanted to scream, 'I don't want you to go. I am not going to be OK.'

I didn't realise it then but it was the first stage of my grief in losing her.

While laying on Mary's bed watching her pack, I pretended to throw a tantrum, tossing one of her folded tops on the floor. I made out like I was laughing but the tears running down my face were a giveaway.

'You're not allowed to go, you silly thing. You're not. *Do you hear me?* I will not have it,' I spat. Mary smiled sweetly, tenderly, like a mother being gentle with her child. She knew I meant it – it was my way of saying I was struggling. And I was. I truly was. The night before Mary flew out, we organised farewell drinks at one of her favourite pubs in Woollahra – a small gathering of her closest friends. The two of us made a pact to leave together so we could say goodbye privately. I'm not going to lie, I bloody hated that party, but I did my best to put on a brave face. The truth was I was happy she'd found love, she deserved it, but once the media got hold of the story – 'The Australian girl dating a European prince' – it just confused what was already difficult enough. 'For Christ's sake, my best friend is moving away. How about you all piss off'?

At the end of the night we made our excuses and headed off. There was lots of hugging and well wishes, with a few friends promising to look after me (the child), while she was gone. I felt dumb and sulky standing among everyone clinking Coronas and chardonnays, bidding final farewells, while Jamiroquai's 'Space Cowboy' played way too loudly. Heading towards Oxford Street, it felt somehow surreal. And unbelievably sad. With Mary plastered all over magazines in Australia and Denmark, awareness of her relationship with Frederik was at an all-time high so she'd decided it was best she go to the airport the next day alone. I didn't like thinking of her doing something so big alone but she was the grown-up and she didn't need to be photographed saying goodbye to her best friend, who was very likely to be clinging to the leg of her jeans, sobbing with snot and mascara streaked across her face, yelling, 'Don't leeeeavvvvvvve me!!!!!!!!!!!'

We stopped at the cab rank and put our handbags down. It was time. I didn't want to rush our last moments but there was also nothing left to say except the word I did not want to say. Through tears in our eyes and a lump in my throat that felt like a tumour I shook my head in protest, 'I'm not saying it. I don't have to. I'll talk to you at the airport, OK?' I'd found a loophole. I held tight in that last curb-side hug. I felt such deep loss but also such gratitude that we'd shared such a beautiful chapter in our lives. And then I broke our stare, jumped in a cab and drove away. I felt crushed and alone in a city that didn't fit me anymore.

There were still so many hurdles for Mary and the fear of the unknown ahead. So much that required my friend to be brave but I knew her tears, for now, were simply for us. This odd-couple friendship, unique, unexpected, and yet somehow, I believe, divinely intended. For me my tears that night were because I felt like I was losing her forever. I knew from that night on we'd never live in the same country again – that all the things I treasured about us, listening to Powderfinger, Alex Lloyd and Grinspoon, being silly and free, with nothing to do but sit and ponder life and its mysterious what-ifs, were over.

So, here's the thing: I was right. They did go the distance. Mary married Frederik in a beautiful, big Danish royal wedding on May 14, 2004, at Vor Frue Kirke, the Copenhagen Cathedral. And I, along with her sisters Patricia and Jane, were standing right there alongside her on the day as her bridesmaids. As I looked around The Royal Danish Theatre from my velvet-covered seat the evening before Mary's wedding day I found if I squinted my eyes, I could imagine being transported back 200 years ago. I'd never seen such a sight, with the stage lit up for the performances there were literally hundreds of tiny sparkling beams of light bouncing off the multitude of diamond tiaras, many worn by the queens and princesses of the other royal houses of Europe – and all worn by queens and princesses throughout history. Call me biased but the most beautiful girl in the room that night, by far, was Mary. Like a porcelain doll come to life she wore a brilliant rose-red, long, silk dress, and the spectacular diamond and ruby parure that had its debut at Napoleon's coronation.

I woke up on the morning of Mary's wedding, utterly cross-eyed with exhaustion. 'Oh my god, thank god, it's here!' I thought, remembering it was about 3 am before I took the last of fifty or so bobby pins out of my hair. A swirling sea of faces and glittering events had led us to this day. There had been many surreal moments during the two weeks since I'd arrived in Copenhagen, many thanks to the creativity and thoughtfulness of my best friend's future mother-in-law – Her Majesty the Queen of Denmark. Amongst all the pomp and ceremony, royal traditions and protocol, Frederik's mother chose to put me in a bedroom across the hall from the bride. On the morning of the wedding, around 9 am, as I woke up looking like something the cat had dragged in (to the Queen's castle without getting caught by the guards), I decided to go and see how Mary was feeling on the biggest morning of her life – a day tens of millions of people around the world had been anticipating and would be watching.

I opened my door and darted my head left and right – no one was coming. I was always terrified of bumping into someone official, no more so than the Queen (despite her kindness). I was a clumsy curtseyer and couldn't bear her having to fear I was about to nosedive at her feet. I stepped across the hallway to Mary's door and put my ear to her door to see if she had company. I heard nothing, so I knocked. 'Come in,' a voice replied. I found Mary sitting alone drinking tea. Everything was so calm – as though it were any other morning. 'Hi,' I said as I a plonked myself in the chair opposite her. 'So,' I said, trying to dial back my smirk, 'What are you up to today? Got much on?' We both laughed.

Thankful for a little lightness in the small window of time before we'd need to let all that go. I shook my head, pulling a stupid, perplexed face, and said, 'How the hell did you get us into this?'

Within a few hours I was standing on the red carpet outside the cathedral next to Mary's sisters, Jane and Patricia. The rapid-fire inner dialogue fuelled by my every insecurity, and heart-pounding emotion, began rolling like a cassette tape destined to tangle and break. *Oh my god, nobody told me they'd be just there. Like, just there. I knew there'd be photographers but there must be 200 of them. It's like a wall of lenses, so close I reckon I could chuck a drink on them. Christ, I wish I had a drink now. Wow. Everyone's so happy. Happy to have her. Mind you, so they should be. She's lovely. They could do a lot bloody worse. All that cheering in the royal square this morning – it's like they were welcoming us all. This motley crew of Aussies.*

Oh, please. How delusional. Welcoming, 'us'? Are you right? You're not her sister. You're not family. You're the one she had to have because you'd have been so broken if she didn't. She could probably smell your fear from Copenhagen to Bondi. Careful ... relax your face. I bet I look really hard. Why do I feel so sad? God, only you would be standing here being all miserable and stupid. I wonder if there's something wrong with me. Why do I always feel sad at the wrong times? Maybe I am mentally ill?

Shit. This is it! They're going berserk. OK, she's coming. Don't cry. Don't cry. Don't over-do the serious face. Stay in the moment. Remember what's real. At the end of the day, she's just getting married. It's OK. You'll be OK. It's just another goodbye.'

WRONG WAY, GO BACK

I couldn't have been in a more challenging work environment when Mary first hit the headlines. Nor could I have had a more awkward one to come back to after being in their televised royal wedding. I went back to my job at one of the country's highest-selling women's magazines but, perhaps unsurprisingly, everything had changed. The fascination with my friend, and by default me, had made things very difficult. I was no longer just staff. I was a person of interest. A person with access to a much bigger person of interest. I'd walk into the office and twelve people sitting in an editorial meeting would fall quiet. Despite an agreement with my boss that my role wouldn't include any questions about my friend, my workplace had become tense.

Mondays were the worst. That was the day I'd get to see what our magazine had in the next issue. Most weeks there'd be a cover with a photo of my friend, taunting me with headlines I knew had no truth to them. The editor was under major pressure from above to churn out a Mary story for the sake of having her there. They used quotes from their 'inside source' – which implied it might be me. I no longer felt I was paid for the worth I once had as an employee. I suspected my real value lay more in just having me there – a pawn in the magazine games checkmating the competition.

Discussions had been going on for some time about me doing something other than my marketing role. When the idea of me writing a column was floated, I was conflicted. *Would I have gotten the column without the royal connection?*

I knew they were exploring a promotion for me from teen titles upstairs to the company's flagship title but now I wasn't sure about anything. *Did you earn this? Be honest. Did you earn this?* I didn't know. Or maybe I did and didn't want to know.

When I eventually agreed to it, with the promise I'd be covering entertainment, events, celebrity interviews and no nasty gossip, the first column was published with a headline above my smiling head that read 'OUR OWN GOSSIP PRINCESS'. I was mortified. The photo made me look smug and now half a million printed copies were making their way around the country. It was precisely the sort of image I wanted to avoid. *How could they?* How could they not.

That was just the beginning of the power games. I decided, rather than retreating from my new role, I'd try to make it work for me. Soon I was travelling around the country attending A-list events, doing photoshoots and 'coffee catch-ups' with a parade of celebrities who I'd had to assure I wasn't like the other people at my magazine; that I was safe. I even ended up in New York hanging out with Chris Noth, AKA Mr Big from Sex and the City. While the connections were mine, I used the magazine to turn it into work. I might have felt temporarily in control, successfully wrestling back the reins of my career but I was playing in the big league for one of Australia's biggest media empires.

Meanwhile, I couldn't have known that my face popping up in print and on TV would put me on the radar of a romantic stranger, who would profoundly change my life. My knight didn't come into my life riding a white stallion. Mine roared in on a black Harley.

Leo predictions for 2006: Close relationships, including marriage (or long-term) partnerships as well as business partnerships, can be tricky this year. Although Neptune has passed its opposition to your Sun it remains in your solar seventh, casting a bit of a veil over your relationships. Your partners may seem elusive, which can be frustrating. Chiron is opposing your Sun (or Ascendant) as well, suggesting that someone important in your life is causing you some emotional pain or confusion.

My stars weren't exactly suggesting I was going to be falling in love with a handsome stranger who'd fly me to Venice, lay me on a Gondola in the moonlight and hum the soundtrack to Ghost in my ear. The reference to 'casting a bit of a veil' should have been replaced with 'talking lots of bullshit' and 'emotional pain and confusion' swapped for 'you'll find out more when you read the Sunday papers'. With the constant celebration of my friend the subject of love swirled around me 24/7. I couldn't escape it. If I didn't talk about it, I looked elitist. If I did talk about it, I was 'riding on her coat tails'. I couldn't win. And all the while I was grieving. I felt left behind. A bit-part player on the love stage. The bridesmaid. Nothing more. I wasn't looking for a royal prince. I just wanted to have my own story. My own fairy tale. The thing I'd never believed in. I wanted someone who saw me. Really. Saw. Me.

Someone did see me. He spotted me from across a room – although I would eventually find out he'd seen me well before that night. Before I knew it, he was right beside me, cheekily flinging his jacket into my lap before flashing a knowing smile. The perfect specimen of the sort of man I'd grown up vowing ferociously never to let into my life. I found out later it wasn't the glimmer of my gold cardigan across the room that caught my future boyfriend's eye that night. He'd been given the old 'the royal bridesmaid in the house' tip-off courtesy of a guy who worked for him, who was previously the editor of a music magazine and one of my regular media calls when I first moved to Sydney.

Some women, healthy women, might have grabbed the stranger's jacket off their lap and hurled it across the room, I, however, found something intriguing about this stranger's brazen approach. It was so bad it seemed funny. And let's face it, emotionally, I was out of steam.

'Are you right there?' I reacted, feigning suspicion.

'I'm hoping it weighs you down so you can't get up and leave. It's quite a heavy wool weave so it should do the job,' he laughed. Annoyingly, I laughed as well. More annoyingly, I allowed the conversation to continue. After an hour or so my new friend James turned serious, whispering he needed to talk 'in private'. I wondered if this was his way of putting the hard word on me. If it was, I could shut that down pretty quick. I followed him to a table in the far back corner of the bar. Sitting opposite each other James began what he called his 'confession'. Tilting his head down, emphasising the importance of the moment, he stared intensely into my eyes.

'I need you to listen to me carefully because what I want to tell you is my truth. I want to tell you my truth right now, right here,' he said, 'because I know you and I are going to see each other in the future. Near future.'

His *truth* was he had a wife and two children – a six-month-old girl and a boy who was two. He appeared sad but resigned to the fact that he and his wife were going through 'an amicable split,' as he described it. Apparently, they'd broken up after their first child but a one step forward, two steps back situation ensued, leading to a second child. As I listened, I tried to tune to his truth. What was real? I'd never been involved with a married man. And, beyond a drunk idiot at a bar, I'd never even been hit on by one. It was the precise situation I'd feared my whole life, scarred by my parents' marital mess, the thing that took my dad away. And yet now, in a set-up I hadn't contemplated, I was on the other side. I was naively heading into *other woman* territory. Less than a handful of years earlier and I would have been repulsed by this guy and his story. Even just the fact he'd taken me into a private corner to confess his lack of appropriate availability. But I'd gone with him. The old me would never have gone to a corner with a guy like him without asking 'why the fuck do we need a corner? But where have my black and white beliefs got me in life?' All I knew at this point was my beliefs about love, people and all the chapters in between had brought only pain – or nothing. I had a new voice directing me now. It was reminding me that everything I'd done until then hadn't led me to joy so maybe new rules were in order? Like going into corners with strangers. To listen to their 'truth'.

The next morning at work a massive bunch of pink lilies arrived for me. My curious colleagues gathered around my desk desperate to know who'd sent them. I was coy, of course. I knew not to share too much in a room full of perfumed sharks. Precisely an hour later more flowers came. This time white orchids, pale pink roses, hydrangea and peonies. Flowers had always felt like such an exciting romantic gesture but something about that day felt strange. And I wasn't sure if I should view it as the work of a hopeless romantic or someone with an agenda. All I knew for sure was it was bringing me a lot of attention in an environment where I didn't want it. The day ended with seven bunches of flowers adorning my desk and the floor. James had ordered a bunch to arrive every hour on the hour.

James's story about the 'amicable' break up with his wife, and the assurance it was under way before we'd met, appeared to come true in a matter of weeks, so I could tell myself it had nothing to do with me.

'Why can't divorce with children be like this?' I asked myself. 'Maybe not everyone needs to get so tortured?'

The gift James bought me in the first week of our meeting was the first sign I felt uneasy about. And yet I didn't slam on the brakes. It was a stunning silver beaded bracelet from one of Sydney's top jewellers. I wore it for one day before I saw it literally explode off my wrist. It didn't drop off my arm – the pieces flew from one end of the room to the next – poltergeist-like. Ego bruised, James replaced it immediately. A week later it did exactly the same thing.

Two months later, as his promises about 'us' escalated, on a warm summer's night with candles twinkling around his pool and a tear glistening in his eye, he handed me a black velvet box.

'This is a symbol of my commitment,' he said, proudly. It was a diamond-and-sapphire ring.

The next week we arrived at one of his favourite restaurants. For some reason, I immediately looked down at my ring. The sapphire was missing. James began freaking out, insisting we backtrack to find it. Then I saw it resting against the chair leg of the table next to us. 'There it is!' I said, scooping it up. My first thought was, *This is another bad sign – a very bad sign.* And then I overrode it, saying to myself, *Or maybe we're just a little off track? We've been fighting about 'his truth' lately. But maybe now things are going to be OK. Maybe that's what the sign means?*

Shortly afterwards James began pushing to meet my mum. Yet again his urgency concerned me. I'd barely had time to think before we were rushing into the next phase of the relationship. I wasn't sold but there was something about his schoolboy excitement I didn't want to crush. He was excited about me and that had a powerful allure. Finally, after three months, I relented, agreeing to a trip to Melbourne to introduce him. Pulling in to the airport, we got out and left the car at the valet. Travelling light, we went straight to security. As I loaded my bags on to the conveyer belt, I noticed two photographers nearby pointing their lenses at us. It was the kind of thing you'd expect for Nicole Kidman and Keith Urban but not us. Not me. Definitely not him. I knew I needed to get away so I grabbed my bags and headed to another line, away from James. I then spotted two more photographers staring straight at me and waiting to pounce at the gates ahead. They were on to a big story – I'd seen it plenty of times in the company of Mary. Now it was me and what I was doing. Travelling with a married man looked bad. Really bad.

James was coming closer, bags in hand.

'Move away from me,' I whispered, bluntly, agitated. 'I'll see you on the plane.'

What the fuck is going on? How did they know we were here at precisely this moment? Are they here for me? They can't be. So why does it feel like they are? I was freaking out. I couldn't understand how I could be having such suspicious thoughts. It wasn't normal to be wondering whether your boyfriend, a guy who's insisted on meeting your mother, might be behind this. Now, with a plane ride ahead, I almost felt like I was having an out-of-body experience and I considered, *Who is this man I am about to introduce to my mother?*

James and I boarded separately. I got on the plane first and sat by the window. I was on high alert. James sat down next to me minutes later. The first thing I noticed was he was jittery. 'What the fuck just happened?' he said. I turned my head as directly towards him as I could, widening my eyes just a little, and then stared at him as intently as he'd done to me on the night we'd met, 'I don't know, James, what did happen back there?'

I refused to blink or look away until he'd answered. He began stuttering and stammering, apparently horrified I might be insinuating he knew something about why they were there. I turned my head away towards the window. I wanted him to think I was ignoring him, taking time out to think. I wasn't. I was playing him – watching his reflection secretly – his every move, his every nervous twitch. I wanted to see him squirm in my silence. A sarcastic voice reprimanded me in my head: *Huh, well, look at you! Off to introduce your mum to your wonderful new man!*

James and I didn't speak the rest of the way to Melbourne. We agreed to get off the plane separately in case there were more photographers at the other end. I turned on my phone as I stepped off the plane. It beeped with a voice message. It was from the Picture Editor at my work ringing to tell me she'd just spoken to the most notorious paparazzi photographer in Australia, 'He has photos of you with your new boyfriend. I need to talk to you about him. I'm not supposed to tell you but your boyfriend tipped the guy off. You need to get away from him. Call me, babe.'

I find it hard to describe how I felt at that moment, standing outside the airport, alone, sneaking a phone call before my boyfriend caught me – receiving a warning by someone whose job it is to buy photos that destroy people's lives. And here I am, hearing my boyfriend, the purchaser of my sapphire and diamond 'commitment ring', may be everything I feared he might be. I'd ignored the warning signs. I knew James was obsessed with the media spotlight. I'd smelt it on a million occasions. It repulsed me about him and yet I had pressed on with us. I told myself I was being a bitch. And yet what the hell had I done to myself? How could I have made this guy more important than me?

As I waited for James to come out of the airport, where thankfully no photographers were waiting, I called my colleague back. She answered quickly. I told her I only had a minute to talk. She reinforced her message that, in no uncertain terms, I was sleeping with the enemy. My head was swirling. How could I have let this happen? James and I barely spoke a word as we drove to Donovan's in St Kilda, my favourite restaurant and my go-to-place for only the most special of occasions. A place now ruined by the memory of this night. Mum was waiting for us at a table. She leapt up, waving excitedly as we walked in. She was so happy to be meeting my new boyfriend. I felt so sad for her but I needed to put on a smile that would buy me time before the awkward moment of presenting James. Just as he'd done on the night we'd met, James went hurtling towards her, grabbing her in his arms like a dear friend. Seeing her in his arms made me shudder.

Mum instantly picked up on my vibe. 'Is everything OK?' she asked.

James leapt in with his version of events. 'You believe him, don't you Amber?' she asked. She thought I was too hard on people, especially boyfriends. James had a willing ally in Mum.

'I don't know, Mum. It all felt just a little strange,' I said, looking over at James, making it clear I wasn't ready to just keep up appearances. I stayed frosty while she and James tried to make dinner as pleasant as they could. Desperate to win me over he slowly picked away at my resistance. My weak side started questioning: *Maybe you're a bitch? Maybe you're too distrustful?* By the end of dinner, I wasn't good and I wasn't better but I had softened. That was my biggest mistake.

It's horrifying to me now that I didn't see how my values and my intuition were being tested. It wasn't that I accepted James's story. I'd never bought it from the start but I chose to move through it, hit pause, while I investigated further. I'd berate him one moment then calmly challenge him the next. I put myself in his ex's path to gauge a reaction that might confirm my suspicions. I wanted to hear her say, 'Thanks for breaking up my family, you fucking bitch'. But she didn't. So, I didn't go. And that's on me, not on her.

By staying with James I'd made a dog's fucking dinner of my so-called life test. My angels, my intuition, call it what you will, had been throwing me signs from the start and all had said 'GET OUT NOW'. But something kept me in and it sure as hell wasn't love. I know now it was fear. But that was the problem – I didn't know that my love story, my belief about love, included fear. It had nothing to do with James – he just happened to be my perfect, toxic match.

James insisted on giving me a vintage Mercedes to drive for a while. It was a convertible and the most beautiful car I'd ever seen, although I was terrified to drive it, self-conscious about being seen cruising around town in it. Vintage or not, I wasn't a convertible kind of girl. At his insistence, and to sate my curiosity, I took it out one sunny Saturday with a friend. The following weekend James took me to Noosa for the weekend. Lying by the hotel pool I was enjoying the afterglow of a romantic evening during which my boyfriend of nearly six months had spent the night encouraging me to leave my job. He knew I couldn't trust the environment any more and begged me to trust him enough to look after me so I could give myself three months off to pursue a writing course. Begrudgingly, I relented, agreeing to trust him. He was so excited that he wrote on the back of the restaurant card, 'Today Amber Petty agreed to let James take care of her so she can pursue her dream.'

Then he dated it, signed it and handed it to me, kissing me on the cheek with another tear in his eye. 'I want you to remember this day forever, babe,' he said beaming. It was in many ways the most vulnerable I'd ever been. Agreeing to someone financially supporting me, even for three months, was way, way out of my comfort zone.

The next day, while we lay by the pool, James started trawling the Sydney Sunday papers – something I'd always found particularly off. I hated the way their toxic gossip columnists held so much power over my self-esteem. I wondered why, on this day of sunshine when we were so disconnected from all the bullshit back home and after the formal love contract of the night before, why the fuck my boyfriend was so eager to dive into its filthy pages?

'Can I have a look?' I said to him, annoyed.

My hackles rose as I felt him hesitate so I snatched the paper out of his hand. And there it was, my fucking face with a story about me driving around in a car allegedly given to his wife on the birth of their first child. According to the papers, and now everyone reading them, I had been brazenly driving around in another woman's push-present. It was about the worst story I could imagine reading about myself. Or anyone else. I wasn't heartbroken, angry or terrified, nor did I feel sick. I felt completely numb. There'd been so many warning bells in the leadup to this and yet I was still there. That was the most horrifying thing of all.

The effect of my relationship with James, what it did to me publicly, professionally and personally, was devastating. One of the things that cut me the most was how hard he'd tried to bond with my dad on a family holiday he'd insisted on joining. Crying over cocktails,

James had had the gall to ask for my hand in marriage.

In one of my last conversations with James as he lay spread-eagled on his couch before I moved out of the house, he'd begged me to move into in the final month of our toxic union – while I raced around collecting my things – I called him out on behaving like something out of The Sopranos. Without missing a beat, he stared at me expressionless and said 'Yep! Series 3. Episode 5.' Or something 'cute' like that.

I'M A SURVIVOR

After I split with James, I spent a lot of time eating tuna pasta, watching *The Hills* and getting really stoned while living on my friend Kate's couch in Paddington. Then the universe threw me a completely unexpected curveball – a lifeline that came with a few bamboo strings attached.

Despite my lack of profile, I was offered a role as a contestant on the 'celebrity' version of the Mark Burnett-produced TV show *Survivor*. Contestants on this first – and last – *Australian Celebrity Survivor* consisted of a menagerie of well-known, reasonably known, and known-for-a-handful-of-minutes types, with the latter including me.

I was well aware my involvement in the show would bring haters, but I had my reasons. Secretly, I needed to find my inner hero. And, let's be honest I was also broke – even after pawning my sapphire 'promise ring' which, fetched less than ten per cent of the value James had implied it was worth. It wasn't an easy decision to get on that plane to Vanuatu, regardless of the cash and hero stuff. Other things were keeping me awake at night – namely the severe paranoia and fear of being on national TV without makeup.

The show's producers told us we were allowed to take just one item to the island. There were a few things this item shouldn't be – a gun, your boyfriend, a hand grenade, a gram of cocaine etc. Other than that, we could use our imaginations. This led to me joining my dots of paranoia – what should I bring that might save me? I decided on ... mascara.

Arriving at the airport on the first day I soon realised my decision might need justification as I discovered the other contestants had brought the likes of a Swiss Army Knife, a bed sheet, a torch and other choices slightly more useful to the overall group.

My next greatest fear was playing the game. Specifically, how often we'd be under water, rummaging for clues, while chained to various things and trying not to drown. I learnt on the job. After dragging myself to the water's edge, somehow still breathing, the next challenge was how not to emerge looking like a sea monster. I hadn't factored this in when I chose mascara, which became painfully clear when I rose from the water looking like an octopus clinging to my face like an old friend's embrace.

But there was another surprise awaiting me on the island. Later I'd find the producers had been cryptically warning us about this all along, telling us we should wear sneakers at all times. The concept of wearing sneakers on what I presumed was going to be a super sunny, hot island, grossed me out. The mere thought screamed *tinea!* I found out what the producers were saying (far too subtly in my opinion) was *There will be snakes!* Four words that would have guaranteed I slept in sneakers for the rest of my life. Out of the twelve contestants and 300 production crew there were only two snake incidents. Both happened to me. The first snake I met while I was standing on a rock. Halfway through the ten-day shoot I was wandering along the rocks at the sea edge, my bare feet in the water, waiting for one of the male contestants to yell 'fish' as he waded out to sea with his makeshift spear. I was wrapped in my bright blue, yellow and black official Survivor top, perched on a rock looking out towards the horizon, feeling like Ginger on Gilligan's Island, when something caught my eye. That something happened to be a tiny, deeply irate, sea snake swimming past me. It was the exact colours of the Survivor show logo. I dared not move. I knew enough about bright things in the wild to know if they chomped on you the outcome wouldn't be bright. Thankfully, after a second or two, it wiggled off. Then it stopped.

'Holy shit, keep moving mate, there's nothing to see here,' I screamed silently. Unfortunately for me, it didn't hear my telepathy. The sadistic bastard chucked a U-turn and came back. Now my little mate had launched half its body out of the water and was seemingly trying to eyeball me. I wondered, *Do I risk trying to leap through the air and hope to land on the other side of the rock, then lurch myself on to the shore, with at least one boob hanging out (which would probably make one of the show promos) or do I wait and try not to vomit?* I chose the latter.

Eventually the exotic little terrorist took off. I then ran dramatically to shore to tell the celebrity white witch about my brush with death. When she realised what had happened, she told me that if I'd been nipped, I would have had about forty minutes to get to a hospital before I ended up a slightly less-vibrant shade of my top.

The second snake (wearing human clothing) I encountered on-set as I sat on a tree stump waiting for the director to yell 'action'. I spotted my soon to be boyfriend at Tribal Council, the place where we'd find out who'd voted for whom and who was getting the boot. With 300 or so people working on the show I rarely noticed them all but the Tribal Council's floor manager caught my attention. When my eyes met his it was like the whole earth had begun spinning slower. I knew I'd just seen the Sexiest Man Alive – and I couldn't take my eyes off him.

The votes were revealed and realisation dawned that the dodgy doctor from General Hospital, my so-called ally, had just read me my last rites. I was relieved my time had come to an end. Still, once I got back to the hotel, after spending my first night back with all the luxuries you forget how much you love – beds, linen, food, floor tiles, mirrors – I decided I wasn't ready to go back to reality. I wasn't gagging to return to my no-fixed-abode address or dwell on all the things I needed to sort out – life shit – a life gone to shit. I was relaxing at the hotel bar enjoying a white wine when the Tribal Council hottie sat down next to me chuckling like the turtle in *Finding Nemo*. One of the production guys warned, 'Be careful, he's horny!'

Despite *Survivor* being excruciating at times – from sleeping in the cold and rain beneath a sagging banana leaf to spooning three blokes while they told fart jokes – I'd come off the show feeling better than I'd done for ages. It was never about winning. The greatest reward, clichéd as it sounds, was (I thought) I'd stopped judging myself. Of course, that didn't quite mean I was ready to pen my first self-help book. Nor did it mean I wasn't subconsciously still ripe to fall for the physical charms of a not-so-sophisticated, super horny, Tribal Council manager. I didn't know it yet but the universe was secretly throwing me another test.

I'd made some convenient sums in my head regarding my new love interest, 'OK, so he's a little unsophisticated on first inspection but he's earthy, isn't obsessed with money (like the last one) and at least he was honest about himself.'

Travis was horny, and that was absolutely his truth. Over the next two weeks Travis and I spent a wonderful, peaceful and connected time with what seemed to be a no-holds-barred approach to getting to know each other. With me due to leave soon we decided to make plans to hang out again in Sydney once he'd finished filming. It would be ten days until we'd see each other again.

Back in Sydney a friend asked if I'd look after her apartment while she and her husband were overseas. This would be the perfect start to Travis and I spending time away from cameras and crew while we decided what was next – what city, what work, what us?

With three nights to go before Travis was due to leave Vanuatu, I called his hotel room for our nightly chat. I knew he'd had the day off so I was looking forward to hearing what he'd done. I tried twice without luck. At the end of the third phone call, which also went unanswered, the phone sounded like it'd been picked up and then hung up. I told myself there was every chance he'd just walked in, tried to grab the phone, then dropped it. I waited a minute or so to see if he'd call back. When it didn't, I called back – same result.

Something didn't feel right. My pulse was beginning to race. I called again. I figured if he was in the room with another girl then I was going to ruin their night with my calls. Maybe one of them would be stupid enough to pick the phone up and tell me to fuck off. At least then I'd know if I was being burnt. My worst fear was that everything I'd thought Travis and I were, how we felt when we were together, would prove to be all in my screwed up desperate mind. But I wasn't going to let it go without knowing for sure. I had to run straight into the fire of truth. There was nothing I could do other than what I was doing. And what I was doing was calling the hotel reception like a detective pumped full of caffeine about to get famous for catching a notorious serial killer. Or a horny Tribal Council manager.

'Hello?' I said, ever so politely. 'I'm trying to get Travis in Room 91 but I can't seem to get through. Are you able to tell me if he's in his room?' I tried to sound super casual and sweet. Not remotely put out. Not ready to punch every single wall in a 10km radius. The receptionist offered to call his room to see if she could get hold of him.

'Yes, ma'am,' she responded, 'I believe he is in his room. I've just walked around to his door and can hear the TV on, which is usually an indication someone's in there. Why don't you try him again? He might have been in the shower?'

I didn't want to tell her that was unlikely considering I'd called approximately thirty-two times. I called again. No answer. Feeling confident I'd built a rapport with the receptionist, I called her back, asking if she might be able to knock on his door.

'Can I ask who's calling?' she said, sounding a little suspicious herself.

'Yes,' I said confidently. 'It's his girlfriend.'

It wasn't a lie. During our last week together, that was exactly what he'd asked me to be. Although I hated the word, I was happy to be something to him. I didn't need my second fantasy relationship in a row. I wanted something real. The receptionist asked me to call back in five minutes. Counting down the seconds, I tried Travis's number again. Still no answer. I called back to the front desk. This time a male voice answered.

'Ma'am, we can confirm he's in the room,' he replied. 'That's all we can tell you. I'm sorry.' He was, I could hear it in his voice. The kind of sorry that meant, 'Your boyfriend has answered the door in a towel while a girl yelled from his bed, 'Who the fuck is that?'

I cried myself to sleep that night. I woke the next day feeling groggy and alone. I wandered around my friend's apartment looking at all the photos in frames of her gorgeous, incredibly fabulous wedding. I felt empty and worthless. All the good post-island vibes had gone up in smoke. My phone rang late morning, 'Hey baby, how are you?'

Travis was yawning down the phone. How the fuck was I? After nine hundred phone calls and a poor, tortured receptionist whose pity was still ringing in my ears? I was pissed off, big time, and yet I had no proof of anything.

'Why would I put it back on the hook if I had someone here with me? Why wouldn't I hang up and then take it back off? I'm not like that other guy, baby, you need to believe more in us,' he said, sounding convincingly disappointed. Was I so profoundly damaged that I was now creating scenarios to sabotage something real? It made sense. I wasn't ready to shut this down because nothing inside me had been solved. I would have to stay in it a bit longer. Even if it killed me.

CHAPTER FOUR.

POKER FACE

'Hi, my name's Amber. You probably don't know me but I'd love to work in radio.'

I didn't think there was much chance of getting a reply to my short and cheeky email to one of Australia's most important men in radio but it was about as creative and honest as I felt comfortable with. I didn't want to be a wanker by dropping bullshit details about myself or fabricating a profile based on everything I thought the Big Radio Boss might like me to be.

As it stood, my CV looked pretty good in terms of media experience but at the time of writing my only employment was with my dad and Myles in their carpet business in Melbourne. It was a part-time job I knew my dad had created to help me out financially – and because he liked having me around. Not to mention I was thirty-six, living back with Mum and sharing my old bedroom with Travis – a boyfriend I didn't trust as far as I could throw him. Lifestyles of the Rich and Famous it was not.

My gut told me things didn't add up, regardless of what Travis tried to feed me about that night in his hotel room. However, I had allowed him to move us beyond it and into the next stage of our relationship, together in Australia. All after hearing from the Executive Producer of *Celebrity Survivor* that Travis – according to crew members who were on the flight back from Vanuatu to Australia with him – had been blind drunk and allegedly joined the mile-high club with a girl he'd met at the hotel.

Mentally scrambled and with my career in tatters the truth was I had nothing to lose, which is when low self-esteem comes in really handy. So, I decided to send an email to one of the most powerful men in radio. Who'd be so bold as to come barrelling into his inbox? Not someone with dignity and self-respect. I had none of that holding me back. Sending a stranger an email and then being crushed by his silence wasn't in my catalogue of fears.

When I opened my emails the following day there was his name pulsating among my new messages. I granted myself all of twenty seconds to enjoy the moment before preparing for rejection. I opened the email, sat back and tensed my stomach ready to take the punch. But I was wrong. It wasn't a rejection at all. Thanks to my recent, slightly embarrassing reality-TV gig he said he 'knew of me'. What that meant I didn't know. He'd answered, and that was enough. Even better, he wanted to catch up to find out 'where I was at'.

Holy shit! Was the bloody universe finally drifting slightly over to my side?

To say a lot was riding on this meeting was an understatement. If nothing came of it, I'd have to continue to hide out in Dad's cramped office at the back of his carpet showroom pretending to know something about office admin while attempting to block out the endless arguments between him and my brother. It was enough to make me want to wrap myself up in a roll of shag-pile and hibernate.

I left lunch on the day I met the Big Radio Boss with a sense of new hope – something I had feared I might never feel again. Finally, it appeared I'd met a guy who wasn't trying to dazzle me with a smokescreen to hide his agenda. He had a plan. He wanted to start me at night at a local station – late enough so if I were atrocious the damage would be minimal. My words, not his. He said he wanted to try me out with different guys to see who I had 'the best chemistry with'.

Bloody hell, I'll tell you who I have the best chemistry with – the guy that's mostly full of shit. That's who I'll click with – my words, not to him. I'd have to keep that side of me secret.

While I'd began doing my night gig locally, I'd also been playing Russian Roulette. I knew that by not kicking Travis out of my life I was sabotaging myself and my radio chances. I was like an addict, not letting him go despite knowing how bad he was for my health.

He'd punched a hole in my bedroom wall during an argument, suspicious text messages kept dinging on his phone at all hours and I was so anxious and sleep-deprived when I'd arrive at the station that I was certain I was a humourless, bumbling mess on-air.

On the flip side I'd been dabbling in a bit of magic – practising this thing called 'manifesting' which is a technique I discovered after a friend urged me to watch a documentary.

'Everyone's talking about it,' she whispered, as though her phone might be tapped. 'It's called The Secret. You need to watch it!' So, I did. I watched that movie like a kid watches *Frozen*. But the crazy thing was, while the boss had been dangling the idea of getting me a permanent gig at his network, I'd written on each page of my diary, 'I AM GOING TO WORK IN RADIO'. I also wrote down my desired salary.

I was, according to The Secret, 'putting it out there to the universe,' and not just when I felt fabulous and ready to kick goals but when I felt so anxious, I wanted to smoke twenty-five cigarettes while forensically examining every reason I'd fucked up my life. Thanks to The Secret I was using the verbal manifesting technique to punch the crap out of that exhausting voice that always piped in, *It's probably not going to happen. Why would it happen to you?*

When the Big Radio Boss called me four months after our lunch date, I was sitting in Dad's office staring at a broken, frosted window with carpet samples hanging off it alongside the fading business cards of companies that had shut down fifteen years ago.

'I finally have an opening for you, Amber,' he announced. 'It's a breakfast radio position in Adelaide and I need you to start in a month.' I took a second to take it in. This was it. It was too incredible, too wonderful, to be real. I was on Cloud Eleven, the VIP section – just up from Cloud Nine. The Big Radio Boss offered me the exact figure I'd written (and said aloud) for fourteen days straight. It was crazy. Somehow, I'd miraculously, almost comically, lured a powerful network into my web. And they, I'd learn, had drawn me into theirs.

With just one month before I needed to be in Adelaide, there was much to do. But I was relishing the sense of purpose it gave me and the confidence boost of being chosen over no doubt a long list of women desperate to land a job in radio.

Dad, who while sad I'd be moving spelling the end of our regular lunch breaks together, was proud of me – as he'd been about me being at Mary's wedding. His Friday lunch buddies often shared with me just how proud my dad was.

'Did you hear about my baby girl?' he'd apparently say.

One of the key events in my calendar was my first photo shoot where we'd be creating the marketing images for our show. On the day I'd arrived at the studio I had been greeted by Jade from the network's marketing team, Harry the photographer and Lisa the make-up artist. My co-host Rabbit, I was told, would be arriving after we'd done my solo shots.

Once in the hair and make-up chair I was reminded how quickly I could ruin this opportunity. My irrational fear of looking hard or plain began eroding my confidence – just as I needed to be fun and playful for the shots. It was always the same, all through the royal wedding, my magazine column shoots and Celebrity Survivor, my inner child would feel sulky. Luckily, I was too naïve to consider that one of the photos from that day would be used on a billboard booked to appear all over Adelaide.

'Can you soften your face a bit, darl,' Harry the photographer urged. I could feel myself smiling like a ventriloquist doll. If he was frustrated with me, god knows so was I. Anxiety wouldn't be a term I'd hear much until years later but it was an ever-present state for me. And it came in trickles, swells and tidal waves.

An hour into my attempts at softening my face my new co-host arrived. His name was Rabbit. It was a radio thing. Rabbit on first impression seemed nice enough – good-looking and friendly although a little reserved. My inner child felt she was on her first day of pre-school. My outer adult felt she was entering an arranged marriage. Whether we liked it or not Rabbit and I were going to expose a lot of ourselves to each other as the months, hopefully years, went on. Secretly I wondered if Rabbit was disappointed he'd scored a co-host with so little radio experience? Hopefully I figured by the time we got into the studio we'd have worked out our conversational rhythm. Right then we just needed to concentrate on creating an image that gave the impression Rabbit and I had been bosom buddies for more than an hour.

I had very little time to decide whether to continue my relationship with Travis or to cut ties. It was a test of my self-worth. In Vanuatu as I was falling for Travis, or so I'd thought, I'd prayed he might provide the karmic relationship healing I needed. I hadn't considered however that Travis had met me on a show where I was positioned as a 'celebrity'. And he was a Kiwi so he didn't question that description like I and others did. I see now that this idea of me, what it might offer, was appealing to him. Confronted with the biggest decisions – new job, new home and all that that entailed – I decided to bring Travis with me because I was scared of being alone. Being lonely with another person felt, bizarrely, safer. So, I didn't invite him as such but I went along with his pleas to join me – to give us a 'fresh start' as he described it.

Given we were moving to a smaller city than Melbourne or Sydney, which provided far more TV opportunities for him, Travis assured me he was ready to make the sacrifice so we could be together. I told myself this suggested his renewed commitment.

The house we settled on, a week before I was due on air, was not in my original target area but a typically savvy real-estate agent could smell I was desperate for a roof and hopeless at Google Maps. But I instantly fell in love with the back part of our new home – a vast light-filled sunroom with a bar that looked out across a pool lined with palm trees. It was very Beverley Hills. I figured if I were to make a fresh start with Travis, in a city neither of us knew, we might as well do it from a peaceful base where we could attempt to recreate the connection we'd had when we first met. The local newspaper requested a photo shoot with Travis and me unpacking boxes as we settled into our new home. I didn't share my hesitation about the shoot with my radio publicist. Given Travis and my history I knew by saying yes it would be more evidence of how stupid I was once the relationship officially hit the wall. Regardless of what went to print, as a radio host you don't rock into town and conveniently not discuss the guy you've got in tow. 'Now, smile for the cameras you two,' the friendly photographer prompted. Oh god, here we go.

In our first official week at the station we planned and performed shows as if we were going to air, with show openers, time calls, ad breaks, music, story topics, celebrity guests, even daily news breaks rolled out during our three-hour show each day.

This was the radio station's first taste of what we were going to sound like. A plus for me was Rabbit was a real pro. He'd been doing radio for years so just seeing him twiddle all of those random buttons on the panel made me feel like someone was in control. But this was also Rabbit's first go at breakfast radio. Beyond throwing to breaks and music and turning all the necessary knobs, he'd yet to prove himself as someone who could relate to an audience skewed more towards women. In the studio after our last trial show of that week, Rabbit asked if I could sit back down for a minute. He said he wanted 'a quick chat'. Leaning back on his chair behind the radio desk, arms crossed, staring at the bench, he was frowning like he was stuck on the last question in a crossword puzzle.

'I'm sorry but I have to ask, what's it going to take for me to get a laugh out of you?' he said, looking at me with his head cocked to the side. I didn't know what was going on. I knew we were having a weird moment but I didn't get why. I waited for him to elaborate. But he didn't. Confused, I asked, 'What do you mean?'

'I mean, what's it going to take for me to get you to laugh at me on-air?' He was serious – deadly serious. My new co-host of all of one week was already pissed off with me because apparently I'd rejected all his jokes. The thing was I thought I had been laughing. I'd naively assumed we'd just finished a really fun, positive, laughter-filled week and I felt good about that. I felt good about us. Clearly, I'd seriously misread it. We weren't off to a good start and now I had the entire weekend to rot in the feeling of being the rejected-new-kid-at-school. While also working out how to transform into my most confident self by Monday.

I must have looked like a terrified puppy the day our show went to air for real – staring across the desk at Rabbit, anxious and desperate for any scrap of attention. Was he going to throw me a bone or would I be off to the vet to be put down after the show? Afraid as I was of him, I was committed to soaking up his radio knowledge. And I still wanted to be friends. After all, isn't working in radio supposed to be fun?

The boss was pretty happy with the results of our first week on-air. Surprisingly, I hadn't been half as nervous as I thought I'd be. Which might have been the blessing of spending the weekend lost in a panic about how bad things might become. The only way was up.

Rabbit mentioned his wife wanted to have me over for dinner. His wording was clear – it was her idea. The invitation was extended to Travis but I quickly decided I did not want us to be on show in front of them, not when I suspected dinner might be an audition. Things were different over at Rabbit's place. Everything appeared very solid. A lovely, healthy, young family doing what happy, healthy young families do. His wife was starting a job as a teacher and their son was at kindergarten. His wife packed both their lunches. Dinner was done by 7 pm – which is 10 pm if you are working breakfast radio hours. I left feeling no less interest from Rabbit in me than when I'd arrived. But also, no more.

There were other challenges in our early days on the air, one of them learning how to talk. One of the surprising and excruciating elements of being new to radio is you need a lot of coaching on how to speak. Just letting words spew out is like playing Jenga. One wrong-word move and your whole story comes crashing down in a heap.

'I saw something in you, Amber, which is why I employed you,' my boss assured me in his super smooth ex-radio-jock voice.

'You're someone that's got a lot of stories, you've lived a lot.'

He's saying you're old, my paranoia immediately said, reminding me I was the oldest of our breakfast-radio team. But actually, it wasn't that at all – he was saying he believed in me. Despite the Big Radio Boss being intimidating he was also one of the best radio mentors in the business.

'Your biggest challenge,' he continued 'is how to tell these great stories in three minutes. You're going to have to learn how to edit. A Headline. A Middle. And An Ending. Three minutes and then you're out.'

If you'd told me this before I began working in radio, I'd have thought, *How hard can that be?* But now I was in it I knew it was going to be a process. I had a lot to say but the issue was pushing past that voice in my head that repeatedly interrupted me mid-sentence, whispering, 'Does anyone care about this?' Listeners had options. One flip of their radio dial and we'd be gone – too many people flipping and we'd be out of a job.

Rabbit and I were called into the boss's office after every shift to review the show. What worked, what didn't? Whether we went to the news on time and all the other nuts and bolts. Every moment had to sound sharp and familiar.

These air-check meetings were awkward. Most air-checks went like this: The boss ushers us into his office. 'Take a seat'. Plonk I'd sink – trying to appear relaxed, nothing to hide, not remotely shitting myself – into his two-seater blue couch that meant Rabbit and I were uncomfortably close. Oh, god, kill me now.

'So, how do you think the show went today?' he asks.

How I hated that question. Loaded much? I mean, what could I say? 'Brilliant. Actually, I think it's some of the finest radio I've heard. Or was I to try and save face by pointing out that at thirty-eight minutes past seven I forgot how to pronounce 'the' and said it three times in a row.

'Let me play you something back.' Away he'd tap on his keyboard, consulting the precise notes he'd taken as he listened to that morning's show. Squirming, I'd have to sit through the greatest misses package – usually me crapping on, all over the shop, until the very ordinary end of a story I was now certain no one needed to hear.

'What did you notice about that break?'

That was my invitation to play program director. Rough as it was it was a genius process of getting you to own your shit. What did I notice about that break? I'd repeat, feeling the pressure as the boss drilled his eyes into me. What, apart from the fact that my voice is annoying and I'm trying to be something I'm not? And then I would admit sheepishly, 'Well, um, the break sounded pretty long, and I took forever to get to the point?'

Nodding, 'And what else?'

What else? Um, that I should grab my lipstick and highlighter pens resting next to my microphone and maybe call that photographer to let him know I'm ready for a 'packing my boxes and getting out of town shot?'

If there's ever a surer way to gauge your confidence levels get a job on radio. All will be revealed. I noticed it wasn't just my air-checks that were uncomfortable. Rabbit was getting a few of his own thanks to his habit of veering off-brand from his 'relatable, married Dad of one' persona. Somehow, he'd find a way to wheel out stories from ten years before when he owned a waterbed with a black leather bed-head and built-in stereo system – alongside all too regular references to old girlfriends. It was odd. But it felt good not being the only one needing a buff and polish – not the kind Rabbit was insinuating he got back in his day.

Another one of the expected parts of being a woman on radio was reading the celebrity news. In my pre-show preparation, I'd trawl the main gossip sites and pull out the big stories. All I had to do was read out a clever little headline followed by a summary of the story then wait for Rabbit to throw in a one-liner. Simple, you'd assume, but for unknown reasons I was continually tripping over my words. I couldn't work out why. Nor could my boss. It took me over a year to work out a technique for delivering the celebrity news that worked for me. I later realised my conscience was getting in the way – sticking its leg out every time I'd start running through a story.

Because the truth was, I wasn't comfortable perpetuating stories at someone else's expense. How could I, of all people, weave sarcasm around a Britney Spears story when it was abundantly clear she was having a mental breakdown. I wanted to hug her, not laugh. Having seen what happened when Mary first catapulted to fame, and my own experiences of being near her spotlight, I knew how hurtful media lies can be and wanted no part of that grimy game. Unfortunately, connection to my conscience had come at an incredibly inconvenient time. There was no way I was going to stay in the job if I heckled every piece of news with, 'Yeah, but to be fair this story probably has about as much truth to it as Santa.'

I couldn't afford to be precious. I needed to keep my job. I was terrified of being without it. I had no back-up plan.

And yet, even then, there was something even more personal putting a handbrake on my mouth. Like Britney I was unravelling in my private life. I was drinking heavily on weekends while Travis would go missing on 'surfing trips' – as he called them. I was taking Stilnox at night in order to sleep, sent to me in regular parcels by my sleep-obsessed Mum. Not to mention I was living with a boyfriend who felt more like a stranger every day. While Travis struggled to find work and I struggled settling into my new breakfast radio hours, my boyfriend preyed on my mental state. He would tell me I was paranoid, angry and 'fucked in the head' when I asked about the constant incoming calls and texts from women he claimed were 'new friends'.

Everything I had hoped was going to fix my life was only making it worse.

PLAYING IN THE DARK

Despite our ratings going up the boss decided our show needed a new male personality involved. He wasn't convinced the chemistry with Rabbit and me was there. I agreed – and I'm sure Rabbit did too. So, on came Cosi – a guy who'd already worked for the network on another show and been flicked when they replaced him and his co-hosts with another team.

Since then he'd made a name for himself nationally thanks to his ballooning weight and his role on *The Biggest Loser*. It was precisely the sort of exposure that impressed the Big Radio Boss. And so Cosi was back in the network and on to our show.

Aside from working in media, Cosi was a former pig farmer and the proudest South Australian you could ever meet. He was the funny guy, Dad of one on the way and stepdad to young Harry. He was in every way the complete opposite of Rabbit, except when it came to his radio ambitions and being a devoted father. For me he was a breath of fresh air.

When Cosi arrived, Rabbit was relegated to the role of show anchor – meaning he was in charge of hooking us in and out of segments, throwing to ads and news as well as playing secondary male host. But I wasn't stupid enough to think he wouldn't put up a fight to get his crown back. No matter how long or what it would take. After nearly nine months on the air. I was happy to sit back and let the boys battle it out. I had bigger battles at home. When I had found that peaceful house with a pool that Travis and I would live in I prayed it would be just what we needed. Over nearly six months of living there the pool water kept mysteriously turning Kermit green – no matter what I did or how many times I called the local pool guy to blitz it with chemicals.

And the hoped-for allure of the black-rimmed bar in our sunroom had descended into the perfect meeting point for two warring lovers with binge-drinking and other addiction issues. It was no wonder I was sick all the time. I was anxious 24/7. Not that I'd ever dare take time off. The Big Radio Boss had made it clear early on we'd need to pretty much be in a body bag before throwing a sickie. I was using all my energy to simply keep up the appearance of being the 'wacky, zany fun girl' on-air – then retreating to a war zone at home. I was running on empty. And empty was just how I felt.

Travis and I had never had a honeymoon period in our new house or our new city. We'd unpacked our bags and got on with our separate lives. Now, six months in, our arguments were getting worse. I was constantly searching for (and finding) evidence that proved Travis was no good. I found emails between him and the Editor of a woman's magazine implying they were in the early stages of a deal involving him talking about me.

I saw photos of a young blonde on his phone which he insisted were taken between cameras rolling on a locally-made TV show he was working on. There were photos of a woman naked from the waist down, asleep on a couch, apparently sent to him by a 'dickhead mate'. And still I let him stay. Even worse, I continued to share a bed with him.

I thought by trusting Travis when we came to Adelaide I had a chance to be proven wrong. I tried to convince myself that somehow I was more in control now I had a job and a house with my name on the lease. But I was kidding myself. All I was doing was enabling both of us. And while I also thought having a public role on the radio meant I could put forward a convenient image of myself I hadn't factored in that I had to talk about the things I didn't want anyone to know about – namely Travis and me. The fact was my boyfriend hated me. And I hated him. Nobody knew how bad things were. Nobody knew there were nights I had to call the police while waiting outside in the dark in my nightie – too scared to go back inside our home.

Some days my anxiety was through the roof. I was so paranoid that while telling a fake 'happy' story about Travis and me one of my neighbours might call up and tell my producer the truth – describing the screaming and shouting coming from my home, report the police pulling into my driveway late at night. Or one of those girls in his camera, the nude from the waist down girl or one of the girls I'd yet to discover, might call in to say they were sleeping with my boyfriend. Fears of humiliation buzzed like a fly around my head every single day. Finally, after another call to the police and Travis taking off to stay 'at a mate's house', I decided I needed help. I didn't know what his limits were anymore. There'd been a look in his eye I'd not seen before in anyone else. Something inside me was warning me: *You need to log this with someone – just in case*. I didn't dare tell anyone back home what was going on. After such a messy few years I wanted everyone to think my chaos was behind me and that I had a new and successful life. Based strongly on a feeling of impending doom I made the decision to make what would be the most excruciatingly embarrassing phone call I have ever made – I called the Big Radio Boss. As I searched my phone for his number, I felt shame that I was letting him down but I had to admit things at home were getting scary.

I chose the Big Radio Boss to tell my secret to because, while he was the person I wanted to impress more than anyone, I also knew he was tough and I needed someone to be alert on my behalf. To know if something happened to me that he would be aware. He could testify. He could get justice for my family.

Calling the boss that day with my confession was one of the hardest phone calls I've ever had to make. Thankfully he reacted in precisely the way I hoped he would. He wasn't emotional, he was practical, protective and methodical. He promised to arrange for me to stay in a hotel for a few days at the company's expense. My shame was temporarily replaced by immense gratitude. I hated disappointing him, not after he'd been the one lifeline I'd had when I thought my life had fallen apart. The Big Radio Boss had put his reputation on the line for me and now the boyfriend I'd promised him wouldn't get in the way of my work was threatening to ruin me – and the boss's reputation.

The boss had been right about me in one respect – I did have lots of stories. I had lived a lot. But he wasn't to know what lay beneath my poker face. I made one more bad decision before calling it a day with Travis. A month after my hotel stint, in which time Travis had gone to stay with a 'mate' after I made it clear I was sharing the truth about us to my boss, I allowed him back home. His tears and pleading and begging for one last try had worn me down. It wasn't long before we were up to our old tricks.

I came home early from work one Friday to find Travis's computer open and still on. It was sitting near the front door recharging. I couldn't help myself. I refreshed his screen, revealing the last website he'd been on. It appeared to be a dating site – a nasty one called 'Red Hot Pie'.

As I waded through the long list of relationship items most women wouldn't have put up with, I chose 'Red Hot Pie' to be most outraged about. When I confronted Travis, we ended up in a *Once Were Warriors*-style clash. He punched me hard in the stomach with a clenched fist. One second I was standing, feeling his spit on my face as he screamed 'You fucking crazy bitch, stay away from my things!' The next I'm in the foetal position gasping for air, terrified it was never going to come.

I lay on the floor near the welcome mat at the front door, inches from where his computer lay charging, wondering how long a body could go without oxygen. When the breath finally came back into my lungs, I realised I couldn't tell where Travis was – but I didn't want to move in case he put me back down. My body hurt. Lying there, not knowing if this was the end or if Travis was waiting to do worse, the world felt like it was slowing down and for the first time everything became clear. I was broken. Mentally and physically broken. I'd just realised this was my life. This was where I was at.

I guess that sounds the worst of it. You'd think so but then you'd be underestimating my addiction to self-destruction. I'd allowed Travis' tales of childhood physical and sexual abuse to excuse him for transferring his violence on to me. I'd fallen for so many sob stories from Travis, my heart desperately wanting to mother him. I'd allowed and enabled him to project his rage on to me, the girl he didn't know how to love. I felt his inner rage at me for not having endured violence or abuse in my own childhood, like I couldn't understand pain.

Travis didn't come for me again that day and I think I went into shock over what had happened. A functioning shock where I could still show up for work and be playful and fun – but I was a shell. I didn't know how to process so I stayed quiet for a week or so. I didn't even know how to tell him to get out of my house. I didn't know who I was dealing with. I didn't know people like him. But yet, here I was.

When my disgust finally motivated me to act, I chose the wrong moment. It unravelled over the bar in the sunroom. To make his final point Travis slammed the candles I had burning along the bar towards me. The hot wax sprayed across my face and cheeks and went into my open eyes. Then everything went black. I couldn't see Travis. But I did hear a voice in my head. Calm, slow and no-nonsense in its delivery, it said, 'There you go, are you happy now? You've kept this going long enough that now you're going to be blind. You stupid, stupid idiot.'

Tears formed. Then I realised my tears were dislodging the wax. I cried, blinking quickly to get rid of the chunks of wax over my eyeballs. So that was the end. How could it not be? I was now clearer than I'd ever been any further chapters would end in a headline no one I loved deserved to read.

I hid our final split for as long as I could. After weeks of not talking about Travis on-air, for the sake of my professional obligations I had to address the elephant in the room. But I wanted to get it out of the way without making a blubbering mess of myself – something I didn't manage. I began crying as soon as I began talking on-air. It made me angry that my tears suggested I was devastated about the loss of Travis. I wasn't. He was a fucking monster.

The months that followed felt like the calm after a terrible storm. Once I left the station for the day, I'd spend most of my time alone. In silence. My phone rarely rang on weekends and I was too exhausted to make new friends. I was, in many ways, avoiding calling close friends because I didn't know what to say. I'd finish work on a Friday and, aside from a shopkeeper here and there while grabbing food, cigarettes or a bottle of wine, there were weekends when I might not see or speak to another person until I arrived back at work at 5 am on Monday. After several of these weekends in a row I felt something I'd never expected. After the silence came the voices. The first voice, which stayed with me for weeks, came as a gentle statement: *Oh my God, you're so lonely.* It took me by surprise because I'd always had plenty of friends. If anything, my biggest problem had been surrounding myself with too many people.

Soon the loneliness was replaced with something more urgent, more aggressive. At night I would lie in bed thrashing back and forth like an addict going cold turkey. My anxiety was so bad I could hardly breathe. I would claw at my bed sheets and pillows, wanting to rip them apart. It was like I was trying to get outside of myself or away from myself. Away from the feeling I didn't understand. I hated the world and I hated that I couldn't find any joy. I couldn't hold any sort of gratitude.

One Sunday night, as I tossed and turned desperately trying to get to sleep, knowing how much worse my anxiety would be the next morning when my alarm clock sounded at 4.20 am, I started sobbing from the deepest part of my heart, words repeating over and over in my head: *If my parents were dead I could leave. But I can't because they're not.*

I didn't know which hurt more, having to stay, or not being able to go. I couldn't have a conversation with myself about suicide without knowing there were two choices open to me – one I was not willing to take. I chose to get professional help to find out if what I was feeling was depression. The thing was I knew, on my dad's side, mental illness (and suicide) was a thing. A very real thing. It's how he lost his mother. It's how she lost her father. So maybe, I thought, there was a chance, *This might just be my time.*

I made an appointment to see a GP with the sole mission of admitting I was scared. I was dreading the appointment. 'What can I help you with today?' the doctor asked once I'd sat down. Suddenly I felt like someone had just turned the MCG lights on in my head, like I'd look up and see a packed crowd in the grandstands staring down, waiting for my reply. I wished the doctor could read my mind and make the whole thing easier. I wanted him to say, 'OK, so you're here to see me today to find out if you're suffering from depression.'

'Yes, I think that's why I'm here. Before I say I've got it, can you tell me how it feels?' But I didn't say that. I answered as directly and succinctly as I could. I used my annoyance at what I took as his robotic process to plough through the awkwardness of saying, 'So, I think I might be suffering from depression, but I want to know if I'm right?'

'I see,' he replied. 'Have you had thoughts of suicide?'

'Yes.'

'How recently?'

'Very recently.' With every answer I could feel relief swelling in my chest. That is until the doctor laid down his verdict. 'I'm going to prescribe you an anti-depressant,' he said, not looking up.

As he scribbled out the details on his prescription-pad I felt overwhelmingly sad and very scared. I didn't know what I thought was going to happen but, as he handed over that prescription, I said to myself: *Oh my god. Is this it? Is this me being fixed by a pill? Now I am fucked.*

I left the doctor's that day feeling mad and more confused than ever. I knew pills were not my answer but I'd run out of avenues to explore. So, I decided to take the pills for a time but I refused to take this as me 'fixed'. I vowed that day that I'd learn how to get happy – on my own.

Two days after my appointment I headed into the chemist to fill my prescription. I would take my first pill later that day. Soon after I swallowed it, I can only describe that it reminded me of an awful night I'd had on an ecstasy pill at the Sydney Mardi Gras. When I say bad, I don't suggest I was running around wanting to cuddle strangers. I mean it made my eyeballs shake in their sockets. After a month or so on the drugs I chucked them in the bin. I could thank them, at least, for showing me what I didn't want. I could credit them for helping stoke a fire in my belly to get well, to stop feeling sorry for myself. As if on cue the solution to getting well was delivered unexpectedly one day in a text message from, of all people, Travis.

He wanted me to know he'd been going to a 'healing energy centre' and suggested I look into it, 'I think you'll like it. It's spiritual, like you.' This side of him was what had made me fall in *something* with him back in Vanuatu. Reading his text, I remembered what it was about the two of us, once upon a time before hell.

I wasn't sure what to expect when I arrived at the healing centre. All I knew was one door had shut and I needed to open another – fast. It wasn't a case of hoping to bide my time so I could ride through my rough patch and feel good again. I couldn't remember when I'd genuinely felt good but if you'd asked me when I started feeling worse it began when I left Julian, shutting the door on pain and running. Back when I was twenty-seven.

I did a drive-by before parking the car. From the outside the healing centre looked like a quaint little shop or café where I might buy a handmade pin cushion or get a toasted sandwich and a hot chocolate. I walked up to the door, opening it to the sound of jingling bells. It reminded me of when I was at primary school and used to stop by the local milk bar on the way home to get ten cents' worth of lollies – a lot back then. The tinkling sound of the healing centre door brought back happy memories and a sense of safety.

A trail of Nag Champa incense floated from the counter. I breathed it in deeply. It was a wonderfully intoxicating smell – the stench of 'bloody hippies', as my dad would probably say, but I loved it. I felt like Alice in Wonderland, moving into a mysterious rabbit hole filled with self-help books, crystals, oracle cards and large chalk-drawn angels hanging on the walls. What wisdom did they have for me? I wondered. What messages did I need? I felt alive. After circling the inside of the store at least three times I decided it was time to do what I'd come there to do – book my first healing. I walked up to the counter as a woman with a kind face and a friendly smile approached the desk. She was dressed in a pretty purple silk uniform and she had the biggest blue eyes I'd ever seen. I explained I had come on a recommendation from a friend. Little did she know the 'friend' had done most of the recent damage I now needed fixing.

'If it's happening to you, it's about you.'

It was time to take back my power. Although it would not come without a fight.

A LOVE STORY

Surely, he's not serious? The boss lingered in the doorway after sharing his big idea for what we might do to get 'get talked about' that week. This had been the filter we'd been reminded over and over again to consider when planning the following week of shows ahead.

The boss's idea was based on a stunt that had played out on-air via the network's most successful breakfast show – in Sydney. The crux of it was they'd pretended their popular female host was dead. I scanned the faces around the room, desperately hoping to find one that matched mine. I knew these moments all too well by now and I could see the only issue with the idea was my issue with the idea. Picking up on my vibe, our producer suggested I head off for the day early.

I arrived back at 5 am the next day. I sat at my desk and looked at the whiteboard where we mapped out timeslots, placing what was happening in each. Ten past seven simply read 'STUNT'. As the show began, I could feel dread building. I had no idea what was going to go down. With songs, ad breaks and a replayed gotcha call making up our first hour of the show you could have been mistaken for thinking I wasn't there, which was precisely their intention. Our newsreader came on, sounding sombre.

'SAFM breakfast announcer Amber Petty has died at the age of thirty-seven,' she announced.

'Amber moved to Adelaide in 2007 after a distinguished media career in Sydney and Melbourne.'

An audio grab played of my dad saying 'We are, of course, devastated. You never want to outlive your child,' followed by one of my brother chiming in with his typical brand of humour:

'I was just happy to see her rise from C-grade celebrity to the B-grade celebrity she was when she died'.

Rabbit included himself in the tributes, 'I remember when Amber and I first met and we went down to the Torrens River. We jumped on the paddle boats down there and I've got this photo I took of her on my phone. Every time she'd call, her face would pop up. I guess I'm now not going to see her face anymore'. The recording ended with a mournful Rabbit signing off, 'Amber Petty, rest in peace.'

I stared at Rabbit, trying to predict where on Earth he might take the break next. He'd executed the boss's idea to 'get talked about' perfectly, but where to now? Would it be '13 1 0 60 when have you pretended someone was dead?' After a perfectly timed, comedic pause, he piped up like a cheeky kid, 'Oh no, she's still here!' Laughing like a brat.

He wrapped up the segment and threw to a song as the phones lit up like crazy. Listeners were calling in distressed, thinking I was dead. They hadn't heard the whole segment because they were making their way to work or in their breakfast routines. Rabbit's big reveal had fallen on many deaf ears so once our producers informed them it was just a 'joke' – they were furious – with all of us.

I just wanted the show to end that day so I could ring Dad. And yet it did the trick. It got people listening – and it sure as hell got people talking. After an inappropriately upbeat song Rabbit reiterated that I wasn't at the morgue and it was all a harmless joke. He got our newsreader back on to get her to playfully back it up, like a prank she was pushed into by a naughty little boy. One break later, while we sat through another song and ad break, our newsreader buzzed back through to speak to Rabbit. This time off-air.

'Heath Ledger's just been confirmed dead,' she said.

'Oh my god,' I said, horrified. I stared at Rabbit. How the hell was he going to go back on-air and share the news after what he'd just done?

Where's your credibility now, mate? I sat back, committed to letting him take over. I was done. All I could think about was Heath's little girl who'd never grow up to know her dad. By the time I finished for the day there were several missed calls on my phone. There were a few from local friends wanting to know what the deal was with my death hoax. But there was one call I needed to return first. I sat in the car park under the station and dialled Dad's number. 'Hi Daddy,' I said, feeling flat.

'Oh darling, that was bloody awful this morning,' he raced back with. 'Your brother and I were listening online. We felt terrible hearing ourselves saying that crap they made us say.' He explained Rabbit had called him the day before while Dad was racing to an appointment. Rabbit insisted he was just recording an innocent prank to stir up publicity. Dad turned him down at first, saying he wasn't comfortable, but Rabbit hounded him, assuring him it was just one of those 'silly stunts the boss was making us do'.

Dad said, 'I ended up being so confused between getting lost, and running late, and figuring maybe I needed to comply with whatever your boss wanted you guys to do. He had a script so I just read that. I'm sorry, baby'. I'd never heard my dad sound so disappointed in himself.

'It's OK, Dad, it's not your fault,' I reassured him.

He replied, 'I'm still annoyed with myself that I didn't tell him to piss off. Anyway, I guess it's a weird job you're doing over there, darling.'

He was right about that.

Getting yourself 'talked about' as a show was one strategy for the ratings. Another way to endear listeners to you, especially in a city as proud as Adelaide, is by creating regular segments so you sound familiar. Rabbit had decided in our first year that he wanted one of ours to be gotcha calls – prank calls produced and hosted by him.

Raymond was one of Rabbit's earliest gotcha-call victims. He was a guy known for making a nuisance of himself outside his kids' school at pick-up. Apparently he'd time how long parents were taking to collect their kids then take it upon himself to bail people up and give them a dressing down. I found Rabbit's method of luring in Raymond and other victims to be fascinating. He'd control them like puppets.

On this particular call Rabbit convinced Raymond he was calling from the local police station and they were looking for someone like him to take up the role of 'sheriff'. As the call went on Rabbit got Raymond to believe a police officer might ring a random bloke with no police training and offer him an American style sheriff's job – with badge, gun and a horse. Raymond agreed to ride the horse to the school and, using an American accent, announce himself as the 'Lone Ranger' (which he happily practiced on-air with Rabbit three times). He then conceded to Rabbit that 'if need be' he'd use the gun to 'encourage' parents to move on. It was some magician shit on Rabbit's part – or perhaps pot luck on scoring Raymond as one of his earliest stars?

Before July 2008, Rabbit's gotcha calls had been focused on the innocent people of South Australia but, secretly, he'd been planning a global attack. The idea was spawned after Blaine Armstrong contacted Rabbit asking him to 'get' his Canadian fiancée Sarah Dickenson. Rabbit described on-air how Sarah was busy packing up her life in Canada, readying herself to move to Adelaide. Meanwhile, Sarah was waiting approval on a de-facto visa from the Australian Immigration Department.

Rabbit set the call up, painting the picture of Sarah. She was a cute twenty-six-year-old yoga instructor living in a share house with girlfriends and excitedly planning her future in South Australia with fiancé Blaine. Their story struck a chord with me, reminding me of what Julian and I'd been through. How stressful and scary it had been being at the mercy of strangers when you're in love. So, falling madly in love in a foreign country at twenty-six? I got it. Having your life put on hold while you wait to hear if you can make solid plans together? Done it. And now, with the backdrop painted for that morning's gotcha call, Rabbit announced he'd be calling Sarah Dickenson pretending to be an immigration officer working on their case.

'Hello?' said a sweet-sounding Canadian girl. Always the

professional, Rabbit launched into performance mode, asking her to confirm her name. I imagined her panic, wondering who the overly serious Australian at the other end of the phone might be.

'Colin from the Australian Immigration Department,' Rabbit went on. 'I've got your file in front of me. Do you have a moment to go through a few questions for your application?' He'd hooked her. Things swiftly took a Rabbit twist as his questions progressed from fair to awkward to downright inappropriate – her fiancé's genitals and her familiarity with them – that kind of thing.

'I'm not sure that's any of your business, I'm sorry,' Sarah responded, laughing nervously. Rabbit stayed silent for a few seconds, just enough time for her to imagine going to the post-box and finding a letter from the Australian government, opening it and reading 'denied' stamped across it. After a carefully curated handful of seconds Rabbit revealed she'd been set up.

Breathing an audible sigh of relief, she squealed, 'I'm going to kill him.'

Six weeks after Rabbit's gotcha call to Sarah Cosi sidled up to me in the office. He told me he'd just walked out of our studio after 'busting Rabbit with that Canadian Sarah'. According to my curious co-host Rabbit was playing his guitar and singing away like Eric Clapton. Realising he had an audience he'd become flustered and stopped.

'Hi mate, what's up?' he'd said. Not one to miss a chance to take the piss out of his co-host, Cosi quizzed him on what he was doing.

'Sarah asked me if I'd share some of my original songs since she's sent me a bunch of hers. Which are good.'

A voice popped up, 'Hey Cosi, how are you?' Cosi recognised the accent. It was Sarah.

Rabbit hated being out of the control seat, literally and metaphorically. Gleefully, Cosi shared how he'd said 'Hi' to Sarah before turning his well-worn sneakers in the direction of the door – making a beeline for me. As amusing as I found Cosi's re-enactment, secretly I felt irked by the whole thing. Rabbit had struck up an instant friendship with this girl on the other side of the world and yet here I was, buggerlugs, having worked my ass off for over a year now trying to get even a breadcrumb of a bond with him. And still I had nothing.

I'd learned by then that nobody trusted anybody in radio, especially if you were on-air. Since Cosi's arrival suspicions between us had tripled. This wasn't just because Cosi didn't mind a gossip or that he had his own agenda, it came because he and Rabbit were 'buddies' on the surface but they both fiercely wanted pole position as the male star. And that, in truth, made them enemies.

Several weeks after the Sarah gotcha, in one of Cosi's fact-finding missions he'd found Rabbit had been trying to get Sarah to help him do a reverse gotcha on Blaine – meaning this time he wanted to prank Blaine. Apparently it hadn't come off because Sarah had gone quiet. Not one to give up, Rabbit decided to go back to Blaine suggesting a video prank on Sarah when she arrived from Canada.

The plan was Rabbit would be at the airport with a film crew waiting for Sarah as she walked out of the arrivals hall, disguised as a limousine driver holding up a sign with her name on it. The limousine was going to be rigged with cameras and microphones and from there he planned to take her on a wild goose chase around Adelaide, pretending to be a clueless driver. The strange thing was, after all the fanfare about his big gotcha production, we kept waiting for him to announce it but he never did. Cosi's inside intelligence had all but dried up – until one memorable morning. We'd just finished planning the show for the next day and Cosi and I were sitting at our desks finishing off emails and getting ready to leave. Before we made it out the door our producer dropped in on us.

'Excuse me, guys, would you mind coming back into the studio before you take off for the day?' she asked. 'Rabbit needs you for something.'

Cosi and I rolled our eyes at each other. We'd both hoped to score an early mark. We got up, dragging ourselves slowly toward the studio. When she got to the door she stopped and turned around and said, 'Just a quick head's up. Remember the girl Sarah from Canada?' 'Yes?' we harmonised, like Nick and Joe Jonas. 'Well something bad has happened to her and Rabbit wants to share it with you. He wants to record her explaining what she's told him. We'll play it on-air tomorrow.'

Cosi and I snuck a glance at each other, suspicious of Rabbit's motives. Rabbit was sitting behind the radio desk looking down at the control panel as we filed into the studio, his guitar leaning conspicuously behind his chair. Cosi and I sat down in our usual seats as Rabbit looked up.

'So, you remember Sarah in Canada who I did the gotcha call on?' We nodded. 'Well she and I have become pretty close mates since then' – flashback to Cosi busting him mid-concert. 'Anyway, I'd been trying to do another gotcha on them. I wanted to get Blaine and then I was going to get Sarah when she arrived. But I wasn't getting a response from either for nearly six weeks, which was unlike Sarah,' he said, sounding serious.

A thought popped into my head as Rabbit paused. I wondered whether Sarah's Aussie fiancé might have told her to tone down the friendship with her new semi-famous radio guy. I mean, how many guys would be happy with their new fiancée chatting (and singing) every day with a bloke neither of them had ever met?

Initially frustrated he couldn't get Sarah or Blaine to sign up to another gotcha, Rabbit said he'd started to suspect something was wrong. Sarah finally wrote back apologising for dropping off the grid. She explained she and Blaine had been coming to grips with 'the news'. Rabbit went silent for a few seconds before continuing. 'Sarah's got stage four breast cancer. She's only got a few months to live.'

I don't know what I thought the Sarah update was going to be, but it wasn't this. It was hard to wrap my head around. This poor young couple we'd come to know through their love story were now dealing with death and losing each other forever. It was absolutely shocking. My thoughts shot back to Julian and me. How would either of us have coped with such a horrific fate?

'I've spoken to Sarah, she and Blaine have decided that she'll share her news with our listeners,' announced Rabbit. My suspicious mind took over as I took in what he'd said. What does Sarah get out of this? Why would she want to share this with strangers on the other side of the world? It didn't add up for me but I dared not share my thought with Rabbit. So, I shut up. Maybe I'll sense her purpose once I hear her voice?

Before we called her our producer informed us that our station would be donating $1000 to them. Rabbit told us Blaine had moved to Canada to be with his fiancé, leaving his well-paid job in Adelaide and was now working out in the snow on a construction site. Apparently the young couple were so broke from Sarah's medical bills that Blaine was forced to wear a pair of old boots in the snow that were taped up and full of holes.

I felt nervous as Rabbit dialled Sarah's number, wondering what to say to a girl who's dying? I wished this wasn't happening, that I could reverse time for her and that she could still be that girl I'd heard on the gotcha call, stressing about her de-facto visa. The call with Sarah was heartbreaking and humbling. As I listened to her tell her story I was struck by just how inspiring she was in the way she was processing all that was happening. Her bravery was overwhelming. I couldn't even manage to get the guts to share my split from a guy that I didn't love and here this girl was talking about how death was going to take her away from a man she wanted to marry. The whole thing blew me away. It gave me a reason to pause and take stock in a way working in radio had never done before. Maybe Sarah had a message to tell the world, and the radio was her channel to share it widely?

When I got back to my desk after the pre-record, there was an email to me from Sarah.

Hi Amber,

I got your email address from the station; I hope you don't mind. I'm Sarah. I spoke with you this morning. I am the one marrying Blaine and who you so generously gave $1000 to. Thank you again for that. I am writing to you because I wanted to get your opinion/help on something. (I know. greedy lil bugger aren't I) So, it looks like Blaine and I are getting hitched on the 24th of January. it's going to be a small thing but we are hoping it to be traditional. Just a tiny lil wedding at his mom's house. It's very much just Blaine's family and friends. His Mum offered that her brother Bruce (who I have met before and has travelling hands) to walk me down the aisle. I really don't want that. I know it may not see like a big thing but it's a very special moment for me … I wanted to ask Rabbit (who is already attending) if he wouldn't mind escorting me down the aisle. I have a lot of respect for him. He has been fantastic to us, and not only would it mean the world to me, we have nothing else to give, and would like that to be a thank you. What do you think? I was going to give him a call at the station on Friday to ask him. What time does he usually leave? Thanks again for everything.

Love, Sarah

I had mixed feelings reading Sarah's email. I was comfortable being part of a group talking to her but one-on-one was a whole other thing. I felt a sense of handling something precious and not wanting to break it. Sarah's situation was so tragically delicate and I wasn't confident I could take care of her. I couldn't even take care of myself. I wondered, too, why Sarah would think to come to me, wanting my opinion on something related to Rabbit? The truth was I was the last person to know what he wanted or thought about anything. I figured I was overthinking. She probably had no way of knowing how to contact his wife. Besides, why wouldn't she presume we were mates? We sounded like it on air. We looked like it in photos.

It wasn't hard to work out how much Sarah's request would mean to Rabbit. It was apparent that morning how much he cared for Sarah and how much he was affected by her news.

I took a moment to reflect on Sarah's predicament. It was so heavy. She'd mentioned she and Blaine still wanted to get married in Adelaide, regardless of anything. What must it be like to be planning a wedding knowing you won't be around long enough to see out your first year together? And then I considered: Perhaps Sarah is planning a wedding and details like Rabbit walking her down the aisle might be just the thing she needs to focus her mind on?

I wrote back expressing how much I felt her request would mean to Rabbit. I reinforced how much her story had touched me personally and that I was around and willing to do anything I could to help them.

It was Rabbit's birthday that Friday so we made a small fuss about that. And, excitingly, it was our last show for the year. Thank god. The thought of getting on a plane to Thailand for a two-week solo trip after heading to Melbourne for Christmas had been my lifeline as I crawled towards the finish line. I'd been fantasising for months about a banana lounge, a pina colada, a self-help book and just switching off from the bullshit at work.

My thoughts had also been on Sarah and Blaine since Wednesday's call. It was hard not to feel guilty about all the great things that were coming up over the next month or so – especially Christmas. While I'd be lounging on a beach, unwrapping gifts in Melbourne and toasting the new year with friends back at home, Sarah and Blaine were facing their last Christmas together.

As our final show of the year reached its last hour it was time to play our call with Sarah after which Rabbit brought her on live to announce we'd be donating $1000 to them. Sarah cried, graciously thanking us before signing off with 'Happy Birthday' to Rabbit. We turned the mikes off for an ad and song break, which was when our producer followed by the Big Radio Boss came filing into the studio. Our phone lines were going absolutely berserk. I could see our assistant producer through the studio window, frantically trying to keep up with callers.

Our producer ducked out to get an update from the assistant. Almost every caller wanted to give money. We hadn't asked for it but they were offering all sorts of amounts. Our team had five minutes to make decisions on how to play the rest of the show. The studio door opened and in walked our Promotions Manager. She wanted guidance on how they should handle the money coming in as pledges. There was no network strategy in place for this kind of thing. I decided it was best to sit back and wait for directions.

The Big Radio Boss made the call on going back on the air, Rabbit recapping Sarah's story, then allowing each caller to come on and say whatever they wanted. It was decided we'd run past the 9 am finish and come back on after the news. We'd never done this but we'd also never had so many callers. And we'd never had a tragic love story unfold on our show.

The calls kept coming, with offers of countless donations. Cosi announced at regular intervals which advertisers were donating their services. There were diamond rings, a wedding dress, wineries for a wedding reception, holiday homes for the honeymoon. It was unbelievable. So were the boys. They were both playing to their strengths. During a music break our producer called through the desk asking me to step out to talk to her.

'Sarah says you guys talked yesterday after the pre-record. She said she has something important to ask Rabbit?' I filled her in about Sarah wanting Rabbit to walk her down the aisle.

'I'm going to bring her back on at the end of the next break to do it on-air,' she said. Wow, this is going to be heavy, I thought. When we got to the big moment, I slowly edged a box of tissues towards Rabbit.

'So, Rabbit, would you do me the honour of walking me down the aisle,' Sarah asked, tearfully. Rabbit broke for the first time as he replied, 'I'd be honoured to Sarah'.

CHAPTER FIVE.

ANGEL SARAH

The coast of Newfoundland in Canada, near where the Titanic sank, was where Sarah Dickenson grew up. I thought back to the afternoon I saw the movie *Titanic*, a year after I broke up with Julian. I sat through all three hours gripped, yet tortured. My friend Kate sat slumped in the seat next to me, unashamedly sobbing, while I sat erect, clenching my entire body as hard as I could. Unconsciously I was terrified that if I let myself succumb to the sadness; I'd unlock something terrible that might never stop.

   Two tragic love stories linked a cold place on the other side of the world. In early January of 2009, during an hour-long phone call with Sarah, she shared memories of her life. She told me her dad, Tony, had grown up in Newfoundland and her mum, Birgitta, was from a small city outside of Copenhagen in Denmark. The two met at the University of Toronto and it was 'love at first sight'. When her dad graduated from engineering, he was offered a job back home so Birgitta agreed to go with him. Eighteen months later Sarah's brother Chris was born – four years later came Sarah.

'We were super close, Chris and I,' she reflected. 'I guess you end up being close when you spend long periods indoors and sometimes we'd get snowed in, which was something we loved and hated. We couldn't go to school so we had to hang out. We always found stuff to do. I used to make jewellery and insist my parents buy it and Chris would paint a lot – but we also did stuff together. I loved my big bro'.

Sarah was living in Toronto in 2000 when her mum called with news that her dad had cancer. 'I didn't know what to say,' she said softly. 'I found it hard to get my head around it. Mum was trying to be strong and said she felt he'd beat it. She was wrong. He was dead in six months.'

Sarah returned home for a few months to rally with the family. 'Mum lost her best friend and, I think, her will to live'. she told me. 'She tried to keep being a good Mum, tried to be there for Chris and me, but she lost her spirit. Like someone had turned her light off. She just didn't shine anymore.'

Sarah's mum died less than two years later. 'It didn't surprise me when she told me she was sick. No matter how much the doctors or our friends would say how unlucky it is for a couple to both contract cancer I felt like it gave me some peace in the middle of enormous grief. It made sense they still wanted – needed – to be together. If not here, then in heaven, and I was OK with that. I guess I'm a lot like my mum. I believe in big love,' she confessed.

I could see how Sarah was able to draw strength from her past to deal with her diagnosis. And it wasn't lost on me that there was a message in her story I needed to hear – the girl who treated Titanic like it was a horror movie, the girl who watched The Notebook and cried so loudly her neighbours called over the fence, 'Hello. Is everything OK?'

Sarah was teaching me about love – that it can't be controlled – and how quickly it can be gone. With dreams of becoming a yoga instructor, Sarah moved back to Toronto after her Dad died and got her yoga certificate while living in a fun share-house. When her mum died three months later, she put her new career on hold and sub-let her room. Her mum's passing apparently inspiring her to fulfil another secret dream of travelling to a remote village in Africa where she volunteered with seven other young women to help build a new school.

'The rewards were incredible and I just felt so lucky to have had my time. I thought someday I would go back,' she said, her voice stained with sadness. Her words hit home with me. 'Someday I'd go back.' Sarah didn't have a someday any more, but I did. And yet here I was, fixated on feeling left out of life. *It's all there, you dickhead. The only thing stopping you is you.* But life has a curious way of redirecting you and if it wasn't for Sarah not going back to Africa, she might never have met Blaine – the handsome Aussie she'd bumped into at a venue called The Music in Toronto. Apparently, Blaine knocked a tray of shots she was carrying back to her friends, cascading the sticky liquid down the front of her T-shirt. She would have been more pissed off, she said, had she not looked up and discovered how 'crazy, cute he was'. 'I looked at him and said, 'You just destroyed two of my shots, now you need to destroy two of yours.'

I'd seen photos of Sarah. She was a pretty, curly-haired brunette. A sassy little Canadian who looked like fun – all five foot three of her, with a smile that looked like it could suck anyone in. Reminiscing about that fateful night when she met Blaine, Sarah described how she veered back to the corner of the bar then playfully demanded Blaine scull two of his drinks.

'Now we're even,' she giggled, 'You may proceed.'

It wasn't long into the night before Sarah convinced her friends to march over to the boys' table and ask if there was room for them to 'merge'. Later, Sarah recounted, her friends were freaking out over the instant chemistry between her and Blaine. 'I think we just fell into our own little vortex for a while.' By the end of the night they were exchanging numbers. It was the start of the biggest love of her life.

I found out later there'd been other loves in Sarah's life. While still a teenager living in Newfoundland, she'd fallen in love with a guy called Josh – *Joshua Jackson*. Years later he'd gone on to become one of the biggest teen stars in the world in his role on *Dawson's Creek*. Sarah seemed to want to play it down a little, saying 'It was just a year'. I thought back to my first real boyfriend, realising how easy it is to play down past love once it's over. Especially if you have found a love that feels larger.

And then there was her ex-boyfriend directly before Blaine who — bizarrely — was another famous guy — comedian/actor Dane Cook. I'd literally just watched him a week earlier in *My Best Friend's Girl*, starring Kate Hudson. He was gorgeous — but an asshole. Shoving popcorn into my face I thought to myself just how close to real life I suspected Dane's character might be — easy to fall for but bad news for the heart.

Sarah claiming not one — but two — famous exes might have set off warning bells for some. Yet I'd learned in life that just because Sarah wasn't famous didn't mean she wasn't special. Hell, she'd even managed to get through the Rabbit-proof fence of my co-host.

Sarah claimed she met Dane through her brother Chris, 'I think he thought I was cute and I laughed at all his jokes, so that helped,' she said with a chuckle. I could see how that would work. I'd be the same. She was twenty-one when they started dating and he was beginning to get attention in Hollywood. Apparently, that meant lots of back and forth between Canada and the US and Sarah was forced to visit him in LA during their four-year romance.

'I hated the LA party scene,' Sarah admitted. Apparently, Dane didn't love it either but knew it was a necessary part of building his career. The way Sarah described it; Hollywood became the toxic third wheel in their relationship. In the end their different worlds tore them apart.

I could hear in her voice how much Sarah cared for Dane, although she was careful to insert a mention that Blaine was the real 'one'. The *last* one.

As she was talking about Dane I wondered if he knew she was sick. In typical Sarah style she read my mind, 'I emailed Dane before Christmas hinting that I'd had bad news about my health. I didn't want him finding out before I got the chance to tell him.' He didn't want to talk about it over the phone. Instead he was going to use a three-day break in his tour to come to her.

'He told me to "hang on".'

I remembered when my stepmother Helen was dying. How she'd hung on to say goodbye to her son Andy. I didn't think she was going to make it. She had seemed breaths away from dying even before Andy had left the US, where he was living. But she did – she hung on until he reached her bed – and then she went. And I wondered, did Sarah need to say goodbye to Dane? Or did Dane need to show her how much she still meant to him? Maybe he was only now realising just how much.

Rabbit had taken it upon himself to set up a Facebook account for Sarah over the Christmas break and since then I'd occasionally received messages on it from her. I noticed she'd included a quote in her bio that read, 'Trying to live each day, smile to smile.'

On the day Dane arrived she sent me a Facebook message. She described how he'd come with Mapleton's organic ice cream, apparently their favourite. I couldn't help but get a little lost in the image of this gorgeous guy arriving at Sarah's house holding a tub of ice cream. *I mean, please ... How had I not realised this was my greatest fantasy?* I was glad, though, that it was happening to Sarah that day. My mind went to Dane and the viewpoint he was coming into this from – seeing Sarah for the first time bedridden, hair nearly gone, drips hanging out of her body, a deathly diluted version of the smile he once fell in love with. What a painfully confronting image. Apparently, Dane was still with Sarah when she sent me another Facebook message. She warned he 'might be reading over my shoulder'. They'd spent the afternoon on her bed talking while Dane finished off the entire tub of ice cream after Sarah had confessed that she had no appetite.

She'd also mentioned in her message that she'd told him all about the gotcha and follow-up calls on-air with us. She said she'd pulled up our show's website on her laptop, describing Rabbit, Cosi and I and the new friendships she'd created with us. At some point, a bit later, she messaged again saying Dane had seen my Facebook profile and had been keen to 'check me out' further. According to Sarah, Dane thought I was 'cute' and she wanted my permission to give him my contact details, given he didn't use Facebook except as a 'fan' account.

Look at Little Miss Matchmaker. It summed up Sarah. She was all about love. And obviously I couldn't help but be just a tiny bit – slash very bloody excited – to think that Dane Cook – *did someone say asshole?* – might be checking me out.

Sarah later told me, after what sounded like a beautiful but heartbreaking goodbye between her and Dane, that he was coming to Australia with his sister in May and then back with his tour around November. 'He's been having a tough time since discovering his brother in law has been ripping him off financially,' she wrote. I suddenly felt protective over a guy I didn't even know. And hopeful that he might contact me at some point that year.

I woke up after our 2008 Christmas party feeling like a squashed crab in a sewage pipe. Was it the recent sadness of Sarah's illness, a general need to drink off an entire twelve months of radio, or a pre-existing binge-drinking issue? But, holy Jesus, did I do a number on myself. Evidence of the night: the delicate new silk dress with silver thread – the one I'd been so excited to road-test – lay in a crumpled, bloodstained heap next to my bed. I'd drunk myself into a complete zombie state. It was as I stood watching the venue owner slam the door in the faces of the last of us party-goers that I discovered I'd left my handbag, phone and house keys inside. It was the usual Friday night (and me drinking) disaster.

Meanwhile, on the other side of the world, Sarah was dealing with shit not of her own making. She wrote that Blaine had come home drunk the night before and began ranting about Rabbit and her having an 'emotional affair'. She said he ended up breaking down about her being sick, angry that he'd be the one left when she was gone.

I felt guilty not writing back that same day – but I needed sleep. I was due to fly out to Thailand the next day and, thanks to my efforts the night before, I was feeling unnecessarily anxious about my travelling day ahead.

When I arrived in Thailand, I discovered the reason I'd scored such a fabulously, cheap deal on my hotel was that it was a shithole. As for thinking I'd be sleeping the mornings away, then lounging poolside, the hotel was wedged between two of the island's major nightclubs. I might as well have been sleeping on the dance floor. I decided not to check my emails for a few days given I was trying to extract myself from anything that would add to my anxiety. In my exhausted and negative state there was a part of me that sensed Sarah wanted something from me and I had to admit the pressure wasn't sitting right. At least for a few days I would accept the side of me that felt guilt.

I did check my emails eventually. I didn't like keeping people hanging, let alone a poor girl dying of cancer. I acknowledged her email about Blaine. I told her Rabbit had mentioned he'd received a 'weird phone call' from someone he thought might have been Blaine. I asked if they'd considered therapy. But there was also a new email waiting from Sarah, this time it was to a group. She was informing the undisclosed recipients that she was changing her email address – now using her married name, Sarah Armstrong.

It made me think. *If I were dying, would I take the time to change my email address? If I were madly in love? Would my desire to take my husband's name for the little time I had left convince me to do what Sarah had just done?* I wasn't sure I'd have the strength to think about it, but she did, and it made me love Sarah's spirit even more. I saw it as a gesture of enormous courage – something I needed to learn for myself.

Over the next few days Sarah sent several emails from her new 'Mrs Armstrong' account. In some of them she seemed to trail off. I wondered if it might the drugs. Or maybe her spirit was being pulled gently above? I didn't know, but I sensed we were losing her.

Hi Amber,

So, friendship is a weird thing. It's a term that's thrown around carelessly by some, and others do value its meaning. It means different things to different people in many different contexts. I mean the whole MySpace 'Friends' thing ... I get it ... but when it comes to my real friends, I hope they know who they are ... To those who I grew up with... went to high school, college ... and people I was lucky enough to encounter in my travels. I hope they know that they mean everything to me ... and whether we still talk or not ... just because we don't, doesn't mean anything happened ... it just means we were in each other's lives for the appropriate amount of time ... and just grew apart ... or as a dear friend tells me all the time 'the universe is unfolding as it should'. Does that make us bad people? I don't think so. I think, and hope that we both gained and learned something from the friendship while we had it ... and thank you for that and for the memories. You have left an impression in me. Those friends whose lives have been cut short... I miss you ... dearly. I guarantee you I don't remember you once a year on the anniversary of your death, but I celebrate your life every day. I like to think that a part of you is in my heart and help me when I need to make decisions in my life. My friends who don't live nearby ... just because you aren't a local call away doesn't mean I don't think of you any less. If anything I think of you more. Thank you for your support, and when you call or message me... it makes me value our friendship even more ... gives me the knowledge that you think of me as much as I think of you, and I do really look forward to our next meeting. To my friends in the city I hope I don't take you for granted, nor do I hope you take me for granted. I appreciate you. I honour you. I look forward to seeing you ... and am happy when we randomly run into each other. To my friends I hope to make in the future... I can't wait. I look forward to learning from you, I look forward to becoming a better person for knowing you. I guess what I'm trying to say is never take anyone for granted. Appreciate everyone and everything. Just because someone is no longer in your life, for whatever reason that may be, value the time you had together and remember what life lessons they gave you. I promise, they left an impression on you somehow.

Love, Sarah Armstrong. x

Two days later there was an email from Hannah, Blaine's younger sister. She wrote advising that Sarah was being taken off all life-support machines.

Scariest moment ever when they turned everything off. It's now up to her. She is doing it on her own. She has been moved from ICU to a private room. They will do nothing. NOTHING if she starts to decline. It's not right. Makes no sense to me.

She mentioned she'd printed off emails people had sent Sarah so that she could read them to her. 'We are told she can hear us,' she said. Hannah described how Blaine had been spending the last few nights lying next to his wife amid her wires and tubes. 'He has full faith she will wake up. He is singing to her, telling old stories. Everything. I reckon he may be strong enough for them both.'

More emails from Hannah came through as I was travelling home to Melbourne, including an update to say Sarah had opened her eyes while Blaine was singing to her. She wasn't talking as yet but she was communicating via a whiteboard and marker next to her bed.

Our show went back on-air by in the middle of January 2009. A few days after my return I got a phone call I didn't expect. It was from Sarah. She was miraculously out of hospital and she and Blaine were living in the basement of Sarah's childhood friend, Sara. Sarah shared details of how the two of them had grown up near each other in Newfoundland. Sara, a scriptwriter for a popular TV show in Canada called *The Hour*, now lived in a large suburban house in Toronto with her husband Jeff, and their three young boys. Apparently, they had a huge basement that was heated and fitted out for guests. Sarah said she'd stayed there when she first moved to Toronto so, 'It feels like home.' It was so nice to hear Sarah's voice, though it was much softer now. As happy as I was to get another chance to talk to her, I worried about the toll it might take on her. Then I asked myself: *Why would you put off speaking to someone you cared about if you might not ever get to talk to them again?*

I loved the way Sarah seemed to know what was best for her. It astonished me how she seemed to offer magical lessons I needed to learn – *Perhaps it wasn't an accident we'd connected?* I thought. Instead it felt orchestrated.

It had been so bizarre; the way I had come to know this beautiful girl I'd nicknamed 'Angel Sarah'. Equally strange was how she was affecting me in such a profound way. Her story was inspiring me to review my own life. I came away from every call with some wisdom. Sarah had come into my life at precisely the right time and I was committed to my new year, my new self and my new friend, to switch the direction of my mental compass. I owed it to Sarah, who was no longer able to plan more than a day ahead.

WHEN YOU'RE GONE

The next day after we'd finished the show, I noticed the boys appeared to have taken off without saying goodbye. *Rude little bastards,* I thought. Then, just as I was about to walk out of the office, something told me to check my emails. There was a new series of messages from Sarah:

Hiya. Sure. I will give you a call after Rabbit calls me. He wants me to record something ... to say goodbye ... have it written down ... feels weird ... tried reading it out loud .... cried. Blaine's Mum is here ...flat out exhausted and freezing. Never seen real snow before ... she thought it was so pretty until she couldn't get warm. Hahah. Loves. Me xo

10.25 am

In fact, if you get this before 11am ... could I fwd you what I wrote?

My heart was racing. *Was I seriously reading this? Surely Rabbit wouldn't be putting his friend up to reading a fucking goodbye so we could play it on-air?* With my adrenaline pumping I prayed I could type fast enough so I could stop her. This time I was not going to tippy-toe around Rabbit's ego. I also didn't give a flying fuck what the ramifications with the Big Radio Boss would be.

10.35 am

It's already done ... on the phone now to Cosi and Rabs right now

It felt right tho. And I'm glad I got to say what I had to say

I was too late. I didn't speak to the boys for the rest of the day. They went their way and I went mine. But the penny was dropping for Sarah in the hours after her crafted 'goodbye'.

2 pm

Hiya ... You around? This thing I did today. That wasn't just for radio was it? Don't tell rabs I'm feeling this way. I'm just wondering. It was because he thought it was best for me. Not radio, right? Loves. Me. Xo

How was I going to tell this wonderful girl that her suspicions about her friend using her for radio entertainment were right? I thought a lot about Sarah that week. It's hard to talk to someone who's running out of time. You wonder if you might be overstepping boundaries of what they need to hear or what might be a good distraction from their impending fate versus being insensitive. But the beauty of Sarah was the way she made you comfortable by reinforcing she had accepted her fate, insisting on me not second-guessing whatever I was going to say. As Sarah's death drew closer, I made more time to talk with her. I was conscious I was being gifted with the wisdom of a person whose spirit was dancing between the physical and spiritual planes.

Rabbit remained put out by the friendship I'd formed with Sarah but I'd stopped caring what he thought. I did wonder, however, if one of Sarah's final missions was to bring Rabbit and me closer? She'd always spoken of my co-host, her close friend, with genuine care and respect. She presented a view of him that was out of reach to me. Whatever she was up to, I trusted her. The next morning, I read what turned out to be Sarah's final email to me. It would, for many reasons, prove to be the most significant.

Hiya. Two of my favourite people. When Sara finally treats herself to that trip ... you two should meet ... Sara you should really meet everyone over there. You will love Amber and Cosi ... and you can make your own mind up about Rabbit ... keep your mind open. I'm flat out exhausted today. Love you both. You two will love each other. Loves. Me

xo

I noticed Sarah was winding things up on Facebook. 'Sarah is ready to let go', her status now read. As well as running out of time she was running out of breath. She'd spoken about her best friend Sara several times. She would spend her last hours in her home. I was worried about Sarah that night, feeling she should have been conserving her energy rather than wasting it on me. She'd finished our last couple of calls by saying, 'You take care of you now? *OK?*'

Towards the end of the call that night there was a heavy pause. I could feel a wall come up between us. The truth was I didn't know what to say. I sat staring at the walls of an apartment that no longer felt like home. I was struggling with everything – where I lived, losing my friend, being left behind (as crazy and ungrateful as that sounded). Things felt like they were sliding. To where, I didn't know.

'Are you OK?' she asked, piercing the silence.

'Yes,' I replied, trying to push out of my sadness. I didn't want her to hear me cry. I didn't want our last goodbye to be about my grief.

'You're crying, aren't you?' she asked, softly.

'No, I'm fine, I promise.' I lied. I felt pathetic as I failed miserably at putting on a show of strength. I couldn't even manage to suck it up for five minutes for a dying girl.

'Don't cry, you're going to be just fine – and me too,' she said.

'OK, see you wherever it is, OK?' I whispered, trying to pull it together.

'Yes, but have a good time in between. *Please* remember to honour the in-between.'

Then we hung up. I felt like I was being pulled down by an invisible weight. My spirit, my soul, yearned to wrench itself out of my body so I could just float towards the stars. Or maybe I was peering into the place where my friend's spirit was preparing to soar? I didn't know. Nothing made sense anymore. I looked at my phone, knowing Sarah would never call again. The girl who we'd thought had so much ahead of her had had it all taken away. I cried so hard that night, as though trying to dislodge the pain.

But it was more than the loss of someone I'd never met – I was mourning a connection with someone who'd encouraged me to open my heart. It had been a long time since I'd shown vulnerability to anyone. With a head full of doubt about my life – graced with health but empty of love – I thought of Sarah, who'd found her soul-mate but was robbed of being with him. Between waves of sadness, and resentment towards whatever god was out there, I felt gratitude for the fact Sarah had chosen me, among a handful of people, to share her last days and thoughts with. I knew there was something bigger out there in the infinite universe at play. What exactly that was I'd have to wait to see. Rabbit called a few hours later to ask if I wanted him to pick me up on his motorbike so we could head to a movie premiere together. This was not standard Rabbit behaviour so I was surprised, and touched. I wondered if it might be the start of a new era between us thanks, of course, to Sarah. It was 6 pm on Friday when I heard the roar of Rabbit's motorbike. *What exactly am I going to say?* I wondered as I walked out to greet him. *Do I check to see how he's doing? How he's coping? Or do I just let it go, be grateful for the gesture – his way of saying, 'We're going through this together, now let's just shut up and ride.'*

By evening it was still sunny and hot, with a warm, soft breeze that felt comforting. I hung on to Rabbit as we rode. It was an intimacy we'd never shared before, flying down that highway, and I could feel we were both somewhere else. Our minds were on Sarah. We arrived at the event and went straight into Rabbit and Amber hosting mode. We introduced the movie, made a few lame jokes at each other's expense, and then sat down to watch the film.

About an hour after Rabbit dropped me off that night, having just lit a candle, incense, and climbed into bed, my phone rang. It was Rabbit. 'I'm just ringing to let you know she's gone. Blaine just emailed me to let me know.' His tone was soft. My heart sank, although the news was no surprise. That night I felt a connection with Rabbit I had never had before. I saw him as a man, and a human in mourning, not the radio host I saw when the mikes were on, and not the guy I saw when they were off. Sarah had left her imprint on us.

The following morning there was a group email sent from Blaine's account, although it didn't appear to be from him – possibly Sara or Hannah I figured – it wasn't clear.

Early this morning, surrounded by those she loved, in Blaine's arms, Mrs Sarah Grace Armstrong found her way to heaven. In what can only be described as a peaceful sleep she fell into, she never woke from it. There will be memorials in Toronto and SA so Sarah's ashes can be with those she loved in the two places she loved. There are no dates set for either. The Toronto memorial will be within the next week and will be held at home where she was last happy. As for the SA memorial, Blaine will be doing some travelling before he heads home. Sarah is survived by her loving husband Blaine. Blaine has the comfort of his Mum and sister here in Toronto. We ask that you please respect this time for the Armstrong family and not call. Emails will be replied to as needed. Sarah wrote a note along with her song, that is copied here.

Well if you are reading this it means I am no longer in pain and in a much better spot and with my family ... so no need to be sad right?? I know. It's sad that we won't chat, share jokes or make each other smile or laugh on this level anymore. But, if you know me, and I'm assuming you did because you are getting this, you know I will always be in your corner. That overly cheesy line or dumb ass comment that comes into your head when you are talking to someone irritating. that will be me. That laugh you hear in your head when you see someone trip and fall flat on their face ... that will be me. Or that song you can't get out of your head sometimes. that will be my fault.

Some of you I have known a long time, some of you a short time. Blaine and his family have only been in my life a short time but they are some of the most important people I have ever met. I won't go into my feeling for Blaine here he has his own letter and right now ... I just can't do that. Canada peeps ... love you all. If you go to Australia ... please visit my friends and family out there. I know Blaine and Hannah have a memorial planned in Toronto before they leave the country so contact Blaine. And when you are in Oz ... he will know how to contact peeps out there. Aussie Mates ... there are no words, love, grace, compassion they don't even start to cover it. If you guys ever make it out to Canada give my Canuck peeps a shout you will have a great time ... I promise. I know B and Hannah are planning a mini memorial for me in Adelaide, Blaine will have all the info ... he will also let you know how to contact my crazy Canuck pals! Hey Rabs: 4389. If I was smart, I would quote my favourite poem by Dylan Thomas ... but this is getting to be long enough ... so I've included a link ... LOL ... How modern/lazy is that?! Please don't forget to have fun and laugh at everything. Smile until it hurts and tell everyone around you that you love them and appreciate them. You don't know what tomorrow holds

Love you all.

Me, Mrs. Sarah 'Sassy' Armstrong X

If there is anyone who did not get this email that should have, please forward on information. We love you and miss you Sarah. Heaven will certainly be a lot more fun with you. Peace be with you. You will be in our hearts forever.

Sarah Grace Armstrong (nee Dickenson) June 15th, 1981 February 5th, 2009

I wrote to Blaine, offering my sympathies. I didn't know Blaine but I could imagine his loss. A few hours later, he sent a cryptic response, '4389. tattooed on her ankle. Her password to everything, the day of the month me, her mom, her Dad and her brother were born. On the phone it spelled out 4ETY = 4 ever thank you.'

On-air the next day 4389 popped up again as Rabbit ended our show by playing Sarah's goodbye message. I hated it. I still believed it was totally inappropriate. It ended with, 'Hey Rabs, don't forget 4389'. It left me wondering: *Was it Sarah or you, Rabbit, that got the final word today?*

A WINDOW OF TIME

Whether it was the new year or the impact of Sarah's passing I was intent on making changes in my life – it was time to buy an apartment and a puppy. Two things I could financially and spiritually call my own. While hot-footing it through a shopping centre one evening, running late to host a movie screening, I noticed in my peripheral vision a pet store on the other side of the centre. I was ignorant at the time about puppy farms but I also can't deny fate. And I do believe it was fate that lassoed me around the neck that day. The pet store window was mostly empty bar one small bundle of white fluff. I walked over to get a closer look. *Where are all its friends?* I put my nose up to the window. The little guy looked up curiously, then looked back down. He looked so sad. I wanted to cry. Then I realised it wasn't just his lonely predicament – I wanted to cry because I'd found him. I had found *the one*. Then the panic set in: *Fuck it, I'm late.* I didn't want to leave the new great love of my life behind but I also knew I couldn't slam down my credit card on the counter, yank my little guy out of his hay-lined bed and then take him to see an R rated movie. I raced inside the store, startling the girl behind the counter, 'Hi. I'm in love with the dog in the window. Is it a he or she, not that it matters?' It was a 'he' and I have no idea what she said after that. I just needed her to understand that he was mine.

'It's OK. I know who you are. We'll keep him for you and you can come back tomorrow.' I wanted to kiss her. It was hideous having to leave the store without my baby that night. My only consolation was I knew that, through that pane of glass, I had met the child I was destined to love. The next day I would collect my baby. I called my friend Bec to tell her I was going to become a mum. Being single herself, and having a dog, she knew just how big a milestone this was for me. She offered to pick me up at 11 am the next day so we could get my baby together.

At 6 am my inner alarm went off. Barely a second clicked over before I was screaming, *Oh my god, today is the day I become a mum! Today is going to be the best day of my whole life.* Overly anxious, I thought I should put a quick call into the store to remind them I was coming. As I finished talking there was an uncomfortable second of silence before the shop assistant replied in a tone I did not like one iota, 'I'm afraid we have some good news and some bad news, Amber. Which would you like first?' She sounded nervous but, quite frankly, not nervous enough. I asked for the bad news first. 'Well, one of the other girls who works here didn't realise we'd put a hold on him for you, so she sold him to a young family an hour ago,' she said. *Another family? Are you kidding me? What part of 'they've already fucking got each other to love' is this moron not getting?* I was ropeable. 'But the good news is they have another dog already so they're just going to give it until Monday to see if he gets along with the one they've already got. If he doesn't, they'll bring him back and we'll call you up. *OK?*'

I will never, with true accuracy, recall what words came out of my mouth before I hung up the phone that day. I was so devastated I may have hung up on her – and I kind of hope I did. I called Bec immediately. 'They've taken him!' I wailed dramatically down the phone. I was shattered. Bec tried to convince me we'd find 'another baby' for me that day. She offered to take me to other stores around town but I had zero interest. I'd already fallen in love and you can't replace love like it's a blown lightbulb. I couldn't take another dog if there was even a sliver of hope that this *family* might return *my* little boy.

Not taking 'leave me alone to mourn deeply alone all weekend,' Bec arrived twenty minutes later. 'Let's just go for a drive,' she insisted, trying to soothe me. After six stores and a succession of adorable furry faces with eyes that said, 'Take me!' I wanted to go home. What was meant to be the most fulfilling day of my life had become the emptiest. The only scrap of respite came when I decided to call Cosi, who didn't answer, thus allowing me to fill his message bank with a rambling, profanity-drenched run down of the day's events that ended with, 'Anyway Cosi, everything's fucked. Like, hardcore, fucked.'

I wasn't looking forward to Monday morning. The last thing I wanted to do at 8.10 am was reveal my depressing update, 'Guess what, guys? I'm still on my own.' But I knew I wasn't going to get out of it that easily. Cosi by then had heard my psychotic voicemail message. He'd also sweetly called me Sunday night to commiserate. Rabbit, however, had avoided involving himself in the drama that would unfold at 8.10 am, preferring to be able to react naturally to my tale. Either that, or he didn't give a shit. Here's how it went:

RABBIT: Rabbit, Amber and Cosi, on 107.1, it's ten past eight.

COSI: Now Petty, we all know you were all excited about collecting your little white fluff ball from the pet store on Saturday morning. It's your first dog and all that and, let's face it, it's about time you had a male in your life. But it didn't go quite to plan, did it?

AMBER: No, it didn't. I called the store Saturday morning, and they informed me that there'd been a mix up and they sold him to a family.

COSI: Yeah, and you were understandably a little bit upset? You left a message for me on Saturday late arvo after you'd been tearing around town looking for another pup.

AMBER: Which I was never going to get. I was never going to get another dog.

COSI: No, you were pretty cut up. Rabs, you want to hear a little about how upset our Petty was when she rang me up?

Rabbit pressed play on my voicemail message. *They're not going to play my message, surely? What the hell had I said?* I could feel my face going purple as I listened to myself ranting about 'this bloody family, who already has each other to love and they also already have a bloody dog, but NO, no, that's not enough is it? They also have to steal the single girl's one fucking chance at finding love.' And so on.

When the voicemail finished, the *Fatal Attraction*/Glenn Close version of me sat silent and mortified. 'Yeah, and you know Petty, it's funny because that family who took your dog, I know them,' Cosi claimed, looking amazed. *Oh god, could it get any worse? I've just carried on like they're a bunch of terrorists who've just bombed the city and thrown a floral wreath over the rubble for a giggle.*

'Yeah, cause that family who took your dog? That was my family.'

At that point the studio door swung open and in came the girl from the pet store, carrying a tiny ball of white fluff in her arms – my baby, with an enormous pale-blue satin ribbon around his neck.

'I'm sorry, Petty!' Cosi laughed.

I couldn't believe what was happening. If I wasn't so incapacitated by shock and joy, I might have leapt across the studio, jammed Cosi's microphone down his neck, pulled it out his ear hole and calmly spoken into it, 'I think it's time we went to a break.' Instead I sat with my mouth open and my hands outstretched. The girl passed me my baby and I pulled him gently to my chest. I couldn't believe he was mine. Meanwhile I had completely forgotten that dead air is never a recipe for radio success but the boys painted the picture of what was going on. *So, they should, little fuckers.* I looked at my baby's tiny face and wanted to cry tears of utter joy. I would protect him and make him happy forever. And I would call him Marley. And yes, I knew what everyone was thinking, and no, I didn't care how clichéd my choice was because finally I was complete.

Talk about change. By the last week in February I was moving into a new home and bringing home a baby. *What was I thinking? Who in their right mind would want to have an eight-week-old puppy running around underfoot as a pair of burly removalists march in and out of my new shell of a home?* It's a wonder little Marley didn't get flattened like a pressed flower.

Three nights later I dreamt of Julian. I was in a cinema with my brother when he'd walked in and sat a few rows ahead of us. He turned around, spotted my brother, his face lighting up as he said 'Hello'. My heart skipped a beat. I felt the reality of his presence. It had been more than ten years since I'd seen him but the old feelings came rushing back. I realised how much I missed him. The next thing I knew I was awake and sobbing. The feeling was like we'd broken up yesterday. The following night I had another dream about him. This time he was standing in a park on his own. He hadn't seen me and I wanted to go up and tell him how sorry I was that things had ended the way they did. I wanted to say I wanted him back, and that I would never let him go again. But something told me there was no way back. That he would never love me as he did before. As I walked towards him, he disappeared. It didn't feel like a dream, but I knew our time had passed. There was no way back. No more us. I woke up in tears again. After nearly ten years I was reliving the pain of our breakup, and it didn't make sense. I thought I'd turned the corner into happiness and yet it hadn't even lasted one week. The next three nights I had similar dreams which left an aching. I couldn't do another night of these dreams so I decided I would put it out to the universe to ask it to bring me the right person who could help me understand and heal. All I needed was the belief and faith that he or she would come.

'When love goes out the window, love comes in,' said the tall, willowy man in the sunroom. I was pissed off and suspicious, which made it hard to concentrate on his words. $360 an hour to be counselled by a guy who'd been recommended by a friend of a friend – a person who happened to be a very wealthy Australian pop star. I couldn't help but think I was being charged on the presumption of affluence. Soaking up his magic while paying enough to get me off a murder charge was a challenge. But I had to have faith. I'd asked the universe for someone, and now I was here. The Julian era of my life was still haunting me. I'd stayed in the relationship way past its expiry date because I loved him, but with the recent dreams gate-crashing a happy new chapter of life, I couldn't do what I did when we split. I couldn't simply run away, throw myself into work, and hope it would go away. Because it doesn't, I was seeing that now. I hadn't taken the time to grieve and heal. Just as soon as I'd found some peace and light it was there waving its hand, 'Hey! I'm over here. My turn now.'

A jackhammer-like noise erupted from outside as a I took a seat in the man's sunroom. I walked over to the window, looked down and realised there was a building site directly below. At precisely the moment we were to begin our expensive chat the boys were picking up their jackhammers. 'You won't notice it shortly,' he assured me. 'Everyone ends up forgetting it.' *What the fuck?* I knew I'd recently signed up for the 'everything happens for a reason' school of thought but what purpose do jackhammers have in this? Or empty wallets? I wanted to knock this guy's annoying Buddha off his expensive hippy shelves in his billionaire Sydney bayside location. I fantasised about pinning him against the wall, putting my face real close to his and whispering, 'Listen Star Man. I'm having an asshole of a time right now and your enlightened words from your elitist, caviar-munching universe, which I've now seen includes people building a nice old block of billion-dollar apartments below, is NOT doing a great deal for my spiritual healing. Are we CRYSTAL clear?'

'Your mother and father, tell me about them.' Star Man continued, unperturbed by the pounding. His first question did nothing to talk me off the edge. Far too broad and requiring too much energy for $360 an hour. 'They split when I was a baby,' I said, enjoying the deflection. *Over to you, buddy.* And then it began. He wanted to know what my mother did right after she left Dad. The question piqued my curiosity because I couldn't tell where he was going. 'She was giving birth to my brother.'

'I see,' he replied, sounding curious. 'So, love went out the window with your father, and love came in with the birth of your brother?'

Interesting, I thought. Next, he wanted to know about Mum and her relationship with her dad. I told him my grandfather had died of a heart attack on a train home from work. Not long after that, my parents had gotten married.

'So, the love of one man left her life, while the other was starting?' he posed. 'I guess so?' I could no longer hear the noise outside. 'And what about your dad? What was happening in his life when he met your mum?' I told him Dad's mum had committed suicide not long after he'd announced he was marrying my mum. I could do the maths on that one. We then moved onto Julian and I told him about my dreams. 'So, when you broke it off with Julian, what happened then?'

'Well, my stepmother died.'

'And what did that mean to you?' His eyes locked on mine.

'I guess I got my dad back,' I said, not expecting to say something that sounded so heartless.

For a second, I felt like I'd discovered I'd ordered her death. But it wasn't that. I was examining my past in the light of his theory about the rhythm of universal flow – love coming in, love going out. He circled back to my mother. 'Could you contemplate this,' he asked, watching me closely, 'that rather than her being a victim of a bad marriage and a hopeless husband who left her with $15 in her pocket and two babies in her arms that perhaps subconsciously she knew the relationship was not going to work? That she needed to make space for the arrival of new male love, in the form of your brother?'

I considered his rewriting of our history. My mother being a single, divorced parent in the seventies, when we knew few others in the same position, had imprinted a belief in our family that we were damaged; that Mum was hard done by. But this framing of the story was giving back to all of us a sense of power. And, for my mother, a heroic, courageous twist. Perhaps, deep down – subconsciously, she knew exactly what she was doing. 'So, what about you, Amber?' he inquired, after a pause.

'Can you consider that you did what you were meant to do too? Because you still had unfinished business and your heart needed more time to heal with your dad?' He was right. My issue was not that I'd made the wrong decision to leave Julian. It was the way I'd gone about it. I'd chosen to hide behind a story that only partially related to why I broke us up. I needed to go because we were over. The visions of Julian in my dreams, that feeling I was experiencing, that emotion, was guilt. It wasn't lost love – it was guilt.

When I left the man's apartment that day, I was $920 poorer but infinitely wiser. His theories about life and love had completely flipped parts of my story, and my parents' story, on its head. He'd taken the misery and the 'victim' out of it. I realised that day there's much more playing out in our actions and decisions than we're conscious of. There's a subconscious compass driving us in directions that our heart needs to go; towards lessons (and healing) we need to have.

CHAPTER SIX.

I WANT TO LEARN A LOVE SONG

Hello All. I would like to first apologise if you are getting this in error. I am not sure all of who are Canadian friends and who aren't. This is mainly for Canadian (but not bad information for those outside of the country). My name is Sara. I have known Sarah for her entire life. Our Mums were friends growing up. Sarah has spent the last few months of her life living here in my home with my family and hers. I have been very blessed in having been part of her life. I will be taking over 'Project Sarah' for now. While we are all very devastated that Sarah is gone it is also somewhat of a relief that we don't see her in pain anymore, for her sake. Blaine's mom and sister are doing well. Blaine crawled into Sarah's bed right after the coroner took Sarah to the crematorium. He has been there with his laptop all day and we do not know when he will resurface. He is online. The memorial service for Sarah will take place on Sunday February 8th, 2009. It will start at 3pm. The address is 12 Doris Drive. I know the proper thing is to say donations in lieu of flowers, but she loved all flowers. So, feel free to send flowers. Blaine's Mum will be heading to Australia on Monday and Blaine and his sister will be traveling to Europe for a much-needed getaway. There are gifts here from Sarah to people. For those of you in Australia (if you are still reading) Blaine's Mum is not able to bring them back over. I will hopefully be in Australia come August for the memorial service there. I will be able to bring the items with me. I would mail them, but a guitar is quite pricey. If there is anything of Sarah's that is not spoken for that you would like, please let us know. We would rather it go to someone she knew instead of donated to charity. If anyone has any questions or ideas or wants to help. Let me know. I hope everyone is coping well, we are doing our best to laugh and stay positive here. Take care of each other, its what Sarah would have wanted. Thank-You

Sara Kelly

We all got the Project Sarah email at work. *What an amazing, brave friend this girl Sara was*, I thought to myself. I replied, asking how they were, and I also figured the small bit I could do for Sarah was to invite Sara to stay with me. I didn't know if she'd take me up on the offer but it felt good that Sarah's presence was still around thanks to her friend. I woke the next morning to find an email from Sara, written at 10.30 pm on the night of Sarah's memorial. She sounded understandably exhausted but said the day had been 'pleasantly chaotic'. Apparently her boys had been very emotional and she'd never seen them cry like they had over Sarah. 'She was the closest thing they had to a sister/female influence aside from me,' she said, remarking how 'proud' she was of 'my little men'.

Hannah and Blaine were apparently passed out on the couch while their Mum was busy packing for all of them to leave the next day. Sara had, since Sarah's death, cleaned out the basement and turned it back to an office. 'I still can't bring myself to go and sit in there to work but it's an emotional work in progress, I guess'. Speaking of which, she was apparently now halfway through a bottle of Jack Daniels, her way apparently of decompressing from a very big day. I liked the sound of Sara. At this point, I liked anyone who launched themselves at a bottle to deal with dark times. It kind of made us blood sisters – blood-alcohol-reading-of-well over 0.05 – sisters. I hadn't always been the type to drink alone. It was a new thing, honed since I'd arrived in Adelaide. I used to think people who drank alone had a problem, but I'd revised that judgement recently. Drinking alone was better than drinking in public, especially when you're messy.

Sara was clearly a busy woman. With losing her best friend, managing a house full of boys, and a husband deployed in Afghanistan, it didn't sound like she had time for grieving. She mentioned in an email that her boys had asked her if she was going to die soon too. Their fears were motivating her to detox their house, throwing out all unhealthy food and soft drink. 'My effort to stay on the planet a little longer for them,' she said. 'The Jack Daniels is staying, though.'

And then another email arrived from Sara that day. It read:

I don't know what it is ... you may have this - 'Sarah's Rules For Life.' For some reason I think you may need to be reminded of them today.'

Here are Sarah's words:

1. To always speak the truth ...except when to do so would injure another.

2. To talk health, happiness and prosperity to EVERYONE you meet.

3. To be so strong that nothing can disturb your inner peace.

4. To be just as enthusiastic of another's success as you are about your own.

5. To remember that God is in the pause.

6. To forgive the mistakes of your past and to strive to greater achievements in the future.

7. To never see failure ... only opportunity. You are no longer a victim.

8. To have NO JUDGEMENTS of others ... No matter what.

9. To live well and CHOOSE happiness. To say I can every day.

10. To make an impact on the world. To live love.

11. To remember your spirit and nourish it daily.

12. To remember these principles above personalities.

13. To always speak of myself in a kind, gentle, positive way. To be nice to me.

14. Progress not perfection. Willingness is the key. And remember to laugh!

I printed off Sarah's Rules for Life and I stuck them on my fridge. I highlighted three that resonated with me the most:

16. To be so strong that nothing can disturb your inner peace.

17. To forgive the mistakes of your past and to strive to greater achievements in the future.

18. To always speak of myself in a kind, gentle, positive way. To be nice to me.

Interestingly, Sara mentioned she didn't approve of Rabbit, that he wasn't good for Sarah and that he didn't 'add up'. In her eyes his only interest in her was that she was cute, foreign and a yoga instructor. I had to hold back from agreeing but it wasn't my place to go bitching to a stranger about my co-host, as desperately as I wanted to. Soon after Sara emailed back apologising for her comments, saying she was feeling a little 'emotionally raw' and admitting 'just because I didn't understand their friendship does not make it wrong'.

Sara and I had our first phone call together a week after Sara's memorial. I was nervous, almost like I was going on a blind date. 'Hey, Amber?' There was a delay before I heard Sara's voice. The first thing I noticed was she had a stronger Canadian accent than Sarah. She had a kind of a no-nonsense tone that fitted Sarah's description of her. We skipped past first-call awkwardness soon enough, speaking for over an hour. I found all sorts of things about Sara, including her boys' names were Joel, Tory and William, her husband Jeff was in the army and she was senior writer on a nightly TV show called *The Hour*. And they'd just had Barrack Obama on the show, which was pretty cool. Further into the call Sara asked, suddenly more serious, 'How's Rabbit been taking things since Sarah passed?' Cautiously I admitted Rabbit and I weren't that close. I wasn't comfortable asking him what was going on in his head, let alone his heart. I said I figured he was probably struggling a little – but then I changed the subject. I didn't want to talk about him. Sensing her disdain, I just thought it safer to move on. Out of nowhere she said, 'I didn't want to tell you this because I didn't want to cloud your view of Sarah, but the world revolved around Sarah. We had to re-mortgage our house because she wanted to die in our home,' she said. 'So, we're $30,000 in debt because of it. Which is fine but I'm just saying, Sarah did what Sarah wanted.'

I was taken aback. This wasn't exactly what I'd expected on our second phone call. Or any phone call to be honest. I wondered if it was part of Sara's grieving process. *Maybe she needs to focus on the less wonderful things about her friend, so it isn't so hard to let her go?* I wasn't sure, but it was odd. I quickly discovered phone calls with Sara, were never dull. From her thoughts on the winner of the first Australian series of *MasterChef*, who, according to Sara, had ripped off a cookbook idea from the winner of Canadian *MasterChef*, to the time her son Tory had a minor snowboarding accident while not wearing a helmet. She'd punished him by taking him on a tour of a local morgue. 'Dead bodies on a few cold trays sure sorted him out,' she recalled, with a sinister laugh. On another call she told me how her other son William had been busted smoking bongs on his first day of high school. After the school principal called her, she'd made a 'surprise visit' to his school, taking him for a 'sight-seeing' trip to a local rehab centre. 'I wanted him to see what it's like for people with drug addictions. I made him spend the afternoon there so he realises how 'cool' it is to dabble in drugs,' she said. 'And just because I don't have enough to do with my days,' she said during one phone call, 'I've just agreed to help out the organisers for the upcoming Winter Olympics.' Being on the 'organising board' for the Winter Olympics apparently meant she was on the hunt for an Aussie band and a couple of comedians to book to entertain the Australians in the Athletes' Village. With a budget to spend on the radio in Australia to promote the games itself, bringing presents from Sarah, and spreading her ashes at the beach where she and Blaine were engaged, Sara's trip was going to be busy.

Meanwhile, I'd had my first appointment at the healing centre that week. I'd purposely made it late enough in the day so I'd have time to process. This in itself was a new way of thinking (and planning) for me. 'Is this your first healing?' Petra, my healer, asked, with a gentle smile. I felt like a little girl following her through the hallways. A peacefulness descended over me as I walked inside the healing room, the walls covered in chalk drawings of angels and master spirits, softly lit by a crystal lamp – and the same incense I'd smelt when I first came to the centre. *I like it here*, I thought to myself. *I feel happy*. There was a massage bed with a pillow set up in the corner of the room covered in a white flannel sheet and a fluffy lilac blanket on top. Petra asked me to sit so we could chat first. She wanted to explain how energy-healing worked. I had no idea what it was, but I was open.

'This process is like peeling an onion,' she said, explaining that after we'd talked, she'd use the *messages* from *spirit* to guide her to where I needed healing and then she'd place me back on the bed and shift my *energy blocks*. 'There's going to be lots of layers, and it will take time to go through each one,' she added, smiling sweetly.

I told her about my job, moving to a new city, my ex, and my recent experience with the doctor. The truth was I'd hoped my dream job was going to fix me. Instead, I was more lonely now than I'd ever been. And I was scared – scared that a part of me was going to give up. My drinking on the weekends was leaving me paranoid and anxious, week after week. I wasn't living – I was in Groundhog Day. 'I'm being told by a spirit you've dealt with a lot of jealousy in your life. It's been a theme,' offered Petra. *Jealousy?* I didn't get that. In my mind, jealousy meant you had something that someone wanted – and I couldn't find a match to that. 'Take me back to the first memory you have of being with your dad and feeling unsure of yourself?' she asked. 'Close your eyes and tell me the first image that comes to your head?' Before I had a chance to presume nothing would come, there I was, in an apricot, V-neck velour jumper. I had shoulder-length, layered mousy blonde hair and I was squinting in the sunlight. Myles and Andy were there and some other kids I didn't recognise, and we were all on a boat in Sydney. That little me had returned – I was eight. That day, on the boat, was during a holiday with my dad and stepmother. The jealousy, Petra felt, was around my stepmother. With Petra's insight I began to understand relationship dynamics I'd never considered. Jealousy was coming from my stepmother, she believed, and no doubt mirrored back at her by me. I don't know what I must have been like as a child to my stepmother but I do know how sensitive I was. I always felt she thought I was a pain in the ass and that my brother was the most magnificent child on the planet; a mini version of Dad.

My stepmother was not only a beautiful woman who possessed a charm I've only seen in a handful of people in my life but she was also what some might describe as 'a classy lady'. She just had that something. I guess you don't know when you're a kid what being intimidated feels like.

'So, let's call her in,' suggested Petra of my late stepmother. 'I want you to think about what it is you want to share with her about that time.' Before I could think of a response, it was out. 'I just wanted more time with my dad,' I blurted.

'And what else?' Petra asked.

I couldn't keep my tears back now as I said, 'I didn't want to compete. I just wanted more time with my dad.' Petra handed me a tissue as I blew my nose hard. I hadn't expected to get so emotional so quickly. Thank god for waterproof mascara. I sat for a few minutes, unable to keep back what I'd unlocked. Whatever it was, it felt very real. Five or six tissues later and it was time to do the energy work. I climbed on to the bed and Petra covered me with the blanket. I closed my eyes while she waved her hands around my body like she was blowing something away, occasionally stopping to massage my stomach. I could hear hers grumbling, and then what sounded like burping. It was a little bizarre but I was intrigued.

I walked to my car after my healing, panting as though I'd just run a marathon. I felt the urge to ring my dad. He was a big reason for me wanting to heal. When Dad answered I played it lightly, sparing him details of the process (he wouldn't get it, and that was OK). And the fact was, a part of me feared he'd reject me. Dismiss my pain. But he didn't. 'I probably should have been more aware, baby,' he said, a little sadly. 'But I guess I just went with it all. Well, if all this stuff you're doing helps, then that's a good thing.' It was enough of admission, and acceptance, for now. I couldn't bear the thought of losing Dad while still hanging onto bitterness, frustration or sadness about the past. I knew my motives were selfish, and I was OK with that. My Dad was not going to die and leave me with regrets about us. That shit would push me over the edge, I was 100 per cent sure of it.

I made a commitment to three months of healing work and with every new session, fascinating new insights and layers were revealed. The dots of my childhood were becoming more evident, so when Petra encouraged me to attend an *inner child* workshop, insisting it would help me understand the dynamics of family, I was in. I didn't tell the boys at work that I was off to 'explore my inner child' that weekend. There were aspects of my newfound spiritual searching that I was OK to share, poke fun at, but there were more I'd keep sacred. I wasn't doing it for 'content' – I was doing it to delve deeper into the unconscious parts of me. I wanted to get back into the real world – where people find love, feel good about themselves, get married and have babies. *Do life* instead of standing still. It was a total leap of faith. There was so much I had learnt that weekend and it began to change the way I viewed my story. It allowed me to see the dots that we all have, stepping stones from our childhoods leading us to where we are now. I came to understand how nearly all of us have our own *victim story* and how we operate unconsciously because of these stories. My parents had a back story, they had parents that consciously, or unconsciously, wounded them, and if I didn't see this, and have empathy, I'd continue to be held prisoner to mine.

It was Dad's story that held the most meaning for me, revealing insights into why he wasn't able to be a husband, why he could only be an absent father. He'd come from alcoholic parents (and a violent father). At twelve he'd been walking home from school one day with a friend when fire engines went whizzing past. Dad flippantly joked, 'See those fire engines, they're going to my place.' When they turned the corner into Dad's street his house was nearly burnt to the ground. I'd always found it hard to imagine Dad as a child because I'd never seen him as a little boy. I was told all the photos of him as a child, were burnt in the fire that day. I'd also grown up not knowing much about his parents. He didn't like to talk about them. I did know that in the year Mum and Dad got engaged, his Mum committed suicide. The only other story I knew about his Dad was one that Mum told me when I was a teenager. She said they'd been at the races one day when Dad said, 'See that guy over there? That's my dad.' Naturally she expected him to take her over to meet his father – but he didn't. The last time he saw his dad was at his Mum's funeral. According to Dad my grandfather was so ravaged by his alcoholism that Dad didn't even recognise him. His best friend Trevor pointed to him sitting up the back of the funeral home. Later, at the pub, Dad saw him standing at the bar next to someone else. His Dad introduced my father to the man standing next to him as 'my nephew'. When he recounted the story, I could see the pain, and the fury, in his eyes.

My inner child weekend taught me about childhood wounds, self-beliefs cultivated in our very early years (nought to seven years mainly), expectations of the world and what we'll receive from it and which when they're left unacknowledged will strive to be heard. I knew my issues were around love. I'd always expected it to knife me through the heart so it felt safer to die by my own hand. At least then I could see the knife coming.

DAISY, DAISY

I work with a beautiful man named Carey. (see attached photos). He may have been privy to a few photos of you and I think he's developed a little online crush. This morning we had one of our typically mature contests where we agreed to both try and make it across the room with a glass of water on our heads (I did say mature right?). The deal was if I made it across without drenching myself my dear friend would have to be my slave for a week. If he did the same then I was required to facilitate an email introduction between him and you … Are you ready to kill me now? Anyway, the fact my mascara is now slightly running may suggest to you I lost … So, tell me to step off if you want nothing to do with this bet but if you can take it in the stupid bit of fun it's meant to be, would you be OK if I did the intro to get the kid off my back?

Sara xx

They'd picked the right person for an infantile three-way bet. Bring it on! According to Sara, she and Carey worked together in breakfast radio years earlier. Carey and Sara sounded like they were doing well for themselves in the Canadian media world, which brought up my aspirations of moving onwards and upwards one day. It was quite exciting having these two new people in my life and I wondered what I might learn from them.

Sara sent more photos of Carey Malcolmson: one with his mum, another with his parrot, called Rebel, and the last was of the tattoo on his arm. It was the picture of an old 1950s microphone with the words

'MUSIC SAVED MY LIFE' running across it. I'd always loved a decent tattoo – I mean one by a talented artist and a design with a meaningful story behind it. Not some bloody doodle you did when you were twenty-one or Tweedy Bird on your butt cheek created at 3 am while you were shitfaced. Carey's tattoo was one of the best I'd ever seen. Carey was getting hotter with every email. Speaking of which, apparently he was also best friends with his mum. Cue a thousand women sighing. *His best friend?* If I could have chosen one thing at the time, outside of being handsome and not a serial killer, having a great relationship with your mother was just about the highest thing on my list at the time. Given my track record with my last two exes, both of whom I believed would've been less damaged souls if they'd had healthy relationships with their mothers, this was more music to my ears.

As for his tattoo, apparently Carey's Dad died just after his thirtieth birthday. They too had been super close and I wondered whether this was another reason for the bond he had with his Mum? *Maybe his Dad told him to look after her?* I might also add his mum looked like the happiest, kindest woman I'd ever seen. She looked, I decided, like the kind of woman who'd make a bloody good cupcake. Then there was Rebel, the green F-bombing parrot! Wow, what a brilliant FM segment that would make? Nothing that a finger on the dump button wouldn't fix to protect little ears on the school run.

Carey's first email to me was an apology for how 'orchestrated' and 'cheesy' Sara's introduction was. Like I gave a shit. His messages were short and very sweet. He'd end each one by asking a question like, 'So, what's your favourite movie?' There was a real old-fashioned innocence about him, and I liked it. We started writing to each regularly and after a few weeks things had stepped up to what I'd call flirtatious banter, which was fun. In one email I'd mentioned that my birthday was coming up and that I was looking forward to Rachel and Dino, two of my best friends, coming to visit, as well as Mum and her friend, Jan. I found out via Carey that it'd be Sara's birthday while she was in Adelaide. I didn't see her as the type that'd want a fuss made but I did promise Carey I'd do something to make her feel special. Carey had a lot of time for Sara, which reinforced to me that somewhere underneath there must've been a softer side lurking.

I envied the friendship they had, the way he spoke of her, especially when he asked me for local florist recommendations so he could order flowers to arrive on her birthday. *What a cute thing to do! The perfect behaviour from my new online boyfriend,* I laughed to myself, well aware of how tragic I was sounding. Feeling playful I decided to sign off my list of local florists with a bit of a 'gag'. I wrote, 'Don't go ordering any gerberas though Sir, no girl wants to receive gerberas on her birthday.' Nothing like a bit of sassiness. *Poor gerberas, they've copped such appalling PR since that* Kath & Kim *episode.*

Carey's email was waiting for me the following morning. He thanked me for the help with florists and confirmed he'd booked a flower order for her birthday. And then he said, 'Sara's favourite flower is a gerbera. Has a full sleeve of them tattooed down her left arm. She got them to celebrate her Nana. You'll see them when she gets there. Love Carey. x'

Oh. Dear. Of all the goddamn responses I could have gotten to one of my *least funny* jokes ever. *How's that for a slap, dickhead. Who the fuck, thinks it's funny to slag off flowers? I mean, really? Flowers?* I waited for days for Carey to pop back with *'GOTCHA!'* But he didn't. I wondered if he'd mentioned my flower bullying to Sara. *Maybe he's taking the piss?* I wondered, hopefully. Obsessing about it for most of each day that followed, I decided to sneakily raise the issue to Sara about whether she had tattoos. 'Yep, got an arm full of flowers,' she confirmed. 'Gerbera daisies. They've been my favourite flower since I was a little girl.' *Wonderful.*

Flower faux-pas aside, my thirty-eighth birthday felt like it was barrelling at me faster than I was ready to receive it. The last thing in the world I wanted was to become one of those women that spend half their life terrified by the subject of age. I'd seen so many of my mum's friends carrying on like the wicked witch in *The Wizard of Oz* after Dorothy douses her with water, the instant the subject came up and it wasn't attractive. Still, something about this one was wearing me down. The week before my birthday the Big Radio Boss had sent one of the promo girls into our daily meeting with an idea for a 'stunt'. Again, like my fake death, it was something one of the other female hosts in the network had done on her show. I didn't hear much past the word 'naked'.

Let me make this clear, I am not your 'get your gear off in public' kind of gal but bringing up the idea of a naked stunt in the very week I'm struggling with the concept that my reproductive organs might have an expiry date, not to mention I'm about as close to finding love as I am walking to the moon, wasn't great timing. As politely as I could I asked if she might provide a little more 'context' to the idea, so I could 'think about it'. I felt for her. I could tell she was awkward doing the boss's dirty work. My loneliness, not having a partner to workshop shit with, my birthday rounding the corner and a team projecting *the hopes of a network* on to my naked bits, didn't make it any easier.

Another thing happened just prior to my birthday. We'd finally done it – we'd taken out the top spot in the FM radio ratings. When I heard the news I wanted to scream, *We fucking did it! Yay, maybe the Big Radio Boss will get off our backs now?* I'd presumed, naively, that he'd come in, high five us all and take us out for lunch. Instead, he came in to see us for about forty-five seconds, tops. 'Well done,' he said. 'There's still a lot of work to do,' and off he went.

His lacklustre congratulations were still ringing in my ears as I drove home, knowing I had about forty-eight hours to decide how I was going to play their nude shit. Later that night it came to me, 'The perfect body is the one you're in.' *That's it! I like that. I can work with this.* This would be my last-gasp attempt at turning what I knew (again) was an unspoken demand from the boss – that said, 'We like team players here, Amber. Remember that.' All I could do was try to turn the stunt into something positive, for me, and other women. I'd never been comfortable about my body. I'd never been like most of my friends who'd happily parade around the beach when we were teenagers. I committed myself to use our radio stunt to heal myself of an old hang-up – and I'd invite other women to do the same. I made it clear to our all-female promotions team that we'd run all aspects of the 'stunt' and the boys were to have no say at all. I was shitty enough that the boss was controlling me but I could at least make sure I was in charge of how it got played out. I told the girls to warn Rabbit and Cosi that if I sniffed even one remotely sexist or sleazy comment, they'd cop my wrath publicly, on-air.

My birthday arrived in the middle of the week. Thanks to being seen as the 'body champion' for South Australian women when we'd launched our campaign, I'd started the week acting way more empowered than I had the previous week. Secretly though, I felt like a phony. There was nothing empowered about me; I'd just become skilled at impersonating someone who was. Thanks to the stunt, however, I'd met a group of brave women who'd come into our radio station to talk about their bodies and their previously private insecurities. These five gorgeous women had committed to pushing through their fears by taking part in our big naked shoot at the end of the week. Meanwhile, the 'leader of the pack' spent her birthday crying at her desk. I'd never cried at work but I couldn't even muster the energy to keep it in. I wanted this birthday, and the boss's naked shoot, like I wanted to insert knitting needles into my ear holes. News of my tears quickly circled the corridor and into the boss's office. Suddenly my phone rang with him asking me if I was OK – and if there was anything he could do. It took one brief phone call from the boss to cheer me up. That's how easy I was.

I was so humbled on the day of the shoot as the more than seventy women filed in the studio door, on their own, each displaying the most extraordinary self-love. It was honestly one of the most beautiful things I'd ever seen. There was such a profound sense of sisterhood in the room that day as we quietly got changed into our robes minutes before dropping them for the big naked group shot. That was until I was approached by one of the girls from the station, informing me that it was time for my 'solo shot'.

Solo shot? My mouth went dry. *No one had ever mentioned a solo shot.* It was one thing to blend into a group shot, another entirely to pose on my own for a photo that could end up anywhere. I was seething, but I had a room full of eyes on me. So, I did it. I gritted my teeth and sat for the camera, wearing only a smile and a tiny, skin-coloured G-string.

When we got the photos back from the studio, the promo girls had enlarged my solo shot for me. They'd also arranged for a black satin dressing gown with my words embroidered on the back: 'The perfect body is the one you're in.' – AMBER PETTY.

What blew me away was what wasn't exposed. Looking at the photo of me sitting cross-legged, my awkwardly small hands cupping my breasts I found it so bizarre that I couldn't see the truth of how I felt that day anywhere on my face. And yet, behind my smile, I was empty and irate.

Another lovely thing happened that week – I got home to a massive bunch of flowers. I hurried to get in the front door, dodging an excited Marley as I scrambled to open the card. *'HAPPY BIRTHDAY MY SWEET AMBER. Have a perfect day. Make sure you feel loved. Carey. Xxx'*

BEARING GIFTS

I wrote to Carey thanking him for my birthday surprise. We'd recently stepped up the tone in our emails to a little (albeit both pretending to be tongue in cheek) romantic. He now called me his 'online girlfriend'. *Maybe we would meet one day? People meet the love of their life in all sorts of unexpected ways, so why not me?*

I got a little kick out of Carey confiding in me. One day he told me something he hadn't even shared with Sara. Apparently he'd been offered two incredible jobs in New York: the first was working back on the radio as an announcer on Z100, an NYC radio station, and the other as a junior writer on *Saturday Night Live*. *Saturday Night, Goddam, LIVE!* I had no idea how talented Carey was, given I barely knew him full stop, and I'm not going to lie, my crush factor spiked significantly when I read those three little words.

I made sure I didn't let on to Sara that I already knew Carey's news. I was conscious of not revealing how close we'd become. I respected their friendship and the last thing I wanted to do was appear to be undermining it. In the meantime, I looked forward to Carey's emails as he transitioned from one fabulous life to the next. With just a few weeks left before Sara's arrival in Australia I confessed to Carey that I was getting nervous. I just wanted it all to go well. Secretly though I also knew, if it didn't, I was in for a hell of an awkward couple of weeks. Carey assured me everything would be fine and that 'Travelling with Sara is fun.' And then he sweetly shared a list he'd made up – 'fun facts' and 'travel tips' he called them – relating to Sara.

- She played Rugby for Canada for four years. Won twice.
- Has broken her nose four times.
- She can be very shy, until she gets to know you.
- Amazing cook ... old school ... everything from scratch. get her to cook for you. she loves it.
- She doesn't have a filter on at the best of times, if she's been drinking, no filter between her brain and mouth at all.
- She has been bitten by a bear.
- She loves being around people, and also loves her alone time.
- Addicted to her Blackberry.
- Does not do well with jet lag, no matter how much she says she does.
- You will always know where you stand with her. She doesn't do the 'oh yeah... sure ... that's OK' if she doesn't mean it.
- She's very self-conscious ... especially about her size.
- She is kind to a fault.

- The funniest woman I know.
- Very protective.
- I think my favourite way to describe her is Mouth of a Sailor Heart of a Poet.
- Very much a mom.
- Always willing to try something once ... anything.
- Very much a small town/country girl ... that mentality. Little old fashioned.
- Pretty powerful in Canadian media/'showbiz'.
- Does not dance. No matter what.
- Loves animals.
- Tends to over pack.
- If she gets stressed she gets flustered. Give her a few mins ... she will calm down. You can't really tell her anything at that moment, so don't try... but as soon as she is over something ... she is truly over it ... whole process takes less than 10 minutes.
- Very kind.
- Loves to laugh.
- Window seat type of girl
- When she says no more shots... she means it. LOL.
- You can leave her somewhere. If you need to take off and she looks like she's having a good time. Don't feel obligated. She will be fine if you leave her.
- She is the type of woman who will put a fresh flower in her hair given the opportunity.
- Loves her shoes and bags.
- Not a fan of 'Rabbit' (good luck with that one ... altho she seems

to think she may end up liking him towards the end ... she has a pretty good 6th sense about stuff).

- Wants to keep the spreading ashes very private and intimate.
- Has not celebrated a birthday in a long time ... over 14 years because her son has a birthday right before hers.
- Give her the opportunity ... she loves a good prank. Look forward to a weekend of emailing and texting. Good morning sweet Amber, I hope the day brings you more than you expect. PS - I have attached a picture of myself and my sisters little white dog Pavarotti and one I don't know if I have sent. When I first started radio.

I looked forward to Carey's updates. There was something magical about getting home after work and finding a new message from a handsome stranger. He was talented, living in the most exciting city in the world and I was alone and single in a beautiful town where things rarely changed. I could count on one hand the number of times I'd met a guy that hadn't lived their entire life in Adelaide, let alone was still single and who I was attracted to. The possibility of finding love, in my city, felt as distant as a star in the back corner of the galaxy. The more I got to know about Carey, and his aspirations for life, the more hooked I got. So, here's the thing, what can become dangerous in this little storybook is when a said fan of said story decides to pour themselves a glass of wine, throw themselves a little 'party of one' and jumps onto a computer. I hosted a few of these parties, so I was bound to come unstuck. And I did so, spectacularly, one night as I sat around overthinking my gorgeous new friend. My trigger (in hindsight) on this fateful evening was Carey's sweet sentiments about his friend Sara. It wasn't even an email about me but he'd stoked my heart into a raging flame with his thoughtful curation of endearing details about Sara, all in the name of helping me get to know a woman he cared about. My idiotic, wine fuelled impatience encouraged me to jump the relationship queue by about six months by pouring out way, *way too many* bullet points about myself, none of which he'd ever requested. The next morning my alarm blared simultaneously with a lightning rod of regret straight through my torturously dehydrated head. *What's wrong? What's happening today?* Then it crept up on me like the Grim Reaper. *The email. You sent a tragically drunk email to Carey. Remember that? And now he knows all that you didn't want him to know about the real you.* I deleted the email. I couldn't bear to see the evidence. If it wasn't there, I could build a strong case to myself that the whole thing never happened. I went to bed that night feeling like a complete and utter douchebag. Bless my fantasy online boyfriend, though – he'd sent me a text message overnight that put my craziness at ease, acknowledging my email and thanking me for sharing all my 'details'. He said he was 'looking forward to learning more about me in the future'. I'd dodged a bullet, fired by my chardonnay gun.

People at work knew Sara, Sarah's BFF, was coming to Adelaide. And most knew she was staying with me. What they made of that I conveniently didn't care to know. I hadn't spoken to Rabbit about Sara's arrival. He'd been notably silent any time Sarah's name came up. I understood there was every chance he just wanted to move on. Cosi, unsurprisingly, was quite the opposite. 'Petty are you a little worried you've got a girl you've never met coming to stay in your house?' he asked the morning before her arrival.

The boys knew Sara was scheduled to come into the station at some point and I'd told them she'd specifically requested to meet us all – the people who'd been part of a sad chapter in the last stages of her best friend's life. We'd fallen in love with Sarah, sent money from our listeners, our station, and Rabbit and I had formed special friendships with her. Sara was also bringing gifts from Sarah for Rabbit and me. It'd been almost eight months since Sara had entered my life and when I woke up on the morning of her arrival, I felt anxious but resigned. I'd arrived early at the airport, so I had to make a couple of loops before pulling up. *This is it,* I said to myself, *She's here. You can do this. You're a nice person.* But I was nervous. There was no denying it. I had a stranger staying in my house for an entire week. Not only that, we were spending a weekend alone together in the Barossa Valley, and then the next week she was following me to Perth. We *needed* to bond. Or break. Sara mentioned she had a few work-related appointments while she was in Perth – something to do with her forthcoming Winter Olympic organising committee gig. She teed up meetings with two of the major radio stations, as she'd done in Adelaide. One of which I'd helped set up.

I pulled my car up outside the Arrivals entrance, with Marley in the back. I stared wide-eyed towards the entrance as an elderly couple sauntered out, then a young blonde surfie dude carrying a board. And then I saw a woman, still too far away in the distance to be sure if it might be Sara. What I could make out however was, if it were Sara, which I suspected it was, she appeared to be carrying a heck of a lot of baggage. The odd thing was I hadn't seen any photos of Sara at this point. I only had Carey's email saying she was a 'big girl' so I'd had to guess what she might look like. And this girl so far appeared to fit the bullet points. The most telling clue would be her tattoos. *How could I forget that?* Sure enough, the woman coming closer with the enormous suitcase – had an inked sleeve of brightly-coloured flowers.

I began waving, a little self-consciously. Sara didn't have a spare hand to wave back so I jumped out of the car to greet her. She was so tall I had to go up on my tippy-toes to give her a quick hug and a peck on the cheek. She didn't give much away. I couldn't get a read on how she was feeling, although I do think she might have been thinking, *How the fuck are we getting my shit into this goddamn clown car?* Marley was bouncing around in the back seat, desperately waiting for acknowledgement. I opened the back door and carried him out to introduce him to Sara. Her face instantly softened. I was relieved to see we at least had a love of fur babies in common. I put her suitcase along the backseat. There was no way we were getting it into my boot. Sara offered to put Marley on her lap. Referencing the other item she was carrying in bubble wrap she said, 'Sarah's old guitar. She wanted Rabbit to have it. I hope he appreciates it because it's been a real pain in the ass to get it here.'

It was nice to get home with Sara to the apartment I was so proud of. I hoped my little 'Zen Den' might be just the thing needed to shrug off jetlag. I had enormous respect for the journey Sara had made. Life had not turned out the way she and her best friend had thought it would and now she was here, in a strange city, on the other side of the world, alone. That night, despite the grogginess of jetlag, Sara appeared in good spirits. She was taken with Marley and he in turn with her. She'd even brought him a small, stuffed Canadian moose dressed as a Mounty. He snatched it out of her hands, clamping his teeth into its antlers before thrashing it from side to side like a lion on a Springbok. 'So, tell me again, what are we doing the next couple of days?' I thought she'd be keen to have a shower and unpack but as I showed her the bathroom and her towel laid out on her bed, she had other things on her mind. I took her directness as a sign of a woman who likes to be in control. I ran through the things I'd planned, most of which we'd already discussed. I told her she was welcome to visit the radio station and 'meet the gang,' and then reminded her of my extra workload that week, thanks to the Royal Adelaide Show. 'So, I guess this is when I'll meet Rabbit?' she asked with a distinct touch of cynicism in her voice. 'You will indeed,' I smiled back, brushing off the awkward vibe.

The next morning, I left the house around 4.40 am while Sara slept. We'd agreed she'd arrive at 11 am. Cosi was gagging to hear how my first night (and day) had gone. Rabbit, however, seemed oddly annoyed Sara was coming in. 'She's got a present from Sarah for you, Rabs,' I said, wanting to remind him there was a Sarah link to all of this.

Meanwhile, Carey had emailed filling me in on his NYC news, which included a bonding weekend away with the Saturday Night Live junior writing crew and a visit by his mother. He seemed keen to hear too how his friend was settling in. I chose to be measured with my honesty but assured him all was going well and that Sara was just about to arrive at the station. Just as I was about to hit send, our receptionist buzzed me at my desk to announce Sara was there. As soon as I saw her, I could see she hadn't brought Rabbit's present but she did have a small gift wrapped in paper and a card for Sarah's favourite 'promo girl' Lucy. I gave her a quick tour of the station, stopping at our studio window to show her where we recorded. To the left was the boss's office. 'We should walk past here fast just in case he decides to air-check me again,' I laughed, nervously. After introducing Sara to the promo team, I texted Rabbit and Cosi to let them know Sara and I were in the girl's office. Minutes later Rabbit was standing at the door. Cosi had already gone home. Rabbit seemed hesitant to step through the doorway. Instead he gave Sara an almost military-salute and said, 'Sara. How are you doing? I'm Rabbit!' Rabbit liked to trot out this wave for people he didn't know well. It indicated 'Hey, I've been told I have to meet you, so here I am. *Happy?* Good. Tick.' Part of me was envious he could pull this off. Sara was sitting down on the edge of the girls' couch and, perhaps sensing Rabbit's distance, she stayed where she was, responding curtly with,

'Hey, Rabbit!' Rabbit gave some polite lip-service, enquiring about her flight, jetlag, the usual pleasantries. It was stiff at best, from both sides. It was a strange dynamic between the two of them and made no sense to me. 'I'll see you at the Royal Adelaide Show next week, I hear?' he asked, in a way that meant, 'That is where I'll see you next, don't come for me prior.'

Sara wasn't done though. 'Yeah, Amber mentioned I should come out and have a look!' she replied, smashing the ball back at him by inferring, 'I've been invited by someone else so go fuck yourself.'

'Great. Well, I'll see you then!' he said, saluting again, then scurrying out the door.

CHAPTER SEVEN.

BEHIND THE GREEN DOOR

Despite being lonely living in Adelaide, South Australia is possibly the most beautiful Australian state. In many ways its nature became my anchor. One of my favourite weekend spots was the Barossa Valley. I'd even managed to have a reasonable good weekend there, once, with Travis. The fresh country air, incredible food and wine, was always a winning recipe to unwinding, feeling cosy and resetting. With a drive of just over an hour, I could fill the time playing music, flicking through different radio stations, giving Sara the lowdown on each one and playing tour guide. It was a successful strategy, deleting any awkward silences or conversations about Rabbit.

I'd booked us into a gorgeous old 1920s bed and breakfast on the recommendation of a friend. Pulling into the long, winding driveway lined with green hedges and blooming rose bushes, the sight of Barossa House, our picturesque home for the weekend, looked heavenly. Proud of myself, I squealed, probably too loudly, 'Ewww, look! It's sooooo cute.' Once parked, and needing to stretch our legs before unpacking, we wandered through an archway (fit for a Jane Austin movie), covered in vines and more pink roses. On the other side we discovered a bird enclosure. Moving closer to the wire to see inside, something on the ground near our feet caught our attention. It was a hen, followed swiftly by six tiny, yellow chicks, marching in single file – *What* a delightful welcoming committee. As I'd seen when Sara met Marley, the animal kingdom seemed to be our most consistent link. It was a beautiful winter's day in the Barossa Valley, with crisp air and sunny blue skies. Our friendly Barossa House hosts soon came bounding out to greet us, announcing they'd put us in the Eucalyptus Room, the largest room on the property. After settling into our room, I suggested an early dinner at 1860; an old favourite restaurant of mine from previous trips. Despite both of us being exhausted it was a surprisingly pleasant evening, the conversation flowed and Sara even paid for dinner – as a 'thank you' she said, for my 'hospitality'. Thankfully, with Sara as tired as me, we finished dessert and called it a night. When we got back to our room, we ended up sitting up chatting on Sara's massive antique bed covered in thick white, embroidered sheets and a quilt cover, and about 400 pillows. I'd given Sara the big bed and taken the single in the corner.

Finally, Sara and I seemed to be connecting as we drank port and polished off local chocolates gifts from our hosts. Then Carey's name came up, which instantly made me paranoid I was blushing. 'He's an old romantic that one,' Sara said of her friend. It hadn't worried me that much, the fact Carey and I hadn't spoken yet. Sara maintained he didn't want to talk to me on the phone. He'd told her, 'The first time I speak with Amber I want it to be in person.' Like other parts of Carey, I'd learnt in the almost six months of our writing, he seemed old fashioned. I loved that about him.

As my thoughts drifted to Sarah, I wondered if she was looking down on us, giggling 'See? I knew you two would get along. Clever me!' Sara shuffled herself on her bed, tossing away a large pillow perched on her knee, sitting up straighter. She wanted to discuss our plans to spread Sarah's ashes at the beach at Glenelg the following week. After all, this was the reason for Sara's visit, not port and choccies and hanging out with me.

When Sarah became ill, she'd asked Blaine and Sara to cremate her and then she wanted them to organize spreading her ashes at significance places (to her) around the world. Blaine was currently in Santorini, where they planned to take their honeymoon, spreading his wife's ashes. And Sara was doing her bit at the beach where Blaine proposed to Sarah. Sarah's ashes were sealed in a Glad Wrap bag and carried in Sara's suitcase. 'I heard Australian customs are pretty rigid,' said Sara, sounding amused. She imagined herself telling the Customs Officer, 'Oh yeah, that's Sarah, she's Canadian. She doesn't have a passport, that's one of the perks of being dead.' Then, just when I thought we were in a productive flow, Sara brought up Rabbit. She wanted to know if he'd be joining us at the ashes ceremony. I had no idea. I was hardly the gatekeeper of Rabbit. As I paused to think of how to politely say 'no fucking idea', I felt Sara's energy shift, which irked me. Here we were finally having a half-decent moment: the last thing I wanted to be doing on my Friday night was talk about Rabbit. I chose to be honest. I told her we hadn't talked about Sarah's death since the day he aired her goodbye. And, even then, Rabbit had played Sarah's message, looked down and just signed us off for the morning. There'd been no sitting around in the studio reflecting or consoling each other like friends. It just ended, and that was it. Mikes off, see ya!

Then again, I said, I had no way of knowing how painful losing Sarah was to Rabbit. I'd never seen him as a man grieving so who was I to know what that looked like? I hoped these insights might diffuse Sara's mission to include Rabbit in anything further. I could give him the guitar once she'd gone but, for some reason, Sara had a bee in her bonnet about being the one to present it.

After a reasonably successful weekend getaway with Sara I felt refreshed and ready to go into our busiest week of the year; The Royal Adelaide Show. For five days we would be doing our usual show in the morning and then heading out to the Royal Adelaide Show for an afternoon broadcast. It was always so much fun getting out of the studio and into the action. Cosi, Rabbit and I bounced off each other well when we had an audience we could see (and play with). Our production team put together a make-shift studio in the heart of the Showgrounds in what they called Sideshow Alley.

Sara showed up while we were still on the air. I noticed her arrive, hanging back in the crowd watching us with what I assumed was a critical professional eye and ear. Cosi's little stepson Harry had come along to see him do his thing with the promise of a proper tour around the show after we'd knocked off. Into the second hour of the show Harry's attention span was waning so Sara offered to take him for a walk. 'Yeah, take him before the kid goes feral,' Cosi said with a laugh.

Hand clasped in Sara's off little Harry went with our new Canadian friend for a wander to kill time. If there was one thing I'd learned about Sara she was used to boys going feral. Having three kids of her own, walking one kid around a show wasn't going to stress her. I liked maternal Sara. Kids and animals brought out the best in her. What didn't bring out the best in her, however, was Rabbit. I was on a mission though. I was determined to get Rabbit alone for a chat between breaks to remind him Sara still had his gift. I found the perfect moment just off the back of a young girl in a fairy costume asking for his autograph. I knew I needed to catch him on a high. It worked. 'Tell Sara I'll pop round to your place Wednesday night. I won't stay long but I will try and get there.' *Hallelujah*, I thought, feeling relieved. Finally, I had an answer.

Rabbit wasn't one to be controlled by a stranger. The only person I'd ever seen Rabbit answer to was the Big Radio Boss. Radio meant everything to Rabbit and he worshipped the ground the boss walked on – some would note he even dressed the same as him, had a matching bald head like him and could also be particularly unemotional at times. The boss was the one in control of my co-host, not Sara, and sure as hell not me.

The next day Marley came bounding towards me as I arrived home from the station around midday. He had his little Canadian Mounty hanging out of his mouth. He dropped it at my feet. Sara's computer was open on my desk but she was nowhere to be seen. 'Hey!', she called out from the top of the stairs. 'Hello, how has your day been so far?' I asked. Sara started making her way down the stairs. She looked sunburnt. My visitor had been sitting out the front in the sun with Marley throwing his Mounty to him.

'He's cute but relentless,' she said with a smile.

'And your meeting this morning with Nova (our competitor), how did it go?'

'A cool team,' she called them, with some 'interesting ideas' about promoting the Winter Olympics. I detected caginess in the way she spoke. I was gagging to ask her more but I refused to play into whatever she was up to. 'He's a very funny guy, that Fitzy!' she said, drilling her eyes into me, waiting for me to buckle.

'Yeah, he is,' I agreed. It was true. 'I think they were careful about what they said about Rabbit though,' Sara continued, baiting me further. *I knew it.* She'd been desperate to try and pull something out of them. But they weren't stupid. Even if they had something negative to say or a great impersonation, they weren't dumb enough to share it in front of a stranger.

I told her Rabbit would be dropping over the next day to collect his present, hoping this might make her happy. 'So, we won't be going out for dinner then?' she said, looking unimpressed. 'That'll be the catch up with Rabbit, hey?'

'Yes,' I said, determined to dig my heels in. 'He's got a busy week, so that's all he's offered.' My answer did not include the ingredients Sara was looking for.

'So, what do you think is the problem with Rabbit? Why is it he's known I'm coming for months, knows I've gone to the trouble of bringing the guitar from Canada, and it takes him days to commit to a quick visit, and that's it?' If Sara was getting pissed off, so was I. Conscious of not escalating it though, I took a deep breath, given I was stuck with her for another week and a half. I also didn't want her running back to Carey telling him I was a bitch. She had control over how I got painted to Carey. I couldn't work out if I was paranoid, but a part of me suspected she knew this.

I decided to write Carey an email that day, given our communication had gone relatively quiet since Sara arrived in town. I wanted to see if he'd mention anything, offer any clues as to what was going on, or tips on how to navigate her. He wrote back a few hours later. The first thing I noticed was from his response was his use of a full stop, right after 'Hello'. Was it my insecurity (again) or was he making a point? He went on to say he'd just finished 'an online chat' with Sara and she seemed 'out of sorts'. He signed off with, 'Thinking of my two girls over there'.

Sara was sleeping in my spare bedroom, which housed my second wardrobe. Before she arrived, I'd made sure I'd grabbed most of the clothes and shoes I might need during her stay, from the room so I wouldn't have to disturb her. It was early evening when I started thinking about the next day and realised that there was one pair of shoes I needed to complete my outfit. Not sure if Sara was in her room or downstairs, I stopped at her door and noticed from the glass panel along the top of the bedroom wall that the light was on. The door was shut but not closed by the latch. I grabbed the handle gently so as not to push it open and gave it two quick knocks with my left hand. 'Hey Sara, you there? I just wanted to grab a pair of shoes for tomorrow from your room, if you don't mind?'

I made sure I kept my eyes down at the floor in case she happened to be changing, aware the door might have drifted open a little. With no response from Sara I reached the door handle again, ready to give it another knock. As my eyes diverted up from the floor, I caught a glimpse of Sara's room through the crack in the door – and what I could see was that the bedroom floor was literally covered in *stuff*. *What the hell is going on in there?* The sliver of what I'd seen had left me strangely confused. There was something about it that felt like I'd seen something about Sara I wasn't supposed to see. And the fact she wasn't answering only added to the weirdness. Suddenly, the door slammed shut in my face. Sara was in there but she hadn't made a sound to acknowledge my question. Instead, she'd cut off my view. *My view of what, though?* I wondered.

I called out again, 'I just wanted to get some shoes from the shelf in there when you're ready. Sorry if I startled you.' I said 'sorry' but I wasn't. I was sorry I'd invited her to stay with me. I was sorry I was too nice and too bloody open with myself and my life. Sara mumbled something I couldn't hear. Something felt off. I decided to re-think my outfit for the next day and just go to bed.

Cosi loved my daily reports on Sara. I'd confided in him about my stand-offs with Sara involving Rabbit. He agreed Rabbit had been a bit difficult, given the girl was Sarah's best mate. When Rabbit got back into the studio Cosi wasted no time fishing for a reaction, 'You're off to meet Sara today, hey Rabs?'

'Yeah mate, I am. I'll be there late afternoon, Petty. I've got a few things to do before I head to yours so I'll text when I'm heading your way. That cool?' Cosi smirked, knowing Rabbit was too busy to look up and see that he might be taking the piss out of him.

'Great, thanks Rabs,' I said. 'I'm taking Sara to the healing centre today so we'll be back by about 3 pm.' Cosi roared laughing, hoisting his legs up on to the studio bench as he did in between breaks, much to my annoyance.

'Oh Jesus, Petty, you're not bad, are you? Off to take bloody Sara to your hippy, witchy mates. Can't wait to hear how that all goes down.'

I amused Cosi no end. While he teased me about my new 'angels, crystals and fairies' lifestyle I'd do the same about his bizarre ritual of eating yoghurt and blueberries straight off a piece of paper instead of a plate. Or his classic Cosi questions, like, 'Is South Africa a country?' Mostly though there was affection between us despite us being like chalk and cheese.

I left the studio around 11 am that day, keen to get home so I could take Marley for a walk before taking Sara to the healing centre. When I got back Sara was at her computer. I couldn't read how she was feeling about our excursion. I decided not to freak her out by making it a big deal. Our fifteen-minute drive was quiet. I could feel Sara had a lot on her mind. I chose to stay in the silence, as uncomfortable as it was. I thought this was a better primer than me babbling on for the sake of it. I also didn't want her to believe she was doing me a favour by coming. She wasn't. I arranged it before she arrived because I cared about her, and she'd asked for it. 'Have fun!' I sang out to Sara as we disappeared down different corridors. *Have fun? Interesting choice of words, Amber.*

My session went for over an hour. When I came out to the front desk to pay, Sara was already sitting at the table by the window. 'I'm sorry,' I said, 'have you been finished for long?' She didn't look happy. She seemed spiritually pissed off.

I needed to use the toilet before we left so Linley, Sara's healer, offered to usher me there. When we arrived at the bathroom, she placed her hand gently on my arm and said, 'I'm afraid that didn't go well. She was very agitated. Very blocked.' Apparently, Sara had taken great offence to Linley's healing style. I hadn't thought to tell Sara that Linley was a burper. I'd learnt over the last year that trapped or dark energy can come up and out through the healer, which sometimes means they burp to expel it. It's a little weird but I knew it worked because, little by little, I'd started feeling better. I was slowly getting more clarity about the good and bad voices in my head. Sara, however, wasn't down with it. She'd been so disgusted that she'd stopped Linley mid-healing and declared she'd had enough. *Oh dear, I should have thought to explain this,* I panicked. I'd hinted it was going to be a bit 'unusual' but I hadn't mentioned burping and now I had a seriously awkward car ride ahead. And Rabbit arriving in an hour.

There wasn't much conversation before Rabbit arrived. I decided I needed to lie down on my bed and check my emails for what was coming up on our Royal Adelaide Show later that day. Rabbit texted saying he was parking, warning again that he couldn't stay long. I got up and headed downstairs. The doorbell rang. Marley jumped up, barking his head off, bouncing up and down at the door. 'Sara, I think this is Rabbit,' I said, as I walked past her door. 'I'll see you down there.' I opened the front door to find Rabbit looking unconvinced about whether he wanted to come in. 'Have any chill-out time this morning?' I asked, in lieu of a greeting. We were always checking in with each other about how tired we were and whether we'd managed to get anything done.

Sara was coming down the stairs, holding a guitar and some other things. 'Hey, Rabbit!' There were no kisses on the cheek, polite hugs or even a businesslike handshake. Neither of their egos would allow them to make the first move. 'Would you like a drink or anything, Rabs?' I asked.

'Just water would be great.' I raced off to the kitchen, delighted to have a job.

'This is Sarah's guitar,' Sara said, handing it to Rabbit. 'It's been well-loved, I know you guys shared a love of music. I guess this is why she wanted you to have it. I'm pretty sure Blaine couldn't play a note.'

Sara seemed at peace, finally presenting Sarah's treasure to the guy her best friend had formed a close bond with. As I was handing Rabbit his glass, she reached down to pick up two other things she'd brought from upstairs. One was a big old rug of some sort, the other small and wrapped in gift paper, 'These are for you, Amber, from Sarah.'

I unfolded the rug. It was a large and obviously well-loved, flannel, cowhide-print blanket. 'It was Sarah's blanket,' Sara said. 'She loved it. She thought you might like it.' I stared at it, not knowing quite what to say. I wracked my brain trying to remember if we'd had a conversation about it. 'Here's another little something for you,' continued Sara, handing over a small wrapped gift. I was glad we were moving on from the blanket because I'd still not worked out why I'd received it, and I didn't want to appear ungrateful. I tore at the paper, hoping to find something more natural to comment on. Inside was a small silver angel bell. I swung it gently, listening to it tinkle. *Beautiful! This is my little 'Sarah the Angel' bell.* This made sense.

'Thank you Sara, this is my Sarah angel, and she can sit on top of the shelf near the stairs to keep an eye on everything.'

'So, Rabbit,' Sara began with purpose, 'Amber and I will be heading to Glenelg beach around 1 pm tomorrow to lead Sarah's ashes out to sea. Would you want to come?' *Oh God, there it was.* She'd cornered him. *I should have seen this coming. He should have seen this coming.* She'd checkmated him. I'll raise your half-an-hour drop-in with a 'You should be there tomorrow if you ever cared about Sarah'.

I'd unwittingly become an accessory to Sara's games. I'd help lure Rabbit into the house so she could pounce. There was no way Rabbit would be joining us at the beach to pay his respects to Sarah. Not a hope in hell.

This, right here, right now, was the platinum-member, VIP, meet-and-greet experience with Rabbit. Expecting more would be access denied.

'Yeah, I can't tomorrow. I've got my little boy's kindergarten play. And then we'll be back out to the Royal Adelaide Show again.' *God, he's good. He's come prepped.* Sara looked suspicious, which wasn't going to be Rabbit's problem. If there was one thing Rabbit knew how to do after twenty years on the radio it was going out on a high. And, while riding that high, Rabbit signed off, bidding us both farewell.

'I've got Sarah in my handbag,' Sara quipped as we prepared to leave the house the next day, headed for Glenelg beach. I acknowledged to myself (in my head) that I had another odd afternoon ahead of me, but I hoped it would be lovely as well. Mother Nature delivered the perfect conditions – twenty-five degrees and not a cloud in the sky. Sara mentioned it'd been years since she'd been to a beach so I was excited for her to see Glenelg. The parking angels (or Sarah) delivered a rock-star park right in front of the section of the beach where we'd planned to spread Sarah's ashes.

First, I suggested a walk to clear our heads and get us into the right space for Sarah's ceremony. We walked for half an hour before stopping to leave our jackets, Marley, and bags under the shade of a tree lining the beach wall. Sara reached inside her giant tote bag, pulling out a small plastic bag filled with Sarah's ashes.

I wondered if Sara would talk me through her plan for spreading the ashes but she didn't. She walked ahead towards the shoreline without stopping, aside from a short jump when she hit the cold water. I followed, hanging back, not sure what my role was. I hoped she'd stop at some point and say something. But she didn't.

Instead, she pulled up as the water hit her knees. Without turning she opened the bag and let the ashes tumble out. With just half the bag of ashes released into the water I watched as a gust of wind whipped up, seemingly just around Sara: it blew the entire second half of Sarah all over Sara.

Oh. My .God. I stood ankle-deep in the water, stunned. *Was this either the worst thing that could happen to someone or the funniest?* I dared not speak in case she turned around with a face of thunder, or tears. As she swung around to avoid the rest of the wind, she had ashes all over her denim skirt and her tattooed arm. She brushed it off like someone who'd just tripped over but was pretending they hadn't. She stuck her ash-covered arm in the water to wash off her friend. Still clutching the now empty bag, without glancing at me, she walked off. Standing on my own in the sparkling waters of Glenelg I couldn't help but feel like an idiot, an intruder even, in a sacred moment I thought I was going to be part of.

I wondered if I should be miffed that I'd been left out, or terrible for Sara that her big moment had gone, literally, sideways. And now it was time to go home and pack for my much-needed holiday in Perth, travelling with a woman who, so far, had been about as much fun as a week of community service cleaning public toilets.

SEND ME AN ANGEL

I decided that since I was off to Perth with the person that I least wanted to go on a holiday with in the entire world, I would start creating some boundaries between us. This was *my* holiday and I'd be buggered if *she* was going to wreck it. As for Carey, I was doing my best to write him off as well. After all, I concluded, if he was as close to Sara as she (and he) made out, then he had very strange taste in friends.

Between Sara and I we had more luggage than Katy Perry on a world tour. When we walked inside the airport Sara mumbled something that I didn't hear then shot off to the counter. I didn't care what she was doing by this stage and the last thing I wanted to do was sit with her on the plane. So, I decided to check myself in at one of the machines conveniently taking her out of the equation. I could see her bearing down over a young woman behind the desk.

I grabbed my boarding pass and headed to the bag drop-off queue. I was enjoying the fantasy that I was heading on holiday on my own. Of course, I wasn't and now Sara was coming my way with an expression I'd come to know.

'They're telling me I'm going to have to pay $30 for the extra weight in my bags! She says she has no record of the conversation I had with her colleague when I booked the ticket.' I feigned mild outrage.

I had naively, (some might say, moronically), agreed before Sara's arrival to share a hotel room with her for two nights in Perth. A decision I was now regretting with every ounce of my being but there wasn't a lot I could do about it except use the three-and-a-half hours of the flight to come up with a genius plan to wrangle us into separate rooms.

Sara had set up meetings with two radio networks in Perth to discuss the Winter Olympics. I thanked God she'd be busy the first couple of days. One of her meetings was with Andy, an old, close friend of mine from my music industry days.

Andy was now the Promotions Director at an FM radio station in Perth. Sweetly, he'd offered to take us for dinner to the Small Creatures

Brewery. Little did I know when I'd accepted his invitation just how much I'd need him. The thought of having an old ally between Sara and I, almost made me misty-eyed.

When we got to Perth, I used the cab ride to the hotel to broach the subject of separate rooms. My disdain for Sara was igniting the ballsy side of me. 'So, I was thinking, given I got such a great deal on the room price, which probably means it's going to be the size of a drawer, maybe we might want to suss out the price of another room? So, we can spread out a bit. What do you think?' I braced for the airbags to go off.

'Sure, sounds good to me,' Sara responded, in a tone that was way better than I'd hoped.

'Let's check it out when we get there. I'm good at negotiating, so leave it with me.' *Negotiating? Is that what they call bullying these days?* I was happy for her to 'negotiate' for us if it meant she'd get us our own space. I'd hang back a little and let her work her black magic. At the hotel, as she liked to do, Sara marched ahead of me to the counter. Our chances weren't good as apparently there was a conference going on, so it was pretty much a full house. I started feeling tense, despondent, forlorn, and a few other dramatic adjectives, as I hung back from the desk praying.

After a few minutes the hotel staffer confirmed there was 'no other room' available. 'Level 3, room 303. Enjoy your stay with us!' the girl smiled, handing over two keys to our one room. *Shit. This is going to be a really long forty-eight hours.* The only consolation was Sara had meetings scheduled and, hopefully, if I prayed as hard as 1000 Christians on Easter Sunday, it would all be over quickly.

We'd be off to Fremantle, another part of Perth, where we'd have our own separate apartments – and I would have my freedom back. Sara opened the door to our new friend-nest – it wasn't the size of a drawer; it was the size of a knob on a drawer.

'This is fucking ridiculous,' Sara snapped. 'I'm going downstairs to have a word.' And out she went, slamming the door behind her. I sat on the edge of the other single bed and stared at my average-sized suitcase. My sudden intense loneliness made me want to talk to it. I wanted to say, *Please suitcase, will you look after me in here? I feel like a cartoon mouse trapped by an angry cartoon cat. And I think she's going to eat me like a piece of cheese in my sleep. Right after she kills the poor love at the reception desk.*

I was still partially catatonic fifteen minutes later when the door swung open and in strolled Sara, looking smug. 'So, we've got our extra room,' she smirked. 'I've always found it works a treat when you mention you work in the media. Gets 'em working a little harder.' She swept past me like an old Hollywood actress drunk with power and gin.

It was a relief to see Andy's friendly face waiting for us in the foyer that night. I gave him an enormous hug, digging my nails into his forearms like he'd just caught me with my captor. I introduced Sara, who was reserved. Dinner was fun, *thank Christ*, and Sara seemed to like Andy. With every drink she seemed to lighten up more.

Bloody hell, if only I'd known she's better pissed than she is sober I would have bought a case of wine for our first breakfast. Back at the hotel I said goodnight to Sara and agreed to meet her for breakfast the next morning before she headed out to her radio meetings. Sara liked people to make her feel important and with the $30,000 she'd mentioned she had to spend to promote the Winter Olympics, she was sure to get the Perth radio teams to make her feel special.

The next morning she messaged saying she'd have to skip breakfast, claiming she had an emergency Skype meeting 'with the team from *The Hour*'. With Carey's absence on the show things weren't flowing on the production front since she left and the host had contacted her for help. This suited me perfectly. I'd begin my tour of the city by finding the nearest place that served the greasiest hash browns I could find to shake off my hangover.

I'd made a plan that night for a quiet dinner in the hotel restaurant with Sara. After an uneventful day exploring downtown Perth I showered and headed downstairs to meet her. By the time I got down there she was sitting up at the hotel's bar with a beer.

'I'm getting a lesson in your weird football,' she said, gesturing towards the bartender.

'How did your radio meetings go?' I asked, sitting down beside her. She looked unimpressed.

'Your friend Andy's team seemed pretty disorganised. I got the feeling they'd just thrown a presentation together to amuse me. I didn't even get to meet the on-air team. The other station was better. They took me on a tour and I met the breakfast hosts. I'd put my money with them if I had to choose.' I didn't appreciate her bagging my friend, although I kept it to myself. It was one thing to be unimpressed in a professional sense but her lack of graciousness given Andy had bought her dinner the night before was extremely poor.

The next morning, I met Sara at reception, ready to check out and make tracks for Fremantle. I couldn't wait to get settled into our next destination and, as usual I nursed hopes that once we got there, we might hit our friend strides. I had equal hopes that, if we didn't, I wouldn't care. 'How did you sleep?' I asked her as she was paying for her room.

'Fine,' she answered without offering the question back.

'I was up late, though. I had a long Skype call with Carey.' I waited for an extension of what felt like an intentional teaser. Sara knew I'd be keen to hear anything to do with Carey, but she gave me nothing. With everything going on since Sara arrived, I was aware I hadn't heard much from Carey. Whatever the answer, the reality was Sara had control over me by dangling the Carey carrot and then snatching it away.

I hadn't even had my first coffee and I was already agitated. So was Sara, it would seem, as she became impatient with the cab driver when his English rendered him a little less au fait with Fremantle than we'd hoped. Sure, he wasn't exactly Morgan Freeman in *Driving Miss Daisy*, but Sara spoke to him like he was a piece of shit. 'There it is,' I yelled as if I'd just seen the Loch Ness Monster through the mist. *Thank Christ for that.* I started extracting myself (and my suitcase) as fast as I could. I practically swiped my credit card across the driver's mouth to get away. Sara pulled at her bag, which appeared heavy enough to contain a dead body. *What the hell has she got in there?* I wondered, not for the first time. *Was all that stuff on the floor of my spare room crammed back in there?* Something about that moment still didn't sit right. I was relieved to discover Sara's apartment was on the opposite side of the building from mine. We agreed to unpack then go for a wander around town followed by an early dinner. After dinner I got back to my room around 8 pm, poured myself a glass of wine and called my friend Diana. I knew she'd be dying for an update on 'the Canadian'. It was on my mind to check my emails too to see if there was anything from Carey. There wasn't. I told myself it didn't matter anymore. I was sending myself crazy worrying what Sara was saying about me. And I started asking myself why was I allowing myself to get caught up trying to please two people who didn't appear to care about me?

I woke around 9 am – officially – the next day, though I'd also woken at 4 am stewing over Sara and Carey. I grabbed my phone off the bedside table. There was a text message from her. She wanted to 'push back our catch up' by an hour. Over an hour later there was still no sign of Sara. I sent her another text checking if she was on her way. At 11.30 am she texted again saying she was 'running late' and that she was 'on a work call' – making no attempt at a polite apology.

Another 45 minutes passed and I was Category 5 pissed off. I'd been sitting around for nearly two hours in my apartment, on my holiday, waiting for Sara. Two hours I could have quite easily, and more importantly happily used exploring Fremantle on my own, at my own pace. But I hadn't because I'd been trying to please Sara and, once again, Sara was treating me like the hired help. 'I don't know what's going on,' I typed furiously in my final response 'but I don't want to waste any more of my day, so I'm heading off.' Not only was this my holiday but so far, despite thinking I'd be able to disconnect from her and play the game on my terms, I wasn't. I was all talk and no action. I left the apartment determined to be free but no matter how hard I tried I knew my holiday was a nightmare. It was windy and cold and I was exhausted and angry.

That night I had terrible anxiety, again, and couldn't sleep. I was furious at Sara, but mostly with myself. *Round and round the hamster wheel you go. People-pleasing; Sara, Rabbit, the Big Radio Boss* – the list went on and on. Not to mention the complete paranoia dropping in and out at regular interviews, at still not having heard a peep from Carey. Thankfully I remembered I'd brought a couple of weapons in my bag – (I'm not talking guns or a knife – thank god because I was ripe) – but sleeping pills and a book I'd found in my mum's collection when I was an angry teenager. It was titled *Love Is Letting Go of Fear*.

I wondered, *Why had I brought this book with me?* Wide-eyed in the middle of the night, anxiety crippling me, I reached down into my bag for the book. I used my phone to make a light so I could read. I said a prayer before I opened it. *Please, God, lead me to the right page that I need tonight*, I whispered aloud. I knew immediately I'd landed on exactly the right page. It was all about the mind and the ego and how it continually seeks negative affirmations about ourselves that keep us paralysed with fear – which is what I was in – fear.

Thank you, angels, I said, smiling up at the ceiling. Whatever was going on, I was convinced, something was protecting me. As I read the chapter, I could feel the words resonating in my heart but then I'd drift back into a panic realising I'd read several lines without taking anything in. So, I'd reset. *OK, see, this is what the cycle is like*, I told myself. *Your ego is trying to distract you from the wisdom. Try to fight back gently. You can do this!*

I woke up the next morning feeling grateful for Mum's book. I was tired but nothing like what I could have been. I checked in with myself. *How do I feel about everything? I think I'm OK, but there's still today. Still, her, looming a few doors away.* All the anxiety I'd battled the night before in bed, my mind racing through the gamut of reasons to panic and doubt myself, were back, standing in front of me like the overbearing shadow of Sara.

It was time to call on my angels again. I made a plan. I'd grab my bag, head out the front door towards the main street of Fremantle and I'd ask my angels to direct me. *Come on angels, I need you right now.*

Please guide me to somewhere that will cure this anxiety that is ruining my holiday. Please angels, please show me you're here. I said it over and over as I walked. Reaching the high street of Fremantle, I glanced around at the quaint tourist shops, thinking there was no hope of finding anything remotely hippy enough to sort me out. Row after row of cafes beckoned me in for some much-needed food, but I couldn't eat. My anxiety had stripped away my appetite. *Please angels, please angels, I know you're going to show up and I'm not going home until you do,* I kept reciting in my head. And then I spotted it. It was a sign, an actual sign and it read: 'The Blue Buddha – Healings, Psychic Readings, Tarot' with an arrow pointed towards a tiny arcade tucked away off the street. *Bingo? And there it is. Thank you, thank you, angels.* I practically skipped towards the sign, flying through the door like Tinkerbell.

At the risk of sounding cliched, a woman in a colourful kaftan with sequins scattered around the neck and sleeves stood behind the counter. She looked up, smiling. 'Hello,' I said. 'Do you have psychic readings happening today?'

'We do. She's with someone but she won't be long. *'Thank you, angels.'* I felt like a junkie about to get their next hit.

'Would you like to come this way, Amber?' the psychic said, leading me into her reading room, which looked just like the ones at the Healing Centre. Relief drenched me. We sat down and the lady asked me if there was anything I wanted to heal or get clarity on.

I told her about Sara and the shocking anxiety I'd been feeling. She closed her eyes, seemingly trying to tune in to the situation. After a few seconds, she opened them and said, 'Yes. This woman you mention, she has very, very scattered energy. This is not about you, though. This is who she is.'

Her words lingered. *This is who she is?* It resonated with me until it didn't. The problem was, I still didn't know who the girl I was travelling with was – and now it was beginning to feel creepy. 'OK, let's get you up on the bed now,' she said softly. I lay down as she covered me in blankets, checking I was warm enough, and then explaining she'd be 'channelling my angels and guides', to assist in my healing.

Apparently, this meant they'd be giving her messages in her mind about me. She also mentioned she'd be placing crystals on my body to settle my nervous system down. After ten minutes or so I thought: *Wow, I think I'm beginning to feel calmer. I do feel calm! Oh, thank God.'* After thirty minutes she told me to open my eyes and slowly sit up on the table.

'How do you feel?' she whispered gently. I felt good. I felt refreshed, and it was fabulous. I just prayed I could hold on to it. 'I want to have a bit of a chat with you before you go,' she said as I sat back down on her chair. 'I don't want to scare you, because it's a great thing, but something happened during your healing that I've never had happen before.' I wondered what the hell she was going to tell me. *Had she seen some sort of demonic presence hanging over me? Had Sara sent some of her evil spirit mates to fuck with me because I wasn't answering her texts?* I want to say I was joking, the dramatic Leo coming out, but I wasn't. I was genuinely paranoid that Sara might sense through a sixth (666) sense that I was secretly going against her.

'Did you feel a point during the healing where there were hands around your ankles?' she asked me. I had. It was a weird sensation because I wasn't sure at what end of the table she'd been throughout our session. *Is she behind my head now? Or is she holding my ankles?* I didn't pay attention at the time, but now I was. A couple of times out of curiosity I'd even slightly parted my eyes, hoping she wouldn't catch me.

'I was at the head of the table the whole time. In normal healings I'll head to the end of the table to anchor the healing but not long into yours I saw a man at your feet. He gave me a nod that I interpreted to mean he'd come into the healing to help out with the power required to ground you,' she said. *OK?* I thought. 'It was amazing. This figure, who I could see more clearly than I often do when guides or energies come into the room during a healing, was a small man, about five-foot-two wearing an extravagant long coat with embroidered edges and a large pointy hat. I could also make out that he had a long black moustache.

The only thing I could think of when I looked at him, when I felt his energy, is that he was like Confucius.' I felt a chill run down my body. Unless she was an A-grade bullshit artist there was no doubt at all in my mind that there had been hands around my ankles for most of the healing. 'I don't know why Amber but whoever this was they came because they knew I needed assistance in grounding you. You have some serious powers on your side.'

I left The Blue Buddha feeling empowered and determined to keep my focus. I contemplated putting off looking at my phone, fearful there'd be a text message waiting for me, Sara's attempt to drag me back into her web. I decided there was no better time to tackle the inevitable, especially while I had the spiritual spring in my step, so I pulled my phone out. There was a text from Sara, 'Just finished up my meeting. Let me know if you want me to come to meet you?' With the ball now bouncing merrily in my court, I looked down at my phone and thought, *I owe you nothing. And nothing is the response you'll get.* I smiled as I switched my phone off and tossed it (and her) into my bag.

My goodness was it nice spending an afternoon (and evening) just hanging out with me. I'd never have thought I'd catch myself thinking, *There's something cool about me.* Not when I was used to torturing myself with tedious, obsessive internal rantings. *If only I could be this chick more of the time. People don't fuck with you if you don't give them air time.* With every hour, every minute, every second that I didn't check my phone and didn't think about Sara, my sense of peace increased and it felt heavenly.

The truth was I hadn't needed to throw myself into any of this. But I had. I'd chosen to. *If it's happening to you, it's about you.* I remembered these wise words that had arrived in my head a year ago. The same words that led me to my commitment to steering clear of men until I sorted my shit out. Somewhere along the line though I'd fallen off the wagon. I'd allowed strangers to come into my life and I'd thrown myself into their story – all their stories. There was one thing I needed to do to cement my 'new fabulous, peaceful me', and that was to confront Sara. My inner warrior, the aspect of me I'd laid to rest for too long, was back, and I was pleased to welcome her. I texted Sara early evening, asking simply, 'Are you at home?' *She won't expect weak little Amber to turn up suddenly. So that's exactly what I'll do.* As a precautionary measure I rang Diana again. She was one of the handful of friends I'd made in Adelaide. I wanted to let her know what I was doing just in case Sara was a fan of Jeffrey Dahmer's work and decided to snap my neck before stuffing me into the freezer. Someone needed to know where I was going and at what time. I wasn't scared of Sara any more – I was sick to fucking death of the girl. She'd underestimated me and it was time she saw the old, tougher Amber, now charged with a bit of Confucius around the ankles. I strolled, purposefully, down the corridor towards her apartment, stopping outside on her welcome mat. I could hear her voice inside talking to someone. *Good, I'll interrupt her. Maybe I'll even interrupt her little chat with Carey.* I knocked on the door assertively – three quick knocks. I felt like an American cop in a low-budget movie. The door opened after a long pause. Sara was standing a foot or so back from the doorway, looking perplexed. She didn't like my random, uncontrollable arrival. 'Can I come in?' I asked calmly. 'I think we need a chat.' Her face remained non-inviting but she gestured me in. I walked into her apartment on high alert, surveying the scene, glancing left and right. Her computer was sitting open on the kitchen table with a paused image of a girl with long dreadlocks on the screen. Now it was just Sara – and the newly empowered, rebooted me.

She walked me out to the balcony. We both sat down. I made a note of the proximity of the neighbouring balconies. *They'll hear me scream if something bad happens*, I assured myself. I decided to cut to the chase. I wouldn't allow her to take control of my moment. She looked at me with a face that looked ready to battle. 'Sara, I need to tell you the way you've been treating me, since the day you arrived, is not good enough. The way you've been behaving as a guest in my home, a guest on my holiday, which this is, is not good enough and I've felt bullied by you. And I want to know why, Sara, you think this is OK?' I sat back, trying to conceal my nerves, waiting for her response. She was gob-smacked. I'd disarmed the mighty beast. She stared at me for a few seconds, her left eye began squinting. I held her gaze, preparing for her reaction. *Expect the table to be flipped any second. Ready your arms to flip it back. You've got this. Someone knows you're here.* I'd recently seen Teresa Giudice flip a table in *The Real Housewives of New Jersey*, so I knew how this shit went.

Sara finally spoke. 'I didn't realise that's what I was doing,' she muttered, unapologetically. She looked pissed off. I could tell I had her but I wasn't stupid enough to underestimate she might still turn at any second. The truth was I had no idea who was sitting before me. It was only then I realised this girl I'd let into my life was a total stranger. On paper my tactic was terrible. There was no contest between us in physical stake, but I was challenging her on the mental stakes now. She could have attacked me. She knew where the knives were. She was six foot bloody four and twice my size but I didn't care. I was ready to go her across the table like a pissed bogan in a pub brawl. Suddenly I felt Sara's energy shift to something a little more girlie, mixed with a light lathering of bewilderment. 'I'm not sure what to say?' she offered in a way I knew was designed to make me second guess my approach. She straightened herself in the plastic chair. 'I'm going to have to think about all this. You've certainly come on pretty heavy in the way you've spoken to me tonight,' she said, sounding sufficiently like a victim.

'That's fine,' I answered. 'I'll leave you to enjoy the rest of your night. I think, probably from this point on, with this holiday, we should do our own thing. And I genuinely hope you enjoy the rest of your trip. I do. Because that's what I wanted for Sarah.' With that I got up from the table and saw myself out. The last image I saw was of Sara's face at the table with an expression that read, 'I didn't see this coming. I didn't see *this* coming from *you*.' The next morning Sara sent a text message suggesting we try to 'get things back on track' by having a 'mani-pedi together'. It was a ritual she'd mentioned she and Carey (my ex-online boyfriend) did together. I declined. I told her *my friend* Andy was coming to collect me to take me out for the day. He wasn't but it felt good to remind her that I too had a male friend that cared about me – someone who had a few 'dot points' of his own.

THE WEATHERMAN CALLED FOR A TWISTER

You know you've had a seriously *shit* holiday when you're gagging to get back to work. Even my alarm going off at 4.20 am felt like a blessing. Unfortunately, however, instead of me having a whole bunch of new stories to tell on-air, as one should after having two weeks off, I had nothing. The holiday had been horrific, and none of it made any sense. On that morning, as was the usual, Cosi and I chatted during our breaks, sharing various bits we weren't going to share on-air. Rabbit would join in between getting ready for our next break. That day was all about how our holidays had gone. Without going right into it I'd teased that my holiday with Sara was a disaster. This, of course, was the perfect hook for Cosi, who kept pressing for more detail. 'Well, she was just kind of mean and a bully,' I confessed. Rabbit was quiet, but his judgment was palpable. Cosi, however, was like a pig in shit – shuffling in his seat with excitement, smirking, as he continued his interrogation. About halfway through the show as Rabbit pressed play on another Pink song for the fiftieth time that month, Cosi blurted out something that almost made me drop my mirror. 'So, Petty, what would you do,' he said slowly, seemingly lost in thought, 'if you found out that Sara and Sarah were the same people?' I stared blankly at him, trying to figure out what he was up to. *What a fucked-up thing to say. What kind of person makes jokes about something that's still so raw?* I was disgusted at his flippancy regarding our dead friend. 'What do you mean?' I said, trying to mask my irritation. Cosi stared down at his jean legs as though he were still formulating an idea in his head. 'Well, you've said she was weird and you couldn't work her out so I'm just wondering, maybe she's not who she says she is? Maybe she's a nutter?' he laughed, pleased with himself.

Despite wanting to tell him he was a dickhead I couldn't find the right words to shut him down. Unperturbed by my lack of engagement, he continued, 'And so, if that were true, that would mean that Carey doesn't exist either? Imagine that?' I glanced over at Rabbit to see how he was processing Cosi's off-air banter. After all, Cosi was suggesting the intense, painful and beautiful friendship Rabbit had had with Sarah, the girl who'd had such an impact on him, was a con. And then I wondered: *Had Cosi been harbouring resentment towards Rabbit because Sarah had brought him attention on-air? Is this his way of restoring his ego?* Rabbit's eyes were lowered towards his radio panel. I got a sense that if the two of us met each other's gaze it might add credibility to Cosi's conspiracy theory.

Rabbit looked up at the studio clock without acknowledging either of us, announcing we had a minute left before our mikes would be back on. We sat silently in the studio as the seconds counted down. I watched Rabbit curiously as he announced the last song, followed by a time-call, then all of a sudden, my mind went completely blank. I couldn't even remember what our next on-air break was. I had no idea if I was leading a topic, a story, or what was happening. Somehow Cosi's words had gotten to me. And then, all of a sudden, it was like a bomb had gone off in my gut.

'Ten seconds,' Rabbit warned again. A voice in my head said calmly: *This is going to be your greatest professional test so far. You're going to have to rise above this. Whatever 'this' is.* Somehow, I managed to get through the show that day but in the days that followed it was hard not to think about what Cosi had said. God knows I wanted to thrash it out six ways from Sunday but I dared not let Cosi know he'd got to me just in case that was precisely his intention. As for Rabbit, there was no way I could bring it up with him. The same old rules still applied between us. Despite Cosi's bombshell I decided Sara being off as a human didn't mean Sarah was on the nose too. Regardless of the unease I felt when I'd think about Cosi's suggestion I knew there was every chance Sarah might just have a sadistic friend – and had absolutely no idea of this side of her. *Or maybe Sarah was just like me and made way too many excuses for people?* In the days, weeks and months that followed I went back to spending a lot of time by myself after work. I needed time to process. My thoughts kept dancing between what might be the truth. I decided I needed to try and maintain some contact with Sara while she was still in Australia. I knew at that point she was spending her last week in Melbourne so I decided to call her and feign renewed care about how she was getting on – just a friend checking.

I launched into detective mode one afternoon – the same energy I'd mustered that day I pulled rank on her at the Perth apartment. I wrote her a friendly text ending with, 'Love a quick call if you have time?' Hours later she responded with, 'Melbourne's cool. All going well.' By dropping my need to please I could now read, in symbolically large font, how I was being played. I'd seen her at her best before she arrived in Australia when the smell of adventure, the anticipation of what I was offering her, was hanging in the air before I stopped being of use. I wanted to scream at her that she was now under my investigation but I had to be strategic. I had to be cold and calculated – valuable lessons I'd learned from her. I'd been easy for Sara – I just kept trying to please her. Two nights after her message I could wait no longer, so I called her. She answered and was surprisingly chatty, presumably still riding high from being in the audience of *Rove* – a nightly TV show (and name of the host); tickets organised by me through Rove's manager. Fan-girling about the experience, she boasted about her 'great seats' and being taken from the audience to meet him. All facilitated by the Queen of the Mugs, *me*. The sadistic side of me was revelling in how good I was at giving the false impression that I was OK with her. All was not fine but I liked being in control – mirroring back her joyful sadism. And I loved that, while she thought I was still an airhead, I was now awake.

A week later I got a text message from Carey, oddly from Sara's phone number, informing me Sara was now home in Canada. Apparently 'her lupus' had been playing up in the last week she was in Australia so she'd returned early and was in the hospital. I stared at the text message that I was one hundred per cent sure was designed to invoke my sympathy – throwing the clueless, compassionate girl a small dead fish hoping she'd eat it like a performing seal. Using Carey to deliver the message was another Sara tactic to pull me back to a place of hope that my fantasy relationship might still pan out.

I wasn't ready to share my suspicions with anyone just yet. I went about work as normal and came home to my usual routine. Nobody around me knew anything big was brewing. In October 2009, more than six weeks after Sara left Australia, I'd begun focusing back on me (I could see how derailed I'd become) but now I felt a calling to temporarily put my mental health and healing campaign on hold – it was time to investigate Sara. I began by googling her name in relation to The Hour. Nothing came up. With this first piece of the puzzle not fitting the urgency was building to do what many others would have done by now. It was time to contact The Hour. I had to rule this enormous chunk of her story out. I called the CBC, the show's network, several times but never managed to connect with a human.

I figured I needed to step it up and send an email, even if it got forwarded to the dragon herself. I emailed asking whether Sara Kelly or Carey Malcolmson worked for them.

Halfway through the email I thought, *Fuck it, I'm going to hook this harder*, so I said, 'Weird things have been going on via a radio network here in Australia, involving one or more of the staff mentioned.' I hoped the suggestion someone was misusing CBC's name might hurry a reply.

Four days later I got an email back saying, 'CBC is a huge corporation' and it had 'several different shows with many people working for them' and offered to pass my inquiry to their HR department. She finished by asking, 'What are these 'weird' things going on in connection to *The Hour*?' I was aware I might be sounding suspicious. I needed to redeem myself by giving more factual detail.

The next day she wrote back, 'I've done a thorough check within the company and can confirm we do not have any record of employment by CBC to a Sara Kelly or Carey Malcolmson.' She signed off with. 'Sorry to hear you've been misled.'

I considered her email. The official denial by the TV network Sara had told me so much about – from the inside scoop on working with George Stroumboulopoulos – to Barack Obama and his Secret Service coming in – to 'goofing around' with Carey in the writer's room. I sat staring at the words on my computer screen, gnawing at my fingernails, recalling thousands of details Carey and Sara had shared about their jobs. Jobs that didn't exist. I was sitting on the same chair Sara had sat on, in front of the desk her silver Mac had occupied. Inside my house where she'd slept in the room next to mine. To my right were the flowers Carey had sent for my birthday – the ones I couldn't bring myself to get rid of. Now they were the dead remains of a guy who'd sent me flowers on my birthday – a guy that may not be real. My body felt like I'd dropped a Valium that was beginning to kick in. Marley was peering up at me, his head slightly cocked, as if to say, 'What, Mum?' The stuffed Canadian Mounty Sara had given him lying face down in the corner of the room. *Could they be wrong? Is there some small piece of this puzzle I'm somehow getting jammed into the wrong place?* Despite the personal work I'd been doing, I still doubted myself. But there was one more email I needed to send to cement the truth – an email to Z100 in New York, Carey's radio station. This one would be short and sweet. My strategy was to assume the fangirl persona, which wasn't an artistic stretch. 'When will the new guy Carey Malcolmson be back on the air?' I typed. A week later I got a reply from a receptionist who was way better at short and sweet. Skipping over 'Hi' or a sign-off, this person left me little to dress up in denial.

'We do not have an on-air host by the name of Carey Malcolmson.'

Questions rattled continuously around my head each day. Whatever I'd been drawn into with Sara Kelly had wasted much of my precious time and, while I wanted to get to the bottom of it, I didn't need to become fixated. She wasn't worth it. I could see very clearly that I had a pattern of jumping into other people's stories when I should have been focused on my own. And I was worth it. I could honestly feel for the first time just how much I was.

The Spring Racing Carnival was on in Melbourne that month and I'd accepted an invitation to the Emirates marquee. I headed straight to the airport after our Friday show, wanting to make the most of my weekend by tuning off, seeing family, and getting lost in the racing abyss. I spent race day bustling around catching up with media friends, people it's easy to say plenty to while saying nothing at all. Later in the afternoon I came across Tim Ross, a radio guy and comedian who used to be part of one of the most successful radio duos in the country. When I first saw him, I completely forgot he was also one of the people I'd recommended Sara contact for the Winter Olympics gig. I was standing alongside his ridiculously glamorous yet adorably down-to-earth wife, sipping champagne and waiting for the main race, when Tim turned to me and said quietly, 'By the way, your mate Sara, she's not who you think she is.'

Oh fuck. That's right, I poisoned him with her. He'd caught me totally by surprise and I could feel myself going red with humiliation and shame. Right up until that moment I'd somehow, managed to forget about Sara for an entire day. 'What do you mean?' I asked nervously.

'I'm just telling you, she doesn't add up,' he replied. 'My manager checked her out because she gave us a bad vibe and I'm telling you she doesn't check out.' My instant reaction was to try to save face. After all, I'm standing there as the dickhead who'd thought it was OK, despite his approval, to hand over his number to a total stranger. I felt like such a fool. Thankfully Tim was more concerned than pissed off.

My Derby Day revelation played on my mind over the next week. I still couldn't share what was unfolding with my co-hosts although by not doing so it built a higher wall around me and the Sara mystery. If I'd made one single decision to not give a shit about what either Cosi or Rabbit might say – might think – I could've quickly demolished that wall. But I couldn't. Or I chose not to. I kept myself prisoner to it all. I decided to contact Rove's manager, Kevin Whyte. I wanted to admit whatever I'd sent his way, good intentions aside, might have been diabolically misguided. He replied almost instantly, suggesting we chat on the phone. *Oh Christ, brace yourself for more bad PR*, this time from the most prominent talent manager in the country. If I'd ever been 'that fun girl from Adelaide radio' I was about to be demoted to 'that dickhead whose referrals are about as reliable as a cheap watch'. Kevin kept it professional. He confirmed his contact with Sara had been so bad he'd decided that – I quote – 'Even if she has a million dollars, we're not dealing with her.' He went on to describe how he'd allocated her a ticket for Rove but when Sara discovered she was sitting in the front row (most likely to be seen on TV) she'd called Kevin from the studio and demanded he 'come down and sort it out.' The poor guy was in the hospital with his sick child but Sara was so ferocious he left the hospital to 'crisis manage her'. She calmed down once away from the front row. 'No hard feelings, right?' Sara said as he left.

I barely slept that night. My anger was keeping me awake. The next day I decided to call Sara's phone number and every email address I had relating to her. I would email Sara, Carey, Blaine, Hannah and even Sarah (both of her addresses – married and prior). With my new sense of purpose, I commenced my rampage, starting with a one-liner to the mastermind, 'Hey Sara, how're things going?'

There was an automated reply when I woke the next day, 'This email no longer exists.' Nervous, yet determined, I rang Sara's number, 'This number is not connected.' I could feel my heart racing as I moved on to the next address. 'Hey Blaine, just checking in to see how you are?' A day later, 'This email no longer exists.' My blood boiled more and more with each reply. I knew it was time to send the one message I did not want to send. A deranged part of me was desperately clinging to the hope the *fairy tale* existence of a guy called Carey. Our first face-to-face conversation, I imagined, might begin with, 'Well, what the fuck have you got to say for yourself? Where was the dot point about your friend being a sociopath?' And so I wrote, 'Hey, Carey, how are you?' That was it. A day later, it bounced-back. *Are you fucking kidding me?* I felt sick. Finally, I was furious enough to stop protecting the memory of Angel Sarah. It's hard to explain why but I'd kept her, so far, in a gilded cage. Sarah was, as yet, uncontaminated by the foul stench of Sara. That night I emailed Sarah. I could hear myself trotting out an excuse: *Yes, but she's dead, so of course, her email address doesn't exist.* But I was testing to see if someone was still behind it — someone who would be mighty unnerved to get an email from me wanting to talk to a dead girl. The truth was I didn't give a rat's ass if any of these psychopaths weren't contactable, or didn't exist. The worst outcome, one that I hadn't allowed myself to entertain, was the possibility that Angel Sarah never existed. Because that – THAT – was somehow so much more than I could bear to consider.

CHAPTER EIGHT.

SOMEWHERE OUT THERE

The last month of the year was a blur. I was like a robot. I didn't care about ratings anymore although, ironically, we were on top. I went through breaks laughing on cue but my heart wasn't in it. All the unanswered questions around Carey and Sara had left my head ready to explode. *Don't be institutionalised by a pay packet.* I knew what this voice in my head was saying – I was surrounded by radio people who couldn't bear to leave their job – radio was their identity. And, for a while, it'd been mine too. I'd arrived in Adelaide with no sense of who I was, in a state of darkness and spiritual death. I've heard it described as 'the dark night of the soul'. But now there was signs of new growth. I was waking up. I'd thought radio was my going to be my dream job but now I could see the universe had had much bigger plans for me. I'd been sent to Adelaide to heal – to find myself.

A familiar voice began whispering something to me one day. It wouldn't go away. *You haven't even tried to find him. Why haven't you tried?* I knew who 'him' was – it was Carey. And the voice was right. I hadn't, and my conscious, my higher self, my inner (good) voice, wasn't letting me off the hook. And, while most people might have assumed when Carey's jobs weren't checking out, his email and phone numbers abruptly disconnected, that the guy didn't exist, something told me he did. There were nights I'd lie awake staring at my ceiling and I knew, with a strange certainty, that Carey *was* out there. I just didn't know *where*.

Of course, along came another voice, one equally familiar by now, and a little bossier. *Yeah, but that's because you want it to be true. And now you're packaging it up as intuition. How pathetic!* I would lie listening to my bitchy inner sister reminding me where my love life was at but the wonderful thing was, I'd begun to recognise the two voices. In my mind I'd swap from one scenario to the other, scanning my body for signs of anxiousness – and signs of peace. I would ask again, *Is this the truth? That he's out there?* And there was no anxiety. The good voice continued to speak to me as the nights went on. It said: *You'll find the answers with him.* It repeated night after night. *You'll find the answers with him.*

Our show was due to finish up in early December and our station's Christmas party was just days away. Just like the year before I felt dread each time I'd think about the party, but this time it was different. This year I knew I couldn't fake it anymore. On the day of the party my head started aching. *Was this my first migraine?* I wondered. I went home after the show and with every hour my head pounded more. There was no way I could go to the party, but I knew if I didn't everyone would be talking and it could spell disaster for my career. As I sat at my desk, phone in my hand, contemplating the text I knew I had to send the boss, I heard the voice again: *You haven't even tried to Google Carey.* I had a feeling I knew what the pain in my head was linked to – it was my lack of action and what I needed to do – not any other night but that night – was get off my ass and find Carey. I texted all the necessary parties around 5 pm, including the Big Radio Boss, saying only, 'I'm sorry I can't come to the party. I am not well. Apologies. Have a great night.' Once I hit send, I had to let it go. They could talk about me, speculate, write me off but I had bigger things on my mind and for the first time I was backing myself no matter the price. My head pain seemed to melt away immediately after I hit send on the text message.

I had zero strategies of how I was going to find Carey but I was channelling something and I knew I was going to find him. Even though it appeared Carey had never worked in radio, certainly not at the station 'they' claimed, something told me I needed to explore radio anyway. I Googled like a maniac, only resting to pull up the photos Sara had sent, staring at them intently, searching every pixel for a clue and turning my psychic radar to full throttle.

Round and round I went for hours. Then I remembered Google Images. It sounds crazy now but people just weren't everywhere online in 2009. Being on Facebook was not a given. Twitter wasn't on my radar. Nor our shows. And Instagram didn't exist. Ordinary people like me weren't Google geniuses or social media narcissists. It was a different world.

After hours of hitting those keys with countless search angles up came a photo of Carey – a photo I'd already seen. The guy in the photo, his real name *was* Carey. I clicked on the picture, pushing back on that long-suffering office chair. This Carey had a different surname. I'd been right all along – he *was* out there and this Carey *did* work in radio. I continued staring at his photo, thinking *Oh my god. Do you know who I am?* Then suspicion kicked in. There had to be a chance this guy, this radio guy, was capable of being part of a prank like the ones we did on our show. *Had I fallen into another radio station's stunt? On the other side of the world? All in the name of getting a leg-up in the ratings? Was this the karma I feared I might catch by being on our show?* It was time to check if this Carey was on Facebook. A few quick keyboard taps and there he was. I sat back and took a deep breath: *If I message this guy, what do I say? What does he know?* Even if this guy was part of the scam at least he'd be on notice that I knew. Not only that, but money had been taken from innocent, caring people – people who'd bought into a tragic love story. If this Carey was in on this elaborate, evil fraud then he was about to find out that karma had just arrived in his inbox. *Or maybe he's a victim like me – of a predator that used his profile to play a game of sociopathic cat and mouse?*

I didn't want to come off sounding crazy in my first message to real Carey. I had to be careful in my approach. I also had to be conscious of my need to protect myself – but also him in case he was a victim in all of it. I had to admit if I found out he was happily married with kids a piece of me would be hurt. But possibly a bigger fear was the thought of being humiliated again – another reinforcement that, when it comes to love, I'll be left out in the cold. It was time to face my fears and send 'real Carey' a message. I chose to go with an air of naïve excitement about finding the guy who was part of my story. I figured I'd be able to tell if he was a 'Rabbit'. If there was one thing I knew by now it was radio guys. I contemplated heading to bed despite my insane level of anticipation at getting an email back. It was now six hours since I'd sent my soul out into the world. Half an hour later, while reviewing some of 'fake Carey' emails and 'real Carey' photos, my heart almost jumped out of my chest when my computer dinged, signalling a new Facebook message had arrived. It was from Carey. *Oh my god, he's alive and on the hook.*

I clicked into his message, leaned in closer, and took a very deep breath. Carey wrote, 'Hi, Amber ... if it's about those pictures with me and the goat, unicorn, umbrella, and cucumber I can explain ... actually no I can't! Looking forward to hearing your story. Thanks for taking the time to search me out to share the story too. Have a blessed Friday!!' he wrote. The first thing that struck me was how completely different real Carey was to fake Carey. *This* Carey was *so* radio. The Carey I'd come to know, or so I'd thought, was more gentle, more reserved and old-fashioned in the way he wrote. It was what drew me in and yet now, given everything, I felt safer with this version – it was familiar. I was blown away by how quickly I'd not only found but got a reply from real Carey. There'd never been a quick response from fake Carey. Whoever this guy was I needed to keep him on the line to get as much out of him as I could. But I'd have to tease him with more facts regardless of whether he was in on the scam or not.

So, I'm guessing you don't know me? And a girl called Sara Kelly? Someone has been writing to me for six months calling themselves Carey Malcolmson and sending your photos. Are you saying that's not you? Do you now work at Z100? And did you work at *The Hour* with Sara?, I wrote.

He replied again instantly:

Hey Amber, sorry don't know about you, nothing personal. I had a short stint of working with Sara Kelly in Winnipeg (Canada). This has happened to me before a few times, with pictures, biz cards and such. Did you at least think he was cute Ha Ha. I hope he didn't treat you poorly or anything. I work in Edmonton (Canada) launching a new station. Sorry about some dude playing with your heart/mind. Once again … SO SORRY!!!!'

Hang on, is he flirting with me? I wondered. 'Did you at least think he was cute?' he'd asked. Whatever he was doing there was no time to play it cool or worry about coming across as a bit intense. I was ready to brain-dump on the poor bloke as quickly as I could type. After all, I'd had months of hanging on to, *What the fuck?* And now I'd arrived. Before long I'd bashed out every conceivable detail of the story – starting with Sarah and Blaine. It was only after I'd read it back that I realised I was never going to play cool and hang back. Talk about unloading on the guy – I was charging forward like a maniac. I just needed to hope he had zero intuition or experience with women with low self-esteem.

'HOLY SHIT!!! I have more to say … can you send those emails? Really interested in this now. SO SO SO SO SO sorry they messed with your heart and brain. WOW!! I'll write more tomorrow, off to a Christmas play. P.S. … how did you finally find the 'real' me?'

Off to a Christmas play? Cute! Maybe this guy is a little old-fashioned after all? I was reasonably sure there wasn't one single guy in Australia currently 'off to a Christmas play' unless they were five. As much as I was disappointed my inbox was about to go quiet there was something else in this last message that I liked and that was, so far, there'd been no mention of a girlfriend. Although that could be still to come. *Maybe the girlfriend is playing Mary Magdalene? Or Santa's beautiful wife? Here you go again. Jesus Christ. Get a goddam grip, girl.* Nativity scene aside I now had one thing to hang my tragic cap on – he'd promised to write again. In the meantime, I would continue to unravel by writing another lengthy and very *un-cool* reply. Falling asleep that night I felt strangely peaceful considering I may have burnt my career in one evening. But it was worth it to have unearthed a small part of the truth. And it was, I had to admit, also lovely to have Carey back in my life. For real-*ish*.

CHECK, ONE, TWO

I woke up the next morning after one of the deepest sleeps I could remember. I slid out of bed while Marley stretched his little legs next to my pillow. What a great feeling knowing one hundred or so of my work colleagues were waking up exhausted, hungover and probably recapping on what they should or shouldn't have done and said the night before. *I wonder what went down about me?* I checked my body to see if it gave me anxiety – it didn't. My next thought was of my newly resurrected Carey. I raced to check my emails. Apparently it was, 'The worst Christmas play ever!' It made me smile. As much as I'd liked the idea of the guy who went to Christmas plays, the guy bagging it was even better. Carey wrote that hadn't read 'all the emails' I'd sent him between fake Carey and me. 'It's too much like reading your diary,' he added. 'I guess I wish I had some words to comfort you and make everything normal and make the old *before amnesia* Carey come back to life, but sadly, I don't.'

Regarding the list of Sara's details about him (fake him) he confirmed that 'most of the points you made about me are true'. His Mum was his best friend ('we do everything together') and he did have a bird called Rebel ('but he doesn't say bad words'). His Dad had passed away but, he corrected, his tattoo had nothing to do with it. And he did grow up in Edmonton but hadn't any bad experiences with an ex.

In the first sign Carey might also be feeling a little insecure he said, 'I feel like you might be playing ME now. Hahahaha.' I'd almost forgotten about my detective work until he reminded me.

'What did the Sarah that came to visit you look like?' he asked. 'This might be a different girl to the one I know?' I noted that Carey had got Sara and Sarah confused. I knew he meant Sara but he'd written Sarah.

It was easy to describe Sara because she had a distinctive look but I wanted to send a photo of her to clear up the confusion we appeared to be having with names. After frantically checking every possible location on my computer, I found one. It was the only one I had. It was of Sara sitting in my courtyard with Marley on the day she arrived.

In the meantime, Carey had sent another email reassuring me he didn't think I was stupid and that he thought it was 'beautiful' that I'd been so open, so giving to all the people in my story. He said he believed people came into your life for a reason and that it was better to be yourself and to have cared than stay protected in a world of what if. It made my heart melt, just a little. *OK*, a lot.

Carey was, however, understandably hesitant about friendships created online. 'Seriously,' he wrote 'you could be Sarah, or a dude, or a very smart dolphin that was trained to type.' He signed off, 'This is by far my weirdest way of meeting someone on Facebook and I feel lucky to have met you. The world is a beautiful place isn't it, Amber?' *Wow.* Carey's words sank into my heart to that magical little space that only fake Carey had reminded me was still there. I considered, either Carey was just one of the sweetest people on earth or there was some kind of bizarre connection forming between us. *Or maybe I'm addicted to delusion?* Or all of the above. I was aware the line between reality and fantasy had for me been somewhat blurry for a while.

Keep it business-like, Amber, I reminded myself as I emailed the photo of Sara. 'Here she is!' I sat back and waited for Carey's reply.

A few minutes later, he returned. 'Just checked, think this is Sarah

Dickenson ... wow.' He'd mentioned Sarah again in his previous email but now he was mucking the surnames up, which I understood wasn't a big thing to him, but it sure was to me. I needed to take control and slow things down so I could reset us. 'Are you saying this girl is Sarah Dickenson or Sara Kelly who you worked with?' At almost the same moment I hit send another message came back. 'Think this a girl who I met through a DJ I used to work with. Let me check.' Ten minutes later, 'I checked. The girl in the photo is the girl I met through a DJ I worked with a few years back. Her name is Sarah Dickenson.'

My brain froze. Carey's words jumped off the screen and slapped me. *He can't be right?* I pushed myself away from the computer, rolling back in my chair. I needed distance, to breathe, to shake myself and re-focus. Seconds later I went back and reread the message, 'Her name is Sarah Dickenson.' And there it was. Perfectly clear, no matter how many times I read it each time it was like a stab through my chest. Stupidly, right up until that second, I'd held hope, prayed, that Angel Sarah was still the only pure, real person, in all of this. I'd completely refused, despite the growing facts, to believe I'd never had a friendship with a girl I'd come to genuinely care for. Now I couldn't deny it any longer: Sarah hadn't died. Sarah had never existed. My head was spinning. If I'd been standing, I'd probably have collapsed. I waited while Carey contacted the DJ he used to work with – Tarzan Dan was his name. Soon Carey was back, saying Dan had confirmed Carey's memory of Sarah and, whatever had gone on, it sounded a very similar situation to what had happened to us – the cute young yoga instructor who dies of cancer and the best friend steps in. Unfortunately, Tarzan Dan didn't want to talk to me about it but it was clear he too had been a victim to the idea of Sarah. I quickly googled him, wanting to see what kind of radio guy he was. *Oh my god, she's got a type!* He was in every way Rabbit's doppelganger – he was bald, had a radio name, and when I played an audio grab of him on-air, he had the cocky, prankster schtick going on, just like Rabbit. *She preys on Rabbit types. Does she do it to take them down?* I wondered. *Or does she do it because she wants to be adored by them?* Whatever it was, there was clearly a method to her madness.

It was at about this point that things between Carey and I might have cooled down – now I had the answers. There was no agreement or discussion after the Sarah revelation that we'd move past our crazy beginnings, but we did. At lightning speed. Within days of our first introduction Carey suggested it would be good for me if we got on the phone so he could prove he 'had a voice' – unlike his fake counterpart. Three days later I answered Carey's call. 'Hey, it's us! How are you, Amber? Wait, meet my mum, Judy. Say hi, Mum!' *Oh my god, he sounds so cute. And he's brought his mother with him.* I immediately felt myself blushing. Things had taken their next bizarre turn in my life as instantly our chemistry ignited. Talking to Carey (and his Mum) was like we'd known each other forever. I couldn't help thinking that somehow I'd been rescued once again by my angels. I'd gone from something hideous to something potentially wonderful. 'Go on, tell her Mum,' he prodded, laughing. 'What did you say?' 'Oh yes, I said, 'Ooohhh, Carey, she's a very pretty woman,' his Mum replied, giggling. Carey's Mum had the most *fabulous* laugh. And then I had a strange thought, as I recalled the last time that I'd heard such an infectious laugh, it was the first time I'd heard Sarah in Rabbit's gotcha call. I shoved the memory to the back of my mind. I didn't need past experiences distracting me from something as lovely as Judy and Carey. *I do deserve something good to come along. Maybe it's this?*

Carey's pet parrot Rebel was quiet but I was assured he was in the background trying to get a word in. 'Sorry, buddy, this is our time with Amber,' he said to his feathery confidante. 'He's a terrible flirt sometimes,' Carey laughed.

Exactly one week after finding Carey he painted a picture of Marley and me sitting together in a forest and posted it on Facebook – it was one of the sweetest things anyone had ever done for me. It'd only been a couple of weeks since we'd known each other existed, not to mention Carey and I lived on opposite sides of the world, so surely it would appear a little early to start planning a meeting? Well, yes, and *no*. Carey wasn't concerned about what society deemed right or wrong – and I believed I was way overdue for my own love story. 'It seems silly that we're both on vacation and all we want to do is hang out together but we can't because we don't know each other well enough. Not enough time has supposedly passed between us,' he said, as I was lying in my mum's spare bedroom, now back in Melbourne for the holidays. *But people don't do these kinds of things? Surely, for a reason? I mean, look what happened* ... I cut myself off. I didn't want Sarah or Sara staining my joy.

'Amber, I'm pretty sure the rules don't apply to us anymore!' Carey laughed, reassuringly.

I guess they didn't. None of this made sense. *Maybe time doesn't make sense any more either?* Speaking of time, holiday wise, I had more left than Carey did given he was due to start a new radio job early in the new year but I wasn't due back at work until mid-January. My logic in considering being the one to make the bold, potentially dangerous, possibly *idiotic*, trip, all things considered was, I told myself, if it didn't feel right, I could do a runner. I'd race to the nearest hotel, stare outside at the snow, order room service and polish off the mini-bar until my flight home. *It'll just be another adventure!* Two days later I had my ticket to Edmonton, Canada. I decided, whatever happened, would be my destiny.

There was something about having a plan to see Carey in the flesh that felt both comforting and utterly *terrifying*. I was sure I'd know instantly if there was something between us once we were face to face. *Had I stumbled into my own freaky fairy tale or was it destined to be just another failed romance?* The answer to that question weighed on me 24/7.

I chose to try and distract myself from the hamster wheel of that question by enjoying Carey's almost child-like excitement – as he appeared to be planning my trip with no less effort than if he was receiving the Queen of England. From the moment I booked my ticket everything felt different between us and, for a brief while, it felt *amazing*. I did, however, confess one night that there was a tiny chance I might start to freak out at some point. Carey promised to coach me through any of my fears. Soon enough, as predicted, my excitement for my trip to Canada and meeting Carey turned into total emotional overload. It'd been so long since I'd felt a guy care enough to put this much effort in, except when they were trying to hide things or manipulate me. And then I worried about what Carey's family and friends must be thinking? This strange girl he'd just met online booking a ticket to come and visit someone she's never even met? Carey, however, assured me that everyone who loved him was going to love me. As my departure date neared my mind started to waver towards matters that I'd previously thought less of, but now seemed to be bearing down on me. In one of our many conversations over the weeks, Carey had mentioned his last girlfriend had been 19 years old. It hadn't sat well with me, even less so now. But I was still in the standard dating, three-month false advertising period so I'd managed to appear unaffected by his romantic history. Yet after discovering his favourite celebrity – 'his all-time crush' – a fact I'd discovered after listening to an audio break from his previous radio show – was Hillary Duff. I started to become deeply concerned that Carey might have a thing for girls way younger than me.

Now, with my crazy-lady adrenaline kicking in, I began to go through all the Facebook photos of mine that Carey had stamped with 'SH' which he'd told me stood for 'seriously hot'. While flattered at the time, now all I could think was how disappointed he'd be when he met me for real. After all, it wouldn't be the first time someone had been in love with the idea of me. Now I was becoming increasingly suspicious and annoyed that I was potentially about to travel *a long fucking way* to meet yet another wolf in sheep's clothing. I fought hard to keep my potentially irrational thoughts in the cage but they were gnawing on the metal bars. I started not to respond as quickly to Carey's messages. I figured it best to make him sweat until I got my head together. That way, I figured, he could get a taste of how it felt to be me. Then again, the other side of me, the slightly more level-headed, less tortured side, was aware that this inner ugliness and paranoia was the last thing I wanted him to see. Finally, after what I considered an admirably long period of restraint, I wrote Carey an email outlining my, let's call them, *hesitations*. I got straight to the point, stating I could *not* understand how a man thirty-five years of age could justify going out with a nineteen-year-old. I ended the email with, 'I'm sorry Carey, the whole thing doesn't quite make sense to me. I hope you understand.'

I felt relieved to get my thoughts off my chest for about ten-and-a-half seconds. Deep down, all I wanted was Carey to dismiss my insecurities, to just say, 'It's OK, I hear you. I'm sorry that's what you think, and I'm sorry your experiences have led you to this place.' But he didn't.

The next morning, as I woke up in Mum's spare single bed, feeling flat, I remembered what I'd done. I quickly grabbed my phone from the bedside table to check my emails. And there it was. Not only did Carey sound like he'd just sat through *Nightmare on Elm Street* twice but he also said he no longer thought it 'a good idea' that I visit him. He said if I had 'so little respect and trust' in him we were never going to work. I was devastated, unable to hold back my tears. I absolutely hated myself for letting my inner *Freddy Kruger* ruin the most magical, romantic thing I'd had since the early years with Julian. My demons had allowed me to enjoy the prospect of 'Carey and I' just long enough that I could feel what it might be like to be happy, what it was like to feel special. In one email I'd burned to the ground any chance of seeing what we could have been. I'd crushed Carey, hurt myself, and now I had a ticket to a destination where the welcome mat had been swiftly removed. I felt sick in the pit of my stomach, anxiety sweeping through my torso. In my dysfunctional thought process, I'd actually believed that offloading my fears would be the way to protect myself, to keep some sort of control of my heart. Yet now I'd given all my power to Carey. And the thing was, I still wanted to visit him. I wanted it more than anything, despite another part of me feeling like he'd come down on me a little hard.

I called my friend Jane, sobbing. 'I've ruined it,' I cried. 'I've sabotaged it and now he doesn't want me to come.' Jane knew my demons. We'd shared plenty of this brand of *shit* before. She was my friend but she was also, conveniently for me, a Love and Relationships coach. She urged me to calm down and step her through the carnage. Jane sounded sad when I got to the end and I could tell she too thought we were over. She offered to contact Carey for me. As pathetic as it was, having a friend that Carey had never met write to him to try and make sense of my premature tantrum felt like the only choice I had left. I was so embarrassed that my only hope left was she might be able to get him not to hate, or think badly, of me. It was two days before Carey replied. He told her he'd been licking his wounds, trying to understand what had gone down. 'He's retreated to his man cave, darling,' Jane warned me. 'But the good news is he's agreed to talk to me on the phone. *It's a good sign.* If he were done, he would have politely thanked me and that would be that.' I wasn't so sure. I suspected he might just want some clues as to how a romantic con had duped him. *How ironic.*

Days later Jane called and said with a laugh, 'Well, you better not forget to credit me in your book!' She'd just hung up after a long conversation with Carey where, somehow, she'd managed to turn him around. 'He still wants you to come but, honey, you need to be nice to him,' she warned. The relief in hearing Jane's update was incredible. I'd spent days feeling like I was swimming underwater, suffocating under the weight of a lifetime of fear and humiliation, and now, it'd lifted. I'd been gifted a second chance.

'We talked about your sabotage stuff and while he doesn't completely get it the fact is, he really likes you and wants to give you guys a go. *So, don't fuck it up!'* Jane was being playful but she meant it and made me promise the minute my sabotage demons started crawling back into my ear – a likely probability – I was to call her immediately. She made me swear on Marley's life that I'd pick up the phone before punching out any further accusatory emails to a guy I'd still never met but already had feelings for. I didn't expect Carey to give me a second chance. He'd sounded seriously done in his last email and I had no idea how I was going to get back to being the girl he'd fallen for before I'd flashed my jagged monster teeth. Jane assured me I just needed to be *me* and not over-think things. Both of us knew this was easier said than done but I had an incentive. I'd drunk from the cup of misery for days as the image of a beautiful man who'd once been ecstatic about me seemed to fade into the distance. I was aware I was being presented with a truth about myself that I needed to see. And I wondered: *Had Carey come into my life to give me a lesson? To hold a mirror up to the ugly side of myself?* A side that lay dormant, easy to ignore as long as I stayed away from love. Still, unless I dealt with it, I was never going to experience a relationship of the kind I knew in my heart, despite convincing myself I didn't need to be in, *I wanted to be in.* Feeling self-conscious and unworthy I answered the phone when Carey called. 'I'm sorry,' I told him. It was all I could think of to say. 'I'm glad I won't have to throw your Christmas present away,' he replied, chuckling sweetly. He was gentle and kind and I could see that what I really needed was this harsh lesson to frighten me into changing.

'You bought me a Christmas present?' I asked, surprised. I could feel us coming back.

'Yes, of course! I've bought you Christmas presents and other presents for when you get here. You deserve nice things Amber,' he said softly. I wasn't sure I agreed but maybe that was the problem. Perhaps I needed to start believing I was worth nice things, so I didn't go jumping to conclusions that all I'd get was an ending. I wanted Carey to be my motivation – I still wasn't quite ready to be my own – to heal my damaged heart.

With Christmas just days away, Carey and I would have a Skype Christmas together that year, and then, who knew? With our plans back on track, now I could look forward to spending some time with Mum, Dad and Myles in Melbourne before heading down the east coast for a few days of lying in the sun with my best friends Rachel and Dino.

By New Year's Eve of 2009 I could do little but think about getting on that plane via Los Angeles for a night to see my friend Kate and then to Edmonton to unite with Carey. And then, of course there were what most people with half a teaspoon of common sense would consider a few other 'minor concerns'. Just the basics, like, *was I going to get to Canada and be greeted at the airport by a tall blonde with intense blue eyes, hiding a sleeve of Gerbera tattoos under a Kathmandu puffer going by the name of Carey?*

Despite my nervous excitement there was a nice old fencing match going on in my head every time I thought about my trip. One side was jabbing, *Why are you doing this? Only a lunatic would get on a plane to meet a stranger let alone after everything that's gone on.* Fighting just as aggressively the other side slicing forward with, *Who gives a shit what's brought you to this point? You're going to meet someone kind and beautiful who so far has made you happier than you've been in years. You have to find out. This is what's great about you!*

The problem was I knew which side I was barracking for but I could still hear the cheerleaders thrusting their pom-poms from the other side reminding me my love life hadn't exactly been my strong point, so one should probably prepare to batten down the romantic hatches.

CHASING A FAIRY TALE

I had to take a little creative licence (a trick I'd learned from my Mother) when telling Dad about a sudden overseas trip I'd not mentioned even two weeks prior. What I told him was I was off to see my friend Kate in Los Angeles – not a complete lie – I *was* stopping off to see her, albeit on route to Edmonton, Canada. I was equal parts excited, and completely and utterly shitting myself. I couldn't decide if I was the bravest girl in the world or if I was about to get tapped on the shoulder by a woman in a white lab coat.

The flight to Edmonton from LA was three hours – just enough time to watch a movie and read a carefully chosen self-help book on how to block out the 'ego voice'. *You're just here to catch up with a friend*, I kept telling myself. *It's no biggie. You've got this!* Before I knew it, the flight attendant announced we were descending. *Right, time for my music. My 'Eye of the Tiger'.* I'd chosen KT Tunstall's 'Suddenly I See' – a song that made me feel alive. Looking out the window I saw nothing but white snow as far as the eye could see. *OK, well, this is it.* It was time to walk in the direction of whatever was waiting for me. *Would it be my freaky fairy tale, or just another, fucking shitfight?* Nerves racing, I exited the gate. I immediately spotted Carey and his mum, waving. My heart skipped a beat as instantly I knew they were everything I hoped they'd be. *I've done it. I've broken my pattern,* I congratulated myself, trying not to spring into the air. Carey raced towards me looking ridiculously handsome and holding a huge bunch of pink daisies (not the gerbera variety). Flinging his arms around me, Carey hugged me tight and said, 'Oh wow, you're even more beautiful up close.' Meanwhile, his mum Judy's sweet, friendly face was bobbing over his shoulder. She looked so happy for us. I wondered, *How did I manage to find the two nicest people on the planet? And one of them happens to be hot.*

'C'mon, let's get your suitcase so we can get you out of here,' Carey urged. 'We're going to drop Mum home and then I want to take you to a bar near my house so we can drink wine and relax. Mum's a little shitty she can't join us,' he said, grinning. 'I've had to remind her you've come to see me, not her.'

Carey handed me a coat. He'd rightly assumed the one I'd bring wouldn't cut it in a Canadian winter. As soon as we got in the car Carey announced he'd made a CD for me that he needed to put on immediately. 'I'm going to brainwash you with music as much as I can so, when you leave, every time you hear one of the songs that you're going to pine for me like crazy. It's all part of my plan to make you fall in love with me forever,' he laughed. Our chemistry was instant. In fact, it was *amazing*. On the road to his house the three of us talked like old friends. Being with Carey and Judy gave me an incredible sense of peace – and pride that I'd followed my intuition and it appeared to be paying off beyond my wildest dreams.

As we dropped Judy off at home, she promised to let us sleep in the next morning before coming to visit. Everything, so far, felt almost too good to be true. Somehow, I'd done it. I'd landed in my very own fairy tale. Here I was in the passenger seat of my extremely handsome, insanely sweet friend's car surrounded by streets blanketed in snow on our way to a warm bar to drink wine. Oh, and pink daisies (not gerberas) on my lap.

Carey's favourite bar reminded me of 1000 dark, oak-panelled bars with soft lighting I'd seen in the movies. I felt so good being with him. I felt safe. That is until an hour later, after a bottle of red, we decided to head home which was, of course, nerve-wracking. *I'm going home with a guy in another country, staying with him, on the first night I've ever physically met him. What the fuck am I doing?* I checked in with myself and somehow, I still felt OK.

Thankfully, from the minute I walked through the door of Carey's apartment I felt peaceful and, once again, safe. It was surreal being inside the house that had become the backdrop of the phone and screen episodes between Carey and me. Now I was on-set.

I looked around the apartment. There was the study and the computer where his first Facebook message was sent, where we'd had our first Skype date. And resting on the floor in the lounge room were the paints and easel he'd used to paint Marley and me in the forest. Suddenly Carey's co-star arrived, waddling out of the spare room and pitter-pattering towards the kitchen. It was Rebel, his pet parrot. Coming towards us he stopped as though to lean against the architrave of the door, appearing to size me up. 'Hey little guy,' Carey said. 'I told you she was coming!' I never imagined myself being intimidated by a parrot but I'm not going to lie, Carey's ten-centimetre green feathered mate, with his royal-blue and red markings and his ankle bracelet had me feeling insecure for the first time since I arrived. I wondered (joking, I think?) *Does he think I look as good as my photos or was he suspecting there'd been some photoshopping at work?* In a bid to save me from Rebel's judgement Carey suggested we head into the bedroom where he had a few 'surprises' – which might have sounded creepy but he was referencing an ongoing joke we'd had around Sarah. 'It's OK, it's nothing that comes in leather, latex or can be worn as a gimp mask,' he laughed. It'd been an early sign that Carey and I had shared a similar sense of humour.

It was around midnight as I sat down on the end of his bed as instructed while Carey opened his closet and pulled out a giant Santa bag full of gifts. 'Here, this is for you. I've been collecting stuff. Some of it I was going to send over to you before you said you were coming to visit and the rest once I found out you were you. Quick, open something!' he said gleefully. Carey was like a kid at Christmas and it was overwhelmingly cute. There was something about Carey that brought out the happy, joyful child in me. I began pulling packages out one by one, tearing off the paper. He'd put in everything from body lotion to face sponges – stuff I might need while I was there – to an enormous Edmonton Oilers hockey jersey, which had my surname embroidered on the back. He'd put so much thought and effort into it and it made me feel enormously loved. Before we knew it, it was 2.30 am. Time just disappeared with Carey. The seven days and seven nights of my stay were going to be hard to slow down. Carey felt uncomplicated, which was refreshing. But I could feel pangs of heaviness in my chest as I'd imagine our week coming to an end. I wanted to curl up in bed with Carey and not let him go. My issues with intimacy dropped away that night, thanks to Carey. It was perfect first night together – passionate but healthy. We fell asleep holding each other, both admitting how indescribably blessed we were. The next morning, I woke up deliriously happy, despite feeling jet-lagged as hell. I could have slept for a week but I didn't want to let exhaustion hamper our plans. We both knew how important it was for us to bank as many great memories together as we could.

As I lay in Carey's bed with the fan blowing gently on my face, my mind drifting through a slide show of possible future memories, the doorbell rang. 'That'll be Mum,' Carey said. Judy was dying to take us out in the snow after I'd admitted I had no idea what a 'snow angel' was – she was determined she'd see me make my first.

Later that day it was off to meet Carey's extended family, who'd sweetly put on a post-Christmas lunch especially for me. With aunts and uncles present his family were as welcoming and kind as he and his mother had been. It was enough to make me think, *Maybe I could live here? Maybe cosy houses, welcoming Canadians, snow-covered everything and a sexy, kind man is all I need?* Thoughts of how hard it'd been with Julian, living away from my family, especially my dad, crept back, and I thought, *But I've been lonely since then, so maybe this is what I have to do for love?*

Carey's family didn't seem to think that me coming to see him after our weird beginnings was strange at all. They thought it was *really* cool. After lunch Carey and I went downstairs to his Aunt's loungeroom where he and his sister used to hang out in when they were kids. Judy and the rest of the family wandered in soon after, taking up positions in front of the fire. The Christmas tree was still up and, with the fire and the snow outside, I could easily imagine what Christmas with Carey's family would be like. Again, it felt a bit like a dream. 'Look out,' Carey warned, nodding towards his Mum, 'she'll want to do the old-wives' tale on you any minute.'

'Do you want to find out if there are children in the future for you guys?' Judy asked, sitting down next to me on the floor.

'Oh. OK, sure,' I said, holding out my palm. Judy hung a pendulum over my hand as we stared at it, waiting. 'If there's a little girl in the future for these two kids, move the pendulum. If it goes right, it's a boy, if it goes left, it's a girl.' I wondered what it was supposed to do if there was no child at all? Judy dangled her pendulum over my hand as all eyes remained fixed on the unfolding ritual. But there was nothing, not even a hint of a swing. *Shit, this isn't a great a sign*, I fretted. *I think I want that pendulum to move.* Just as I was getting uncomfortable the pendulum moved. It started moving wildly to the left.

'It's a girl!' they all shouted in unison. Judy looked at me proudly, like I'd just given birth, before clenching the pendulum back into her fist. 'I think he'd be wonderful with a little girl, don't you think?' I smiled and nodded. I did think he'd be fantastic with a little girl. He was gentle and sweet and he'd be present. He'd be just what little girls want their daddy to be.

After kneeling around the coffee table waiting for the pendulum to seal my fate, I sat back on the floor while the smiling faces of Carey's family beamed towards me like I was an angel that'd just jumped off the top of their tree. *Could I have found myself in the middle of everything I've ever dreamed of? With a man who could be everything I ever wanted for my future daughter. A man I could love. A man who can break the cycle of my pain.*

My last days with Carey loomed like a dark cloud. We both knew how hard it was going to be to say goodbye. I was grateful, however, that I cared enough not to want to say goodbye. Leaving and feeling terrible, I could see now, was the downside to all this love stuff, which by the way, was now official, we'd both said, 'I love you'. And it felt perfect. It was a sombre last morning in Edmonton. I was sad but trying to stay positive, Carey, however, was struggling.

When it came time to leave for the airport, I turned at the doorway of his bedroom and said, 'Don't let any other bitches in here while I'm gone.'

Carey squeezed me tightly and whispered, 'Don't worry baby, there won't be any other bitches in here ever again.'

Standing at the Departure Gate, Carey and I held each other until I broke away, keeping him at arm's length so I could look into his sad eyes. I said, 'Hey, I love you. Thank you for every second of the last week. We can do this OK?' Carey was crying, he looked so lonely and yet somehow, I felt stronger than ever. As I turned and walked away, I didn't want to dwell in that last, sad space. I wanted to stay in the gratitude of what we'd been given. Carey and I were now a real couple and in love – and I had an Oilers jersey with my name on it to prove it.

But there was one other thing on my mind as I left that day – I had to go back and tell my radio team that Sarah, that girl we'd all fallen for, was a con artist. And that we'd mourned the loss of nobody, rewarding her financially. Once back at work I emailed the bosses hinting to an issue with Sarah. A closed ranks meeting was called with a handful of people – the station manager, the promotions manager, the Big Radio Boss – and Rabbit. 'So, let's go back to the start,' the station manager said. 'What was the first contact that resulted in the gotcha call?', he asked. I waited for Rabbit to take over but he didn't. He just sat there. I couldn't believe it. It was like he thought by not making eye contact that someone else might take responsibility for cleaning up his mess. It was a move, I realised, I'd seen him do before. With no words forthcoming I turned to him and said, 'I don't know *Rabbit?* How did it all start?' Begrudgingly he muttered his end of the story from the inception of the gotcha call idea with Blaine and jumping to Sarah's so-called death.

'So, did you ever speak to him on the phone?' the Big Radio Boss asked, eyes fixed on Rabbit.

'No. It was always via email.'

It was at that precise moment that I nearly fell off the goddam couch. *What. The. Fuck?* I knew not to question Rabbit about his precious gotcha calls but we'd all been led to believe his communication with Blaine had included at least one phone call. It was an assumption of a crucial detail that had influenced everything. We ended the meeting that day with the bosses delegating the job of checking Canadian death records to the head of our promotions department. Days later it was confirmed there was no record of a Sarah Dickenson dying in February 2009, in Canada. Apparently neither country's police departments had jurisdiction over a fraud like the one Sarah had pulled off. I told Carey that night about the meeting. It was nice, finally, to have someone to share my latest work weirdness with. Carey, however, was more interested in planning our first Valentine's Day. Twenty-four hours before Valentine's Day my producer asked me to step out of the studio. Standing in our guest green room was Jane and her two beautiful daughters, Tara and Zoe. 'We were instructed to get three bunches of daisies for you,' Jane said, the three of them beaming. They were from Carey. The card read:

Sweetest Amber, if I could have talked Jane into cutting down a forest for you, I would have, that's how much I love you. But since she didn't have time (has to drop the kids off to school), these daisies will have to do. Know this very second, and forever more, you are loved. Happy Valentine's Day. x

I did feel loved, gloriously so. *Oh, what a difference twelve months can make!*

I thought, thinking back to my last Valentine's Day – spent on my own. I felt truly blessed. My Valentine's gift from Carey was a heart-locket necklace, among the many thoughtful things he'd sent. It was an heirloom from his Auntie Peggy. It was the kind of gift the little girl in me had longed for, and now it was mine. Now, it was ours.

One of the most important days on the Adelaide calendar was the Skyshow, which was on the following weekend. Cosi, Rabbit and I were charged with hosting it. It was an event that held enormous nostalgia for our listeners and everyone in Adelaide. I, however, was excited to have my friend Kylie fly in from Sydney for the weekend. I'd thought hosting in front of literally tens of thousands of people would be terrifying but there was such an incredible vibe in the air that night that there were no nerves at all. It turned out to be one of the best days I'd had since I'd started on the radio. The morning after the Skyshow I Skyped with Carey. It was the longest time we'd not been able to speak and he was dying to hear how the show had gone. I was dying to introduce him to Kylie. It was the first time one of my friends would get to meet the man behind my big (and bizarre) new romance. Kylie jumped in front of my computer, delighted to meet my new man. 'Hey Carey, Amber's told me so much about you. It's so lovely to meet you,' she said, smiling and waving at the screen. Unfortunately, on the day, Carey had a severe case of man-flu and, while he was polite and sweet as always, he wasn't his usual self. We agreed to rain-check until the next day. 'Sleep well. I hope you wake feeling much better. Love you,' I said, trying to sound soothing.

The next day when I spoke to Carey he was still sounding flat and sick but he was keen for me to recap on the Skyshow. He wanted to know what had it felt like being on stage? How did the crowd react? How did Rabbit, Cosi and I get on? Given we'd talked about it the day before I didn't have much else to say. It reminded me that the novelty of being on a radio show had worn off me. That night, as I was getting ready to go to sleep, a text popped up from Carey. He said he was disappointed with our earlier chat and wondered if I thought we were running out of things to say. I had to read it twice to check if he was serious. I wrote back asking him if everything was alright. I wanted to keep it simple so I could get a clear answer. He replied saying he felt I didn't bother sharing something with him that was 'such a big event' and that if I 'couldn't be bothered sharing' then maybe 'something was wrong with us?'. He was referring to the Skyshow. The whole thing baffled me but I put it down to man-flu. When I got to work, I saw an email he'd sent with the flight details for him and his Mum attached. The plan was for Carey to come for a week leading into my 40th birthday party and then his Mum would join us for the last week. As I checked the flight detail on the itineraries, I noticed that, contrary to our plan, he and his Mum's flights were the same. Carey and I would not have one single day alone. I chose to leave this out of our text-message given things had gotten frosty overnight. It did, however, prompt me to wonder if there was something more going on. His message fired back, fast, and furious. In further confirmation to Carey that our love was waning he pointed out that on our last Skype call I'd failed to notice his haircut. For a second, I wondered if he was right? *Had I become so blasé that I hadn't noticed he'd had his hair cut?*

Now, this may sound a little abrupt, because it was, but the relationship between Carey and I was over just twenty-four hours later. It was two text messages before we were done. 'I'm sorry,' he wrote. 'I don't think it's working. I wish you all the best, Amber. Goodbye.'

I was completely blindsided. It made no sense at all to me. After everything we'd been through, all the words, undying love, promises of waiting for each other, even the suggestion that he wanted to get up at my fortieth later that year to ask for my hand in marriage, all up in smoke in a matter of minutes. It was so extreme it almost felt like a stranger had taken over his body. In the days that followed my dramatic and yet totally undramatic break-up with Carey the emails back and forth outlined just how out of whack we were. The lightning-speed demise of the two of us left me reeling and devastated. This time, however, I was not going to blame myself for the ending. None of my usual racing to gather evidence to build a brutal case against myself as to why he'd called it off. As much as I was hurting, something had shifted in me, and it was a good thing.

I soon realised the truth about Carey and me was that we were both equally chasing a fairy tale. Carey wanted me to be Princess Ariel and I wanted him to be my handsome, old-fashioned saviour – the man who would see all my wounds, hear my lion's roar and gently pat down my fears. In finding Carey I'd found my ultimate shortcut. I knew how damaged I was and I wanted an easy out. I wanted to dip my toe in the water of healing then be miraculously transformed without having to swim the English Channel.

With my new personal revelation still sinking in I was asked to drop by the boss's office for a chat. I sat on his couch as he delivered the news that my contract was not being renewed. I was blindsided. As I sat on his couch, processing the shock, I felt humiliated and stabbed in the back. Two days after being told I was being let go my replacement was merrily chatting to my producer right outside my office. 'Hi!' she said, grinning, as I left for the day. I felt like a discarded piece of trash.

Driving away from the office on that last day on-air, after tearful goodbyes from listeners, and an audio 'tribute' for me, produced by Rabbit and starring Rabbit, a voice inside my head said, *Don't mourn the loss of something you didn't want. You made this happen. Just because it's not exactly how you thought it would look don't pretend you didn't ask for it. Don't ruin your gift of freedom by falling into victim energy.*

CHAPTER NINE.

THE LONG GOODBYE

I could see Dad across the room, surrounded by a bunch of mates as they all laughed. I'd seen the sight a 1000 times. Dad smiling cheekily, basking in the glow of one of his naughty one-liners. But he wasn't laughing this time. Instead he looked confused, his body swaying like he might topple over at any second. His friends seemed oblivious, which made me angry. 'Why can't you people see he's dying?' I yelled across the room. No one turned. 'For Chrissakes, why can't you people see he's dying?' I screamed again. It was like they couldn't hear me like, I wasn't even there – and no one could see me crying. I woke up with my chest heaving under the covers from crying in my dream. I told myself it was just a symptom of being frightened about Dad's recent health issues. It'd been a tough year since I'd moved back to Melbourne. The thought of him dying had stepped up since his recent Type 2 diabetes diagnosis. Dad's mortality had always haunted me but now it was getting more real. The truth was my dad was a junkie – a sugar junkie. Which might sound a little cuter than saying he was on crack. His dealer was Darryl Lee, not Darryl running a meth lab.

Dad's drugs of choice were liquorice all-sorts, Rocky Road, Cornetto, Weiss bars – all of the above and way more. I counted thirty-two different confectionary brands after raiding his fridge (during an intervention), his coffee table bowl (sharing rent with five TV remote controls) and his bedside drawer. Most of them were back two weeks after my raid. Dad didn't seem to care if he died. He wanted a quick fix and shortcut to happiness and I struggled not to take it personally that he didn't fear breaking my heart. He had two toes chopped off that year. It was morbid confirmation that the trade-off for his lifestyle was losing body parts. Dad expected to die young. He'd always said he believed fifty-odd was a 'pretty good innings' for someone who wanted to enjoy life.

As Dad stumbled lopsided out of the hospital the day that I took him home, sans toes, he'd promised to take his health more seriously. I hoped it was the start of something new. A promise inspired by the misery of sharing a public hospital room for two weeks with a bedridden (by day) elderly woman who'd mysteriously come to life at night. Standing at the end of Dad's bed at 3 am she'd scream like she was in a heated debate with the devil. It took one car ride home, and me suggesting I stop off to get us a salad sandwich, that saw Dad immediately turn. 'Don't think I'm going to start eating that shit,' he snapped, angrily.

Months after Dad got home from the hospital, I went to my cousin's engagement party. As I climbed into bed at 2 am I felt a pain on the left side of my chest. A strange thought came to me: *I hope Dad's alright.* I looked at my watch before I turned the lamp off in case I needed to cross-check the moment I'd felt pain. I wanted to call to find out if he was alright but I imagined Dad picking up the phone, totally fine, and having to explain my call was based on my own chest pain – and a dream. The next morning a doctor at the same hospital Dad had been at a few months before called me. He said, 'We have your dad here. He's been admitted with signs of heart failure.' The doctor reassured me that Dad was OK, despite what sounded like grave news. I asked what time he'd come in, 'Around 3 am.'

Dad sounded flat when he got on the phone – not scared, just flat. How else would you feel when you can no longer plan stuff you used to love? Dad loved golf – the playing, the frustration and victory. Laughing about it with your mates and having a drink afterwards. What happens when that's gone? And it was for Dad – he survived his failing heart and the Type 2 Diabetes gangrenous toe incident but it shifted the dynamics between us – and not in a good way. I'd fight with him about his health and while I understood, to an extent, his addiction issues, I couldn't sit back and watch him kill himself. I loved him too much. But sugar drove a wedge between us.

I was his daughter and I wanted to save him. Yet I became *the monster*, the sergeant major, in his eyes and the eyes of his friends. Some of his mates waged war back by replenishing his stash of sugar as quickly as I'd cleared it. It took a while for me to get it – they were also acting out of love. Dad became the child and me the parent. He wanted milkshakes and lollies and I wanted him to stay alive. Since I'd returned from Adelaide, we'd spent every weekend hanging out, having breakfast, eating lunch. Our relationship had always revolved around food and had always been on his terms. Food was the thing that brought us together – and the thing I feared would end us. One of our favourite places was a café by the bay called Ricketts Point. We had some great times there – and some that were bad. On the weekend after his toes were removed, I'd stormed out after he'd ordered a milkshake. His friends who'd joined us that morning were left sitting at the table looking at me like I was the most revolting daughter in the world.

I drove off that morning crying, feeling shameful and embarrassed but mostly misunderstood. The words *I only have one Dad and I want him here forever*, kept going round and round in my head as I drove away in tears. I felt like a child again. Same shit a bunch of decades later. I resented my dad that day. *When will he care how I feel? When will he feel the pain I'm in?*

Weeks later Jane came to visit me from Adelaide for the weekend. She was happy to join Dad and me for our weekend breakfast ritual with Roxy (Dad's dog) and Marley. Dad didn't like women paying for food so, as was the drill, he gave me money for our order and I asked him what he wanted. 'A vanilla milkshake,' he said without making eye contact. I looked at Jane, who winked at me affectionately. She knew the deal and I wasn't going to ruin a rare, special moment with two of my favourite people. I went off to the counter to order, leaving them to chat. When our food and drinks arrived, Dad raised his vanilla milkshake to his lips like a cheeky little boy, took a big sip from the pink straw hanging out of the old-school metal milkshake container, before thumping it down victoriously. After a second or so of silence Dad stared somewhere in between us both, looking lost in thought, and said, 'I want you to know I've had a great life. I've done everything I wanted to do. There's nothing I've wanted to do that I haven't done.' He lowered his head slightly as he did when wanting to make a point before turning his gaze towards Jane. 'And, you know, I've had some time recently to do a lot of thinking about whether I might not make it out of the hospital. Or if my time's up sometime soon. And, you know, the only thing I really can't bear,' he said, gesturing toward me 'is the thought of not seeing her face again.'

I couldn't keep Dad's gaze. I couldn't bring myself to match his vulnerability. Instead, I looked down at the empty chair at the table next to him, my stomach feeling like a vacuum was sucking out my insides. And I realised, pathetically, that all the love I felt for my dad, the endless depths of love I had, I'd only ever articulated in my head.

I'd continuously thrashed it around expecting everyone – him – to get it and to hear it. Until then I'd also never heard my dad express his love for me in the way he did that day. It made me feel nauseous.

I wanted permission to fall apart at that café. I wanted to throw myself on the floor and scream and smash every piece of furniture. I wanted to rip my hair out, to let out the ugliest of cries held back too long. I wanted to cry for every moment I'd felt I had to keep my feelings in for fear I might humiliate myself in front of some adult that didn't understand how much I loved this man.

I realised I'd never been able to express in words to my dad how much I loved him. And here I was, in a rare moment with him, right down the line, he's sick and I'm middle-aged and I'm still strangled by fear of the inevitable goodbye.

Jane, sensing my energy shift, jumped in with a gentle voice and said, 'Well Ian, you know your daughter and I have some pretty weird ideas about all that and we believe we will see you again and that we're never really gone. We all go somewhere pretty magical.'

Dad did this nod thing where he also shakes his head at the same time, his way of saying, 'I hear you but you know you might be insane.' I could sense a strange, uncharacteristic openness from my dad. 'So, when the time comes and you do leave the planet and you discover that we were right,' (Jane and I both laughed, enjoying the lightness of us ganging up on him with our 'hippy shit'), 'Why don't you come back and give Amber a little sign?'

Dad smiled, unable to resist the charm of a loving woman. I had to break the ice, unable to sit in the heaviness of the moment struggling to hold the space of what felt like the saddest, and yet most beautiful conversation I'd ever had with my father. I took a second to store away what was the most indescribable joy and affirmation of having the man I'd loved more than maybe anyone else in the world qualify that his love for me matched mine. Finally, I said, 'Yeah, do Dad. But don't make it too creepy.' The three of us laughed. It was a moment that felt a lifetime in the making. And it wouldn't have happened had my friend Jane not been there as our divinely placed meditator.

We headed down to the beach after breakfast, scooping up Roxy and Marley who were both waiting impatiently outside. They ran around excitedly, cocking their legs on everything except us. Jane took a moment to capture a photo of Dad and I as he leant on the rails of the wooden walkway leading to the sea and I nestled into his big arms as he kissed me on the side of the head. Jane proudly presented the picture from her iPhone. As I stared at it, I was struck by the evidence of how much time had passed, that we'd shared a long life together, and I was just so profoundly grateful that the man standing next to me that day had been my dad. What I didn't know was that, on that day, Dad was already dying.

I was at work at my PR gig in Melbourne when I got a call from Dad's doctor. Keen for some privacy I quickly excused myself from a conversation and headed into the boardroom on the fifteenth floor, shutting the door behind me. I walked over to the window looking down at the park below where staff from our agency and neighbouring companies were sitting lunching in the sunshine. 'OK, sorry, I can talk now!' I said, giving the doctor my full attention. I pictured her, given the background noise, standing in the hallway of a busy hospital ward.

She began explaining they were doing some tests on Dad. Then her voice went a little quieter as she added, 'We expect at the end of this process to confirm your father has Alzheimer's.' I knew in that moment that doctors don't make predictions like that until they're sure what those test results will be. As if reading my mind, she confirmed my thought. It was on that day, as far as I concerned, that I learnt Dad was dying. Dad's Alzheimer's had been buried under the layers of other health issues that were more obvious. It was easy to assume when he'd been raced to the hospital, again, with a complexion that looked like third-degree burns (brought on by him stopping his diabetes insulin injections), that his sugar levels were to blame. It was also easy to be distracted by a heart that repeatedly kept slowing down. I excused myself from work, called Mum on the way home spluttering the news and trying to speak while my grief erupted. Mum met me at home by which time I'd opened a bottle of red wine, a packet of cigarettes and was sitting alone at my outdoor table working my way through both. I was going into shock. My mind swirling with the doctor's words and a thought that utterly terrified me – one day Dad might forget who I am.

The next day my friend Tim called. We talked for over an hour. With a sick father himself, I knew he got it. He told me something that would guide me through my next chapter, for however long it may be. He said, 'This is your time, sweetheart. This is what you always wanted.

I know it's hard to process right now but you have more time with your Dad. Try and make it count.' I understood what Tim was saying but I also knew it was without a doubt going to be the most difficult and painful challenge of my life. But I could either plunge into fear and grief about losing him or I could be grateful that what I'd been gifted was a little more time. It was the start of our long goodbye.

LOVE COMES IN, LOVE GOES OUT

Love comes in, love goes out. The words of that strangely brilliant, albeit diabolically expensive healer from years earlier came back to me. I spent years excavating myself spiritually which at times was painful – and ugly – but I also fell in love with the process. The sense of discovery it brought to my life ignited the curious mystic within me – but also my practical side which simply wanted me to sort out my shit.

If it's happening to you, it's about you. This statement kept returning in my head. Unlike many of the other words or voices that would come to me this one didn't feel judgmental, mean or leave me feeling anxious. There was something about this particular voice and what it was suggesting that I instinctively knew meant I needed to park and reconsider. Soon enough I decided I had to put the bad experiences I'd had with my exes, and all the shit that seemed to have gone wrong in my life, through the filter of this statement. I know now it was my higher-self trying to guide me. One of the things I decided to do as part of working out the pure essence of who I am, and who I wanted to be as an adult, was to go back to my childhood and remember the things that I naturally loved. It was through this that I recalled a promise I'd made to myself when I was very young, maybe eight or nine. I'd said to myself that one day I'd adopt a child instead of having one of my own.

Recalling my unusual childhood commitment made me wonder if, instead of thinking I'd failed in having one of my own, that maybe I'd forgotten what I'd always dreamed of motherhood looking like for me.

With adoption being tricky, financially restrictive and a process that might go on for years, in late 2017 I started looking at becoming a foster carer. But I kept it to myself, conscious I might not be approved or, if I was, I might be bloody terrible at it. I also kept it from my friends and family. I didn't need opinions or advice. I was sure about this one and it was too precious to taint with judgement or fears from those that didn't share the same dream. But as much as I wanted to become a carer, the thought of having a stranger's child at my door and a tiny human sleeping in my spare room was unnerving. So too was the concept of going from living alone to sharing my life with a child. But I also worried if I'd be strong enough: *Would I be biting off more than I could emotionally chew once I knew what they'd been through?* Especially given the journey I was now on with Dad. On the other hand, I hoped I might be OK given I'd been such a sensitive child and now was an adult with an ever-present memory of being a child at odds with their world. My childhood had never involved abuse – there was plenty of love – but it had nonetheless left me with emotional pain and trauma. So, I figured I could at least use what I knew about kids unconditionally loving their parents, especially their dads, no matter what the dynamics and what they got back. By taking on a child I was walking into completely unknown territory but I had to have faith that I was driven out of a deep desire to be part of the cycle of life. I longed to be the creator of happy memories for a child that might have had too few – or none.

Everything with Dad had now become limited to merely preserving what he had. But there was no joy for him anymore. New memories were forgotten as quickly as they played out. Dad was safe, he was being fed, but he was losing his mind every day. I'd been living back in Melbourne for nearly seven years. I had my own apartment in the gorgeous seaside village of Elwood and was working part-time at a media agency while writing this book. I had little time for a love life – Dad was my focus – my social life had wound back to a bottle of wine on Friday night and a phone call with a friend interstate. It made no sense on paper to want to choose this time to honour my dream of becoming a carer but my intuition was telling me that it was the antidote I needed. I could feel that old voice calling me softly again: *Hey, are you sure you're not getting depressed? You thought you'd never go back to that place but maybe it's always there? Just waiting for a comeback.* I couldn't risk letting myself go into a space where I could hear the voice more clearly.

I went through several months of the vetting process for becoming a carer, attending the foster caring briefings and then rounds of home visits where a case worker dug into my history to gauge where my trigger points might be in dealing with a traumatised child. It became clear, according to feedback, that the work I'd done on myself might now be an asset in navigating a foster child. After a couple of false starts with two little girls who were eventually placed elsewhere – a decision by the foster agency to place them with seasoned carers due to their specific high-level needs – I agreed to take on a five-year-old girl called Lilly. I was told she'd spent two nights with emergency carers after being removed from her home in the middle of the night. When I heard a knock at the door on the morning of her arrival in late January 2018, my heart started pounding. *It's time*, I said to myself, *Just go. It will be what it will be.*

I opened the door to my apartment to find a little girl with messy, brown, curly hair, standing flanked by two female, child services (DHS) staff. Lilly was wearing a grubby white singlet, black shorts, grey sneakers with no socks, a pink backpack with red ladybugs on it in her hand. She was staring at her feet.

The first five minutes alone with Lilly were strange and beautiful all at once. She stayed silent as I showed her around my apartment, introduced her to Roxy and Marley, and then settled her into her new bedroom. After an hour or so Lilly suddenly erupted, going from saying nothing to talking non-stop – every thought repeated exactly four times each. The poor little thing was wound up like a top. Her nerves were completely shot. I chose not to imagine what Lilly had experienced in her short life. It was my job just to make her feel safe. I adored Lilly from the first day she came to me. She was curious, funny, sensitive and she took to her new routine without one hint of attitude. I sensed she was craving an adult to care about her, to tell her when to go to bed or when to have a bath. I found her openness to me, to whatever I was offering her, a total stranger, to be a sign of her extraordinary spirit.

I'd limited the number of people I had told about fostering. I didn't want to fall flat on my face because I'd never been a parent I worried, *Would there be things I'd forget to do that the rest of the world knows? Maybe I'd finally find out I'm simply not cut out to be a parent.*

Two weeks after Lilly arrived, I was sitting on the shore of Elwood beach watching my beautiful little friend splashing about in the water and chatting to herself. I was in awe at the joy of a child discovering the beach for the first time. Hiding under the brim of my large sunhat, trying so hard to hold it in, I started crying. I was shattered. I'd gone from living alone, caring for my father and my dogs, to overnight caring for a traumatised child. I no longer had a second of peace, just a sense of guilt that I wasn't doing a great job of caring for anyone – including myself.

Juggling Dad and Lilly was intensely difficult. Despite Dad now living in an age care home, locked in a secured dementia ward, I was the only person monitoring how he was, getting him out to see his mates at the pub and making sure he had visitors like me and the dogs – and now Lilly. It'd been uncomfortable enough for Lilly visiting Dad with me, where patients worse than him wandered the halls like tragic, innocent zombies. Trying to get Dad in and out of his room to take him for a walk or to a café and into my Mazda 2 – with a wheelchair, two excited dogs and a happy but still traumatised child – was overwhelming.

Six weeks after Lilly arrived, I woke from a dream feeling heartbroken. In it I'd been standing on a bridge in the sunshine watching a group of friends huddled together under the bridge talking and laughing. I turned around and began walking away just as a woman came striding towards me. I thought she was going to pass me but just as she reached me, she smiled and put out her hand. 'Hi, you should come with me,' she said.

Taking her hand, I followed the woman as she led me toward the entrance of a building. She vanished when we got inside. My feet seemed to be walking of their own accord, taking me further inside into a large, dimly lit room with rows of seats like pews in a church. Now I was standing in front of a mirrored wall that stretched along the front of the room. I stopped in front of it, staring at my reflection for a moment, and then suddenly it hit me – I was at my dad's funeral. *Oh, no. God, no. This is it.* I doubled over to catch the blow of grief, tears that seemed to have no beginning and no end poured out of my soul. Then I woke and realised where I was. *It's OK, he's still alive*, I reassured myself. And yet it felt like he'd already gone.

The sound of the television was humming in the next room where Lilly had slept. It was the Sunday before Easter and the four of us (Roxy and Marley included), were house (and dog) sitting for a friend. Coming to, I felt like I'd just crawled through the door at 5 am after a massive bender. *Get up. It's 8 am. There's a child in the other room.* I scolded myself. *You need to go and check on her. She needs to eat.* I walked into the main bedroom, almost staggering. Bless her – she couldn't have been happier propped up in her 'big girl room' watching cartoons, surrounded by four dogs, sitting at a small antique table, busily drawing Nemo in the ocean.

I hadn't slept well the night before. Old spinal injuries and someone else's pillows didn't help. But I also felt something else was out of whack that day. Feeling guilty, I asked Lilly if she was OK if I went back to lie on my bed after giving her a plate of toast and a Milo as a treat. Falling asleep, I woke an hour later feeling even worse. I checked my phone – there were seven missed calls from Dad's nursing home. I sat up in bed, shaking as I called reception, too terrified to call Dad direct in case he didn't answer. I braced myself as a voice answered – it was Roger, one of the nurses. He said, 'Your Dad hasn't been good during the night. We think it's his heart again.' They wanted to call an ambulance at 3 am but Dad had refused. Roger was standing next to Dad's bed, so I asked him to put him on.

'Hi baby,' Dad answered, sounding defeated.

'Hi Daddy,' I replied, feeling the sad heaviness between us. 'Dad, they can't care for your heart where you are. Please, let them send you back to the hospital,' I pleaded. Dad had spent a handful of days in hospital the week before after admitting he didn't feel right. His breathing was terrible but, even then, I'd had to talk him into letting them call an ambulance. I understood he didn't want to go to a hospital but what if you don't care about dying anymore? How does going to the hospital offer anything but a much less uncomfortable place to be? Yet, *we* needed him to go.

There's a sad numbness you get when you've got a parent whose been sick for a long time. You run out ways to help. What follows is a struggle to find things to keep them hopeful, to throw a positive light on life. You know the spin feels like bullshit. I called my brother Myles to make plans for the three of us, including Lilly, to visit Dad in the hospital that night. Part of me was trying to disconnect with the seriousness of what might be unfolding. I had a little girl in the equation – a kid I couldn't help falling in love with. I needed to consider how to include some 'fun' into our crappy final destination. I knew how much Lilly hated hospital – certain events in her life had left scars – and now I was taking her to a place she was trying to forget.

We stopped at Biggie Smalls hamburger joint in Collingwood on the way. I really hated leaving Dad alone and if I hadn't had Lilly, I'd have been there in a second. Lilly adored my brother Myles – the two of them brought something out in each other that was beautiful. Hamburgers and Lilly dancing on the edge of a stool doing an impromptu freestyling rap routine was the perfect stepping stone to our next stop.

Dad was in the emergency ward when we arrived so I had to put Lilly in a small waiting-room with a colouring-in book and pencils. I wasn't good at asking people to help out with looking after her – I hated admitting I was struggling. My guilt in subjecting my little friend to the hospital made my head even more all over the place.

Myles and I spotted Dad on a bed with the curtain open, lying in the middle of the emergency chaos. The sight of my beautiful Dad, so vulnerable, uncomfortable, and so sick, tore my heart apart. As usual when someone other than me was around, Dad tried to put on a brave face. Playing up to Myles he smiled and made a joke about what a 'great time' he was having while simultaneously making a flirtatious comment to the nurse as she came to check on him. As she walked away, I said, 'So what's wrong, Daddy?' He looked tired and whispered,

'I'm still not feeling right baby.'

A woman with a clipboard appeared at the end of his bed, introducing herself as the head doctor of the ward. She wanted to know who we were. Then the doctor directed a look towards me indicating she wanted to talk privately. I took her cue to excuse myself, saying I needed to check on Lilly. It was the worst kind of juggling act. When I rounded the corner from the waiting-room I could see Dad laughing with Myles. They were good at doing light, making jokes at each other's expense, but I knew I had to get Myles away so we could speak with the doctor together. Myles looked up as I signalled him to join me. He walked over as the doctor approached us. As the three of us stood out of Dad's eyesight I suddenly had a very bad feeling. It hadn't gone unnoticed that the doctor seemed disconcertingly aware of our movements. And then, all of a sudden, it was like I'd just stepped into a strange kind of vortex where everything became quite surreal. Like a movie scene where everything speeds up – swirling bodies – nurses, paramedics, people visiting patients, all darting left and right in a sea of desperation and focus.

I made sure Dad couldn't see us as the doctor stood in front of us. I didn't want him to see my face. And then she spoke, 'So, your father's heart is working at just five per cent. I'm afraid his liver is also failing and so are his kidneys. Which means he's in Stage 4 shut down,' she said gently. I stared at her silently. Blame it on denial, shock, whatever, but the little girl inside me didn't want to get it. If she'd left it at 'five per cent' I might have known. Even with my lack of mathematical genius I would have landed on 'this isn't good.' But there were three parts to what she'd just said that dulled the impact and left me clinging to the idea that this was an emergency and we were in the right place. 'I'm sorry,' she said, 'but he's in the process of end of life.'

Bang, there it was. And everything, time, me, stood still. I think I stopped breathing, as though somehow it might delay the truth. But it didn't. We were in The Moment – the one I'd feared my entire life. My Dad was dying and there was nothing I could do to remove its brutal truth. I turned to Myles, hoping he was about to ask something that'd give hope or more time or that I'd misinterpreted her words. But there was nothing – just the face of a boy who'd been told his Dad was dying. Then a thought flashed through my head, *This is not supposed to be for us. I thought we got the slow goodbye that maybe would never end.* With all Dad's illnesses and ailments, we'd been lulled into a false sense of death. I thought, somehow, what we had with him, as shit as life had been for him in the last few years, meant there was always just a little more time for all of us. I felt nauseous as I thought of my beautiful Dad lying in a fucking awful, uncomfortable bed with steel frames under fluorescent lights. *This can't be a place to die. What was the point of bringing him here?* The thought he didn't know he was dying horrified me because I didn't want him to be scared. And I couldn't look into his eyes with both of us knowing this was our goodbye. I just couldn't. The doctor continued her verdict, 'We expect he's probably got three to six months left, more likely three.' And there it was, our sentence. *Your dad will be dead this year*, a voice inside me said. It was that moment that haunts humans. That moment you realise nothing will ever be the same and nothing can save you from that pain. The doctor was wrong – three to six months turned into four days.

Two days later, on Easter Tuesday, another doctor announced Dad probably wouldn't make it past the holiday. I knew I needed to notify my stepbrother Andy and a handful of Dad's close friends. Dad was in a room with four other patients, one of whom had had a recent heroin overdose. I left the ward for five minutes when a fight broke out between the boy's mother and a nurse. As my auntie was consoling me, I could hear smashing and screaming from the room and I wondered: *How can his life end like this? My Dad, everyone, deserves more than this.* Wiping my tears, I went back to the room and sat by his bed. He was fumbling around for his phone. As I picked it up the phone lit up – there was an old text message displayed on the screen from me to him; it read, 'Hey Dad I was just thinking of you. I love you.' And a reply from him that hadn't gone through that read, 'We're in sync baby. I was just thinking about you. I love you too.' I couldn't even recall when I'd sent it. Without mentioning it, I hit 'send' on Dad's reply back to me.

By early evening Dad was moved into his own room. It had an enormous window with a view of the dome of the Melbourne Exhibition Centre and a magnificent dusty pink sky. It was so beautiful it looked like a painting. The relief of knowing he could die in a space that he deserved felt divinely orchestrated. While Dad's friend Liz was talking to our new nurse Grace, I took this as my cue to leave the room again – to have another cry.

While standing in the hallway crying, I noticed there was a song playing in my head over and over. *Jesus Christ, haven't I got enough going on? How is there even room for this annoying song?* No matter how hard I tried I couldn't make out what the song was. It became an irritating constant in my head. When I went back into the room Dad's bed had been positioned lengthwise towards the window. Liz described how Grace had moved it then whispered in Dad's ear, 'Look at that beautiful sky. I want you to look into that gorgeous, soft light and I want to take that picture with you on your journey.' For the first time in many hours Dad opened his eyes just a little and smiled.

'It's time,' Liz whispered as I lay in a bed beside Dad. It was 1 am on Good Friday when I sat up and looked across at Dad. The room felt so calm and peaceful. I got out of bed, perched on the chair arm next to him, and placed both my hands on his arm. I needed to feel his skin, the hair and shape of his arms, so I could imprint it all into my memory knowing it would be the last time I'd touch him. Liz put her hand on my shoulder, whispering again, 'You can tell him it's OK to go now. He needs to know you're OK with him going.' I felt like someone was strangling me. *Could I do this? Do I have to?* I knew I did. I had to do it for him. I had to do it for me. I stood up, putting my arm across his chest, and whispered, 'It's OK Daddy, you can go now. I'll be OK. I love you.' But I would not say goodbye.

I watched as my dad's face suddenly looked peaceful. In my mind he looked like a little boy again. And then, like the last bit of a candle flame floating off, Dad's spirit was gone. I realise now that I was in shock for most of the week before Dad died and for many months later.

I finally learnt how to ask for help that week, calling on my friend Melanie to look after Lilly for a few days. While I'd been in the hospital with Dad and spent a night at home alone trying to collect myself, Lilly was collecting no fewer than 130 tiny eggs at an Easter hunt put on by Melanie's husband Daniel.

If I'd known that three months after receiving Lilly at my door that Dad was going to die, I'd never in a million years have signed up to be a carer. But now I knew what an incredible gift Lilly was for me. Because I wasn't alone, I had this feisty little rapper who would make me laugh when all I wanted to do was cry. In me wanting to heal Lilly, save the little girl that she was, I'd healed the little girl in me. And I realised that all children, whether they be biological or in our care, all save and teach us as part of a divine and loving exchange.

On the night I, alongside Lilly and Myles, left the hospital after getting the doctor's verdict. I stopped in the street on the way to the car to let Lilly know why I was crying. 'Little one, I just want you to know why I'm sad right now. I've just been told my dad is not very well and he might go to heaven soon,' I said, crouching down in the rain so I could look into her beautiful big eyes. I tried to use words that didn't make it sound scary.

As we walked to the car, the rain getting heavier, almost shouting, Lilly looked up at me and said, 'So *your* Dad's going to die?' Rain and tears drenching my face, I shouted back, 'Yes darling, my dad's going to die. But it's OK, I'll be fine. I'm just a bit sad.'

Lilly kept going, asking, 'So when's he going to die?' I looked at her again, amused at her matter of fact delivery, and said, 'I don't know sweetheart, I guess when he's ready to go.'

On the way home, Myles stopped at the petrol station to get me a large slab of chocolate. While Lilly and I waited in the car, with me trying to hide the tears, she suddenly appeared from the back of the car. Perching herself on the console, she hooked her head around in front of mine, so close I could feel her breath. With eyes widened and patting me like a dog on the side of the face, she said in a caring tone, 'I know [pat, pat] your Dad's going to die, [pat, pat] and you're never going to see him again. That's why you're sad.'

I wiped my eyes, trying to get it together. 'Yes. That's right,' I replied, knowing the kid had broken it down to its basics. I almost started laughing, the last thing I'd have thought I'd do on such a night. There was something about Lilly, her child-like innocence, mixed with an almost emotionless mini gangster approach – born of her life experiences – that brought a black comedy flavour to the situation. Lilly became my reason to get out of bed each day. She needed me and I loved making memories with her. I wasn't supposed to fall in love with her, but I did, with every ounce of my heart. My friend Jane commented weeks later that she felt Dad knew he was able to go because he could see I'd found love.

Thanks to Lilly I was reminded how lucky I'd been to have a father. Sure, he wasn't perfect but we'd expressed love to each other and, because that love had been so great, so too was the pain and loss. But there was another thing I was blessed with, something not afforded to many others whose loved ones develop Alzheimer's or dementia. My dad never forgot who I was. For that I am forever grateful.

Myles picked me up from Liz's house the day after Dad died. I felt numb and deeply sad but resigned to Dad being gone. In many ways I'd been prepared for Dad leaving – my dreams had forewarned me about what was ahead and the sorrow and grief I felt in them had been genuine. I had started the grieving process on the day I'd been told of his diagnosis but also through my dreams.

I slept a few hours at Liz's that night Dad died before waking around 4 am, wondering where I was, and remembering that Dad was gone. In the awake part of my consciousness I noticed the mysterious tune from earlier that day was still playing in my head. In a way it was like it'd been waiting for me to wake up and hear it. It was there again as Myles and I drove to Mum's house but this time, rather than be annoyed, a strange feeling was rising inside me: *Was something trying to get my attention?* 'Do you recognise this tune?' I asked Myles, humming the tiny bit I could get. 'It doesn't make sense that it just keeps playing. I need to work out what it is,' I told him.

When we got to Mum's place, she'd prepared some food which we ate outside in the sun, all of us too tired to talk. When I'd finished eating, I went through every song in my Spotify playlists – until I found it. *'This is it!* This is the song that's been playing in my head,' I cried excitedly, quickly googling the lyrics. 'Oh my god. I think this is from Dad.' With tears pouring down my face I read out the lyrics. They spoke of a heart exploding, being alone in the atmosphere, at the beauty they had just discovered but never known: *This is paradise, here in paradise.*

The next day we met Paige, Dad's goddaughter, and the daughter of his best mate Trevor at the Brighton Baths café so we could start planning Dad's funeral. She'd brought along a photo of Dad and Helen to put on the table. I told her about the song and that day at Rickett's Point with Jane. I said I wanted to tell the story in my speech at the funeral. I wanted everyone to know I suspected Dad was somewhere wonderful. I pictured the faces of a room full of 70 plus year old's trying to get their head around that one. But I didn't care. As far as I was concerned, Dad and I were on the same spiritual team now.

Just as we were discussing Dad's favourite music, a song playing overhead in the café distracted me. It sounded familiar but I had to tune in over the wind to pick up what it. *It can't be. Am I hearing things?* But I wasn't. 'Oh my god!' I practically shrieked. 'This is the song I was just talking about.' They both looked at me like I was going crazy as I asked, 'Have you ever heard this song?' Neither had.

ALL MY LIFE'S A CIRCLE

In the year after Dad died, I found that when I tried the hardest to deny my thoughts of him, as the swell of grief would encompass me, that somehow I'd be led down roads that had the most significance to both of us. Sometimes the grief comes at night and sometimes smack bang in the middle of the day. I had one night, among many, where the wave smashed down on my heart as I was lying in bed. It seemed to come out of nowhere and kept escalating to the point that I could feel my heart burning. I woke the next day feeling fragile and worn out. My only saving grace was that I'd scheduled a grief counsellor appointment that day. Her office wasn't far from my dad's last home, so I planned my route to make sure I wouldn't drive past it. I could not endure any more sadness that day.

My friend Karina called me on the way to the appointment wanting to know how I was. I described my grief tsunami the night before and said I'd been trying to make sense of where Dad was – and how to navigate grief – by listening to podcasts on death, grief and the afterlife. Because we were talking, I'd forgotten my planned route and, before I knew it, I was passing the park where Dad and I would go with Roxy and Marley. It had a bench close to the opening where I'd park the car, making it easy for Dad to get out of the car and sit down. Out of all the parks Dad and I went to in the last years of his life, this was our favourite. It was small, filled with orange and red flowering gums, and it rarely had anyone in it but us.

As I drove past the park and recognising where I was, I gasped, *Oh Jesus, not that park! What are you doing? Get out of here.* Minutes later it happened again as I found myself driving right up the street to Dad's last house. I was so furious with myself for not concentrating and driving up the one road in the entire city I was supposed to avoid. And yet, in all my hysteria, something wanted me to slow down and pull up outside his house. So, I did. I stared across the road to the window of Dad's bedroom, the place he'd slept every night for nearly twenty years.

But he was no longer there. He was no longer anywhere.

I told my grief counsellor that day I'd considered I wanted to stay in pain because I wanted to stay close to him. It was irrational, and I knew it, but I was struggling to understand the point of time, our human experience, the afterlife and the powerful connections we have in life, like the one I'd had with my dad. *How can we be so intertwined and affected by someone and then one day they are gone? Why does love leave us hurting so badly?*

When I left the appointment that day, I chose to drive the opposite way I'd come, determined to avoid more memories. I was tired, hungry and irritable – like a worn-out child. I just needed to eat. I remembered there was a little sandwich shop a few streets away across the road from my brother's carpet business, the one he'd shared with Dad years before. Enough time had passed that it wasn't a place that triggered me about Dad. The shop was closed. *Oh, c'mon? All I want is a goddam tuna sandwich.* I walked away from the shop trying to suck back in a tantrum. I decided to cut my losses and stop at the supermarket around the corner but I managed to overshoot the entrance. *Are you joking?* I screamed, slumping at the wheel. *Why is the universe working against me today?* Then I remembered a bunch of tradie cafes on the other side of the road. I swung a hard right. I chose one, walked up to the food counter and I ordered a tuna sandwich. When I was comfortable the man had put the salt and pepper on the tomato and not the lettuce, I glanced at the bain marie. I had to hide my disgust as I viewed its contents – large chunks of sweaty pork next to a pile of crackling, steamed and fried dims sims, crumbed chicken strips, spring rolls – it was Dad's idea of heaven. Then all of a sudden, I could feel Dad standing next to me at the counter. *Hang on, we've been here together.* We'd marched in on at least one occasion and headed to our respective sides – me on the right for the salad sandwich and him to the left for everything else. 'Oh Dad, that all looks so gross!' I'd whispered. 'What are you talking about?' he'd whispered back, 'this is the good stuff' – smiling as he viewed his greasy prize as if it were a diamond the size of a baby's head.

The connection to my dad in the café was so vivid that day, so immediate. I was on the verge of tears for about the twentieth time that day, desperate for the man to hand over my sandwich so I could flee. Despite fighting to block Dad out that day I'd stepped into a memory of him that felt so alive. I got into my car, ripping open the paper sandwich bag as the memories flooded in. Salty tears streamed down my face. I chewed slowly as I plunged further into a vortex of lost memories. Now in my mind I was back working for Dad, embarrassed to be back in the carpet warehouse after my career (and reputation) had fallen apart.

I could see the broken frosted window with faded business cards stuck randomly around its edges, hiding out contemplating the disaster of my life. My father providing me with a weekly pay cheque while I sifted through the debris, still believing *I had nothing left to lose*. Now it's nine years later and I'm in a car crying and I'm having one of the most profound (and painful) moments of my life – and it came like a sucker punch to the gut. I'd been so wrong. It wasn't true I'd had nothing to lose, not when the most important person in my life was still right there. A dim sim's throw away.

During that window of time, working for my dad, we'd lunch together every day. We'd jump in his car and drive down the street to our favourite cafe. I could see the inside of the car, covered in form guides, the console brimming with coins, lollies, nail clippers, golf tees and other assorted blokey paraphernalia. Sometimes we'd dine in and other times we'd eat together in the office. It was a simple time, despite how complicated the rest of my life felt. Dad and I had a routine. We weren't distracted by other people or any sense we were on borrowed time. It was everything I'd ever wanted as a child and now I'd give anything for one more lunch break together.

A part of me feels that when I try to push away the memory of my dad, as I fall into the darkness of grief, he, or my angels, keep nudging me back to a connection with him. I sense I'm not supposed to shut him out. That he wants to stay with me. He wants me to heal and he wants me to know he was always with me, and always will be. My human story with my dad came to a beautiful circle of completion. At the end of our time together on this earth all that was left between Dad and I was love – no regrets – just pure, in-sync, love.

I lost another great love of my life in the year Dad passed. After nine months of living with me Lilly went to live with her mother. It shocked me at just how close the level of grief I felt losing Lilly was to that of losing my father. Different, but deep.

And yet, despite the pain that moving on without her caused, it taught me perhaps the most beautiful lesson of my life. Because no matter how much it hurt not knowing if I'd ever see her again there were no regrets. I wouldn't have taken back meeting Lilly for all the money in the world. She taught me that in order to experience love, to receive it, I have to allow myself to be vulnerable. I'd taught myself as a child that in order to protect my heart I must control the part I play. I was still doing that while grieving Dad. And now Lilly, a child of the same age as I was when I thought I had the answers to love, had shown me that love can't be controlled and that being vulnerable is simply the price of love.

CHAPTER TEN.

TAKE IT TO THE BRIDGE

'Give her the opportunity … she loves a good prank.'

It was Easter of 2015, a glorious, crisp, sunny day in Sydney's Blue Mountains when I read fake Carey's email from back in 2009. Lying on a banana lounge next to my friend Rachel, looking out over the valley, I'd begun sifting through the Sarah folder on my computer. Rachel had been in my ear that weekend about me writing a book on my 'Sarah saga', as she called it. It was Rachel I'd called, freshly mortified, when I'd thought I'd made a dickhead of myself after slagging off gerberas to Carey. And it was Rachel (and Diana) with whom I'd logged my location before I headed off to confront Sara in her Perth apartment.

With time to kill and a glass of white wine close by, I decided that day in the Blue Mountains that I'd check what I'd kept from my radio and Sarah days. To my surprise I'd saved hundreds of emails, from the whole slew of Sarah's characters: the cute, five-foot-four yoga Sarah, the hunky Adelaide fiancé Blaine Armstrong, his slightly self-involved 20-something sister Hannah, Sara Kelly the powerful media mogul bestie, mum of three, and my old-fashioned electronic squeeze Carey Malcolmson.

I thought back to when I'd first started referencing my hypothetical book when Sarah was (supposedly) dying but I'd had no idea what it would be about. I just knew that years earlier I'd written a bit of stuff about Sarah telling myself then that her story was the only meaningful thing I had to share. Sarah Dickenson, to me, was a courageous and gracious young woman, with so much love to give to the world, before her dreams shattered overnight. Inspired by her strength and vowing never to forget 'Angel Sarah' I'd tell friends, 'I'm going to include Sarah in my book one day.'

Nearly six years on, with Rachel on the next banana lounge, I let out something between a squawk and a squeal. *'Oh, my god...you are not* going to believe this!' Sitting up straighter I read out an email from Carey, pausing for dramatic effect as I delivered the last bullet point of his message, *'Give her the opportunity ... she loves a good prank.'*

'Wowwwwww,' we both sang in unison. Cunningly crafted, it was one of Sarah's most telling emails under the guise of one of her leading men – the endearing, thoughtful, handsome and romantically unattached Carey. The character she'd designed just for me. But now I could see this final *tip* and sadistic slap had also held a warning, 'Give her the opportunity...' God knows I'd given Sarah that, constantly jumping out of my story and into the labyrinth of her fictional world. It was only when I'd moved back to Melbourne that I'd committed to staying focused. I could now see I'd become addicted to worrying about how people viewed me, constantly on high alert for bad news – negative voices, external or just in my head, I gave air time to them all. From my best friend's royal wedding, my magazine column, competing on *Celebrity Survivor* and my radio gig – they all shared the same outcome – would I be voted in, would I be voted out? And among all of it my greatest critic had, in fact, been me. I'd been placed in environments that encouraged a rating of my popularity and my relevance in the world. My lack of self-esteem had given me dangerously flimsy boundaries so

was it any wonder I became a hot favourite for predators who could smell my vulnerability a mile (even another country) away. But the big question was, why had I let them all stay?

We repeat what we don't repair. If anything in my childhood was incomplete or lacking harmony it was my relationship with my dad. You can spend your adult life trying to rewrite a happy ending. The one that you longed for. For me, I wanted time with my dad. And I wanted to be validated by him. As a child I believed Dad chose other people that had something I didn't. Fear became my driver when it came to relationships with men – the fear of being rejected. It was a narrative that said, 'When it comes to love you'll always be left out in the cold, love will be traumatic, and it'll end in goodbye.' And it had, so I'd built a *fabulous* catalogue of evidence to prove I was right. Three strikes and you're out was more than just a saying. I recognised after Travis that I needed to put myself on a twelve-month love ban. I knew if I'd continued dating, with the negative energy around me, I could end up dead. It was my way of placing barriers around me while I worked on cracking the code to my love patterns. The universe, however, had one more test for me just to check how solid those barriers were – Sarah. She got in via a loophole in my contract because she wasn't a romantic partner, she was just a sweet girl with a love story, and so I let another stranger in.

Nearly a decade and an almost finished manuscript later an email popped into my inbox. It was cryptic, lacked formal pleasantries but it had a distinctly familiar flavour – *it was Sarah* – my old friend back from the dead. After five years of chipping away at my book I'd resigned myself to the fact I may never get the truth about Sarah nor the opportunity to ask her 1000 whys. And then she was back offering 'to speak' and demanding 'no recording devices'. In a twist I didn't expect I discovered my curiosity for getting her truth was playing second fiddle to my unprocessed anger. *Who the hell does she think she is, barrelling back into my life telling me what to do?*

Eventually I reminded myself that I wanted something from Sarah

– an end to my book. In my mind that put control back in my hands because I had an agenda. I chose not to respond until my resentment settled enough so I could muster the energy to play the game. I needed Sarah to know I was in charge now, that she'd knocked on the door of a very different me. I took a week to get back to her, offering a date and time to speak via Skype. But when it got to the day she didn't call. I was furious Sarah was pulling the strings again. After a lukewarm apology from her days later, I locked in another date only to have her ghost me again. A week later a Skype message popped up randomly from Sarah while I was online. 'If you're free, let's do this,' she wrote. I'd had three hours sleep that night thanks to a full moon so when I saw her message I thought, *Fuck it, I don't care anymore, let's get this shit out of the way*. Exhaustion had stripped away my nerves and anger.

The first thing I noticed about Sarah's voice was that it was Sara's, albeit notably less tough. Breaking the ice, we launched into a round of small talk, her asking about the Australian bushfires then mentioning the recent Canadian ice storms. We played the two old acquaintances game. When I asked Sarah what had inspired her to reach out she claimed, 'it was just time' – that it was part of her 'healing process'. She said she'd thought about coming forward many times over the years, worrying how her actions had affected my life. 'I wondered if you'd ever be able to trust anyone again?' she said. Lately, though, I'd been showing up in her dreams. An indication, according to Sarah, that it was time to make peace.

I went along with Sarah's *truth* – but I didn't buy it. It was a little hard to swallow given only twenty-four hours before she'd messaged me a journalist in Adelaide had contacted her. The guy had been investigating the story after I'd reached out to him. I was fed up. It was ten years since the gotcha call and still no one who donated money had learnt that truth about where their money had gone.

Sarah and I spoke for about an hour during that first call. She claimed that back in 2008 when Rabbit did the gotcha call on her, impersonating the Aussie Immigration Officer, she was undiagnosed with bi-polar, drinking heavily and using cocaine. I was curious to find out how she'd heard about our show on the other side of her world.

She claimed she'd had a friend travelling around Australia who had listened to our gotcha calls and sent her a podcast of one. Intrigued, she'd then worked out how to contact Rabbit to pitch an idea. That's when Blaine, engaged to Sarah Dickenson, was spawned. I asked how she'd reconciled taking money from our listeners and if she thought about reaching out to offer to pay it back. She said she hadn't but claimed that on her birthday each year she hosted a fundraiser for local charities in her community. We wrapped up the phone call by agreeing, at Sarah's suggestion, to check-in via email with each other in a couple of weeks to see how we'd been processing our reconnection. Sarah and I had only just begun to scratch the surface and, although I didn't let on, I was torn about leaving the door open. Sarah coming back into my life had brought up residual anger but what was more surprising, after all these years, was how little I cared.

If it hadn't been for my book, I might not have bothered with the first call, let alone others. It wasn't that I wasn't open to hearing Sarah's apology, or even accepting it, it's just that after so many years of healing myself in all areas of my life, I didn't need it any more.

I wasn't Sarah's victim. I wasn't anyone's victim. My determination to not live with that label had fired me up to commit to trying to join the dots of my life so I could break my vulnerability cycle. *Things come in threes.* James, Travis and Sarah – the latter being my car crash moment and my time to discover the lessons of my hideous hat-trick.

The answer didn't come overnight – there'd certainly been plenty of rounds in the ring fighting through my fury towards Sarah thinking *how dare she?* and visualising a dragon-like showdown between us one day. Later I'd question my motive for writing this book: *Be honest, is this about revenge?* I knew if there was even a remote chance of 'yes' I'd be inviting bad energy back into my life.

At times I wrestled over what role my sense of compassion had played in me falling for so many smiling assassins. I had to decide whether it was a quality I should own or whether it was a sign of weakness? I concluded it was both and, going forward, I needed to become more discerning when offering it. Ultimately though I knew that to rage and hate over Sarah was to pretend I didn't understand a mind under the attack of mental illness. To not wish her well, despite everything, was to say I didn't care for the child she might have been, one wounded enough to become a woman who preys on strangers for fun.

Sarah and I spent nearly five months talking on and off. Prolonging these calls, for me anyway, was the fact Sarah had agreed to be part of an interview with the US podcast series Love+Radio. Two years earlier the host, Nick Van Der Kolk, had interviewed me for an episode called 'Gotcha' after hearing my story via another podcast host, Barry Lam from Hi Phi Nation. Nick and another producer from This American Life had contacted Sarah to be part of the episode but she'd denied knowing anything about the story or ever visiting Australia.

I didn't expect Sarah to agree to do the Love+Radio follow-up interview. She didn't owe it to me. But she did it anyway, for which I was grateful. We both knew her being part of it greatly increased her chances of being recognised by the people in her new life who knew nothing of her past. Sarah gave me more time than I'd ever imagined she would. And in turn I gave her more of my time so she could unpack her *truth*.

I found myself genuinely liking Sarah – she was engaging, compassionate and thoughtful. She was funny and a great story-teller (the irony not lost on that). In another life we might have been friends. Quickly I found myself falling into a comfortable relationship. I had to face the fact I was swimming in a sea of Sarah's truth and it was easy to drown in the detail. If it hadn't been for sitting on the sidelines while Nick took over the questioning, I might have dropped the ball altogether. It soon became clear Sarah might have developed a softer, more aware version of herself than the one I'd experienced twelve years ago, but she was not out of the woods. Not when it came to telling the truth.

Here's the thing about *truth*, it's not always black and white – until it is. Sarah claimed, 'I reached out to you because it was time,' and yet this might not quite be *the truth* while also being *the truth*. The driving force behind Sarah reaching out was likely triggered by the fear that I wasn't going away. But what was behind that slightly less virtuous reasoning may genuinely have been her desire to do good. So that's a kind of fluid truth.

I grew up thinking that all marriages end in divorce and that influenced me in relationships. My brother was right beside me during my childhood but he didn't see the world like me. He didn't interpret things about Dad in the same way. Despite sitting in the next seat, he didn't believe we were going to die in a plane crash, like I did. That wasn't his truth so he didn't carry the residual fear like I did.

When I'd asked Sarah whose ashes were in the Glad Wrap bag she'd brought to Adelaide, the one she'd sprinkled out to sea (and worn the rest), she said it was one of her closest male friends who'd died when she was twenty-three. So, either it *was* her friend in that bag or she was *full of shit*. I may never know the truth but I did get closure with Sarah and there was enough truth in it for me to be OK.

In the first year I moved to Adelaide I remember sitting on my bed in the apartment I'd first spoken to Sarah in. I was watching Rachel Zoe on TV talking with fashion designer Diane von Furstenberg. Diane said, 'I am lucky to have become the woman I hoped to be.' That sentiment hit me. I looked at the incredibly elegant woman that Diane von Furstenberg is and it wasn't that she'd built a fashion empire that impressed me, it was the love and pride she held for herself. I realised in that moment just how far away I was from feeling like that about myself. I was just thirty-eight years old and yet somehow, I believed that any chance of me becoming the kind of woman I'd hoped to be was already dead.

As I head into possibly the greatest milestone of my life so far – turning fifty – I know I am finally closer to becoming the woman I hoped in my heart I would one day become. Where once I'd been held hostage by my fear, my mind is now gentler and hums a more loving tune. I still have bouts of anxiety but now I listen. I understand it's my body giving me feedback. It urges me to listen and consider what needs my attention. Sometimes I feel anxiety and suspect it's just the energies around me shifting and making way for a change I've asked the universe for. At times it's much more intense, as bad as the old days, and can last for a day, days, or at worst, weeks. But I don't dismiss it anymore or think it's just my state of being. I see that anxiety is often linked to past events and earlier environments which created neural pathways in my brain that are triggered by current events that my brain recognises and perceives as dangerous. And yet the danger may not be there at all.

I know I can create *new* neural pathways in my brain. Much like learning a musical instrument it can feel difficult, as though no matter how much I practice I'll never quite get there. But the brain, I've learnt, needs patience and my commitment to regular practice, which I do by trying to see every event that happens to me as a chance for new growth. By using gratitude, among other things, in time I have seen that the experiences that once ignited anxiety have slowly lost their burn.

Where I am now in life, if it were a song, is at the part they call the bridge. I can see the past for what it was and how it has given me wisdom but through therapy, and a commitment to self-love over time (we are all works in progress), I have cleared enough space in my mind (and my heart) so I can finally visualise the things I want in my future. Perhaps most importantly I am able to feel, and truly appreciate, precisely where I am. My *happy ending*, at the risk of sounding like an entire cheese platter, has been *finally* falling in love with me.

In loving memory of my Dad, Ian Sinclair Petty
27.12.41—30.3.18

www.ingramcontent.com/pod-product-compliance
Lightning Source LLC
Chambersburg PA
CBHW071730080526
44588CB00013B/1976